Quake™ II

Authorized Strategy Guide

Other Titles from GW Press

Order information: Contact The WizardWorks Group, Inc., 2300 Berkshire Lane North, Plymouth, MN 55441 USA. You can also call toll free 1-800-229-2714.

Visit our Web site at http://www.gamewizards.com

Quake™ II

Authorized Strategy Guide

John K. Waters and Michael Koch

GW Press
A Division of GameWizards, Inc.
7085 Shady Oak Road
Minneapolis, MN 55344

Publisher Shel Mann	**Quake II--Authorized Strategy Guide**
	Published by
Associate Publisher Scott Grieve	GW Press A Division of GameWizards, Inc. 7085 Shady Oak Road
Project Manager/Senior Editor Michael Koch	Minneapolis, MN 55344

ISBN: 1-56893-959-0
Library of Congress Catalog Card Number: 97-81437
Printed in the United States of America
97 98 99 10 9 8 7 6 5 4 3 2

Design and Layout
B. J. Shull
MK Publication Services

Contents at a Glance

Contents

Acknowledgments

We couldn't have put together such a comprehensive guide to this great game without the help and support of many talented people. From start to finish, this project was a real team effort, and we want to acknowledge and express our appreciation to the other members of that team.

First we would like to thank Shel Mann and GW Press for giving us the opportunity to work on this project. Our deep appreciation as well to Todd Hollenshead, Barrett Alexander, Christian Antkow and all the others at id Software for their support and for putting out another cool game. Mike McClure and John Golden at GameWizards have been most helpful in giving us a head start on the maps. Many, many thanks also to Talon for his help with the multiplayer section. The cheats come courtesy of Kuhas and the QuakeMarines.

Finally, thanks to our friends and relatives for putting up with us during a most stressful Holiday season.

About the Authors

John K. Waters is a freelance writer and veteran computer game book author. He has written strategy guides for many popular games, including the best-selling *Diablo: The Official Strategy Guide*. A full-time journalist, he regularly contributes news, features, and commentary to *The Java Report*, *Object Magazine*, *Web Apps*, and a wide range of regional and national publications. He recently completed work on the script for a documentary film entitled, *Silicon Valley: A One Hundred-Year Renaissance*.

Michael Koch has been developing and editing computer and computer game books for many years. The former editor-in-chief of *German Life Magazine*, he has held editorial positions at GW Press, IDG Books, and Prima Publishing. As an editor, he has helped bring a number of popular game books into the world, including *Total Annihilation— Official Strategy Guide*, *Duke Nukem 64—Official Strategy Guide*, *Duke Nukem 3D Construction Kit*, *Conquest of the New World—The Official Strategy Guide*, and *Bad Day on the Midway—The Official Strategy Guide*. *Quake II—Authorized Strategy Guide* is his first turn as an author.

Introduction

The pre-release buzz was deafening. News of its impending release circulated endlessly on the Net. Anxious gamers speculated on its rumored features in newsgroups. Previews appeared on the coolest Web sites. In short, the tremors preceding the release of *Quake II* nearly knocked the dishes off the shelves. How could any computer game live up to all this sweaty anticipation—and from such a notoriously demanding audience? How could a mere sequel to one of the most popular 3D shoot-'em-ups in digital history possibly measure up? We don't know how id Software pulled it off, but *Quake II* is everything we hoped it would be, and maybe a little bit more.

Beyond the hype and the standard gaming cliches, we're here to tell you that this is a hot game. In the words of PC *GameSpot*'s Michael Mullen, *Quake II* "goes one step ahead of *Quake*, spins it around and nails it to the wall." This is a totally new tale of war and savagery, fully outside the story line of the first *Quake*. The developers have come up with a new cyborg enemy—the awesome and many-facetted Strogg—and a huge, totally cohesive, and often gruesome alien battlefield that fans of the first game will love.

And this thing is huge! With 8 missions and 44 objectives, it's easy to get lost in its immense alien landscape—and even easier to get chopped up for spare parts.

Which is where we come in.

Quake II—Authorized Strategy Guide has everything you need to make the most of your gaming experience. We stayed up nights, worked weekends, and alienated our friends and families to bring you the *most complete and comprehensive guide* to this great game. We're not complaining, we just want you to know that we cut no corners and left no cyborg unturned. If it's in the game, it's in this book. We didn't miss a thing. Turn the page, and you won't either.

How to Use this Book

Quake II—Authorized Strategy Guide is your ticket to a hell of a ride. This book has it all—maps, tips, strategies, secrets, and cheats.

Part I, *Quake II* Basics, briefs you on some general **single player tips and strategies**, your arsenal and military supplies, and enemy profiles.

Part II, Walkthrough, is a **step-by-step guide to all levels** of this labyrinthine game, complete with **custom maps with detailed callouts** that will point you to all secret locations. Keep in mind that the levels in *Quake II* are not strictly linear, and there are various ways to accomplish the goals in each level. Subdivided by missions and mission objectives, our walkthrough is just one way of finishing the game.

Part III, Multiplayer *Quake II*, covers wicked **multiplayer tips and strategies** that will help you make it through the most challenging deathmatches.

Appendix A contains summary listings of all **cheats**. Appendix B tells you how to use the **exclusive CD-ROM with add-on levels**. Appendix C gives you the **maps** to these exclusive add-on levels.

Now, Marine, it's time to quit stalling and kick some serious ass.

Part 1
QUAKE II BASICS

THE FOLLOWING SECTION IS DESIGNED TO SERVE as a
reference guide. It includes a few general
tips and strategies on how to play the game,
detailed weapons and equipment stats, and
profiles of the creatures that populate
Stroggos. We've done our best to cover everything you'll find and everyone you'll meet
between the pod crash site and your final
confrontation with the Makron.

Quake II

GENERAL TIPS AND STRATEGIES

WELCOME TO STROGGOS. What a lovely planet. So warm. So welcoming. The inhabitants are so very glad to see you. They want you to stay. They want to make you part of the family. They want to pull off your arms, eat your liver, and drop your screaming carcas into a meatgrinder. To make the most of your stay on Stroggos, we've put together some vital tips, slick strategies, and indispensable intell on the natives.

Quake II

MISSION STRUCTURE

Quake II is made up of roughly eight missions, each divided into a sequence of objectives and goals. As you complete each objective or goal, your field computer will flash a brief message that will advise you of what you need to do next. It will also show you a list of potential kills (which translates into the number of monsters coming after you) and secrets. The only detail left out of this message is just exactly how you're supposed to do any of it!

You must complete each mission before you will be allowed to move on to the next one, and most of the objectives are interdependent, following each other in a sometimes convoluted, but ultimately logical sequence. Once you complete a mission, you won't be allowed back to any of the locations in it.

Your ultimate goal is to kill the Makron, leader of the Strogg. When you terminate the big guy, the game is over. In multiplayer deathmatches, your goals change a bit. Forget about Strogg and the Makron and anything else—in multiplayer *Quake II* your goal is to kill everyone else and be the last one standing when the smoke clears. You'll have access to every weapon in the game, but so will your competitors. In short, multiplayer *Quake II* is a different ballgame, and this guide's multiplayer section will give you the info you'll need to defeat your opponents.

THE INTERFACE

The manual does a good job of providing everything you'll need to install, start up, and operate the game. For clarification, we added a few additional points.

Skill Levels

You can play *Quake II* on Easy, Medium, or Hard. Each setting adjusts the reaction, health, power, and number of the monsters you face when you play at that level. For example, Medium sends a greater number of tougher monsters at you than Easy. Most gamers will want to start at Medium, but the Hard skill level is where you'll find the real game—while proving your worth and testing your gaming mettle.

The missions in Part 2, Walkthrough, assume the gamer is playing on Hard. We didn't want you to miss any monster or items as you proceed with your mission, leaving a trail of blood on the surface of this charming planet. **note**

Options

The sound and video options are covered adequately in the manual, and each individual player can select preferences as far as keys and macros are concerned. But two of the other *Quake II* options need further explanation.

- **Always run**--With this setting on, you'll be going at your maximum speed whenever you advance. We recommend using this setting. Without it, you just won't have the speed you need to cope with fast attacks from multiple adversaries.

- **Freelook**--This setting is a must when you know you're going to be fighting a lot of airborne monsters. It's equally useful when you're going against Barracuda Sharks (they're in the water, but it's the same principle), and snipers. It gives you quicker responses to attacks from above, and it enables you to aim more accurately than the "look up" and "look down" keys. Many players use it all the time, which is fine, but those who generally prefer a more stable mouse should switch this setting when they see trouble in the sky.

GENERAL GAMEPLAY TIPS AND STRATEGIES

You can count on the walkthrough and the maps in Part 2 to give you everything you'll need to complete each mission in *Quake II* successfully. Here, we'd like to offer a few general tips that summarize the most successful strategies for pummeling the baddies.

- **Keep your eyes and ears open**--Of course you have to stay alert in this game. There's a Vegematic with legs around every corner and outcropping on this damned planet. So you've got to be on the lookout for the enemy. But you should be *listening*, too. Each monster on Stroggos produces a specific sound: the squeal of the Icarus, the harsh gutteral shouts if the Guards, the lumbering of the Tanks, the moaning of the Iron Maiden. (Oh that moaning!) The sound is one of the coolest aspects of this game; noticing it will give you an edge.

- **Crouch and cover**--Your mother told you to stand up straight, but we say on Stroggos *crouching* can save your ass. Do it to hit ducking monsters and to make yourself harder to hit when there's no cover. The move actually helps in both cases.

- **Look up**--The creators of *Quake II* went to a lot of trouble to give you a 3D experience. So, experince it, dude! But don't do it just because the sky is pretty or the ceiling tiles are fetching. You've got bad guys to watch out for, and you

shouldn't wait for them to tap you on the shoulder with a spray of bullets or a grenade. That's how you weaken and die before your time! Also, many of the game's secret areas are accessed through impact switches and cracked pipes that are above eye level.

- **Look down**--When you're not looking up, look *down*. Walking up to (or jumping on) the ledge of a platform, ledge, or walkway and looking down below (into a pit, river, or canyon) will give you important recon information about enemy size and strength. You might even consider raining on their parade by dropping grenades down below.

- **Climb the crates**--There's only one size crate that you can jump up onto. If you see one of those little ones shoved against a stack of big ones at floor level, you've found a surefire clue that something is up there. If, when you climb up, you don't find anything, keep looking around and shooting at things until something happens. The makers of *Quake II* rarely give you a step stool for no reason.

Part 1: Quake II Basics

- **Leave the beaten path (even if it's slimy)**--You won't find the secret areas on the main trail. Okay, you'll find some of them, but a lot of the really good stuff is hidden off the edges of the walkways, back in the corners of dark rooms, and under the water and toxic slime. There's so much going on in this game that nooks and crannies are easy to miss. To get the complete experience, you've got to wander off the beaten path.

- **Master the fine art of jumping (including rocket jumping)**--In this game, you've got to jump. It's that simple. Some of the jumps are easy; some are maddeningly tricky. Developing this skill early will make the later missions that much easier. And while you're at it, save a game somewhere and try a rocket jump or two. There is one secret area that is inaccessible by any other means. Rocket jumping is accomplished by firing a rocket at your feet, and jumping up just as the explosion happens. This enables your player to jump much higher than normal, but there's a price to pay—you'll take a hit for around 20 percent of your health. That's a constant, so if you're only at 20 percent health, you'll splatter yourself all over the area.

- **Prioritize your enemies**--You can't shoot everybody at once, even when they're all coming at you at once. As a rule of thumb, always shoot the Berserkers first, especially if they're close. When one of them whomps you with that hammer, your aim will be shot to hell and you won't be shooting anyone. After that, shoot the monsters you can't get away from. If there's no roof or ledge to duck under, you've got to knock out the Flyers, Technicians, and Icaruses. After that it's anybody you can't run away from.

- **Keep track of the location of military supplies**--Oh sure, you're healthy now. You're 100 percent. In fact, thanks to a few stims and that shot of adrenaline, you're more than 100 percent. If there's one thing you can count on in this game, it's that you won't be healthy for long. Therefore, it is in your absolute best interest to take careful note of every medkit and first aid kit you see. You will need them all. Similarly, keep track of any ammo or other military supplies you had to leave behind, because you couldn't carry any more, or because your guns were loaded. Guns don't stay loaded for long on Stroggos.

Quake II

- **Queue up alternate weapons in the Inventory**--When you run out of ammo with the gun in your hand, *Quake II* automatically hands you another one from your inventory. Do not let the game make this decision for you or you'll find yourself in the middle of a flock of Icaruses with a blaster in your hand. You should always watch your ammo level and avoid getting caught with a dry clip; but for those occasions when you do, have your next best weapon queued up in the inventory.

- **Pick up every weapon**--You may already have a hyperblaster, but that hyperblaster twirling up there on the stack of crates is a *loaded* hyperblaster. Extra weapons mean extra ammo, without using up valuable inventory space.

- **Try a bank shot**--Grenades bounce. With a little practice, you can get them to bounce where you want them to, especially when you're using the grenade launcher. This is a particularly useful maneuver for nailing cyborgs around corners, and for getting behind the force fields of the Brains.

- **Use and respect explosive barrels (and crates)**--Barrels are great. You can blow them up with a blaster shot. And they really *explode* when they go. Used strategically, they can cripple an enemy, and they often hide ammo, entryways, and other secrets. But if you're standing too close, an exploding barrel can do a lot of damage to you. And a barrel is sometimes the only means short of a rocket jump to climb up onto a stack of crates. By all means, shoot every barrel, but look around first to make sure you're not blowing up your only means of reaching a power-up or secret area. Also, stand back before you blast one.

WEAPONS AND MILITARY SUPPLIES

THIS SECTION PROVIDES A LIST OF ALL the weapons, ammunition, and military supplies you'll find during your sojourn on Stroggos. We've included statistics on firing rates, maximum clip counts, and damage; everything a well-heeled Marine should know about his hardware.

WEAPONS

There's nothing quite like being dropped into the enemy's camp with little more than a pea shooter in your hand. Fortunately, the Strogg are not big on housekeeping. These cyborg slobs leave their stuff lying around *everywhere*—which is good news for a Marine in need of the tools of his or her trade. The array of weapons you will come across during your mission is considerable. Whatever weapon you use, first you must have ammo for it. Six types are available to you, including:

 Shells--used in Shotgun and Super Shotgun, 10 per box

 Cells--used in BFG and Hyperblaster, 50 per battery

 Bullets--used in Machine Gun and Chaingun, 50 per box

 Grenades--thrown by hand or used in Grenade Launcher, 5 per item

 Rockets--used in Rocket Launcher, 5 per rack

 Slugs--used in Railgun, 10 per box

The weapons themselves range from backwoods buckshot blasters to digital-age death dealers. All damage statistics listed here are "raw," that is, they do not take into account the effects of armor, quad power, or shielding. Firing rates are approximations with the trigger held down. (For the hand grenades, the standard was repeated pressing of the trigger.)

 Blaster--The first and only weapon you arrive with. The good news is, your ammo is unlimited; the bad news is, the weapon isn't very powerful. More good news: it shoots very straight and keeps going until it hits something. More bad news: it leaves a trail that your enemy can see and dodge, effectively giving away your position. All in all, a good weapon to replace.

Type of ammo:	Energy
Firing rate:	2.5 rounds per second
Max clip count:	Unlimited recharge
Damage inflicted:	10 per round (15 in deathwatch)
Effective range:	Equally effective close and long
Most useful against:	Guards, Enforcers, Impact Switches, far-away enemies

 Shotgun--Lots of bang at short range, but nearly useless against distant enemies. A definite step up from the Blaster. Get in close on the early monsters, and you'll do some real damage, but on the bigger critters you'll just mess up the paint job. The toughest thing to get used to is the time it takes to jack in a new shell.

Type of ammo:	Shells
Firing rate:	one round per 1.25 seconds (one shell per)
Max clip count:	100 (150 with Bandolier)
Damage inflicted:	up to about 40
Effective range:	Close
Most useful against:	Guards, Enforcers, close-up Flyers

Quake II

Part 1: Quake II Basics

Super Shotgun--Now you're talking! Bring out big brother and put a serious hurt on somebody. Same basic scattering design, but with a much bigger bang. Still deadliest close up, but with more firepower at a distance. The weapon of choice for discriminating cyborg killers.

Type of ammo:	Shells
Firing rate:	1 round per 1.5 seconds (two shells per)
Max clip count:	100 (150 with Bandolier)
Damage inflicted:	up to about 100 at close range
Effective range:	Close to Medium
Most useful against:	Guards, Enforcers, Parasites (but it'll hurt everybody)

Machine Gun--Your first automatic weapon. Light weight, easy to use. Just point and spray. But the barrel migrates up as you fire. It drops right back when you let up on the trigger, but you have to watch it or you'll waste a lot of ammo. Most effective technique: fire in short bursts. Not great at long range, but a real gutting machine at medium and short range.

Type of ammo:	Bullets
Firing rate:	3 rounds per second (one bullet per)
Max clip count:	200 (250 with Bandolier)
Damage inflicted:	8 per round (6 in deathmatch)
Effective range:	Close to Medium
Most useful against:	Guards, Flyers, Enforcers, Parasites

Chaingun--This one is a real weed wacker. The weapon of choice for cyborg shredding, but it chews up ammo at an alarming rate. Its rotating barrel starts up slow and keeps rolling a bit after you release the trigger. Takes some getting used to. You'll want to release just before your opponent dies, so you don't waste ammo on a corpse. Great for sustained attacks.

Type of ammo:	Bullets
Firing rate:	about 28 rounds per second (9 bullets per)
Max clip count:	200
Damage inflicted:	8 per round (6 in deathmatch)
Effective range:	Close to Long
Most useful against:	Tanks, Brain, Gladiators

Hand Grenade--Grenades are both ammunition for the Grenade Launcher and weapons in their own right, though some players forget that. You can select them from your inventory and throw them yourself without making a sound. The longer you hang onto it (hold down the trigger) the farther you'll throw it. Be careful; they *will* explode in your hand if you wait too long. They explode on or about the fourth loud "tick," so release them after the second one.

Type of ammo:	Grenades
Firing rate:	1 per throw at about 3 seconds each (they explode about 4.5 seconds after you hit the trigger)
Max clip count:	50
Damage inflicted:	up to 125
Effective range:	Close to Medium
Most useful against:	all

Grenade Launcher-- The grenades used by the launcher are a little different from the ones you throw by hand. If you hit an object, they will bounce around for about three seconds before exploding; if you hit an enemy, they will explode immediately. And they pack a bit more punch. Great for doing damage in hard-to-reach areas, but you don't want to shoot it in a confined space; the bomb may bounce back at you. In fact, the blast radius is a good-sized one, so make sure you've got some distance between you and your target. Tip: For maximum distance, get a running start, aim slightly up, jump, and fire.

Type of ammo:	Grenades
Firing rate:	about 1 round per second (one grenade per)
Max clip count:	50
Damage inflicted:	up to 120 per grenade
Effective range:	Medium
Most useful against:	Tanks, Brains, and surprise attacks

Rocket Launcher--

Some real fire power here. Great for big, distant bad guys. The rockets go straight, but slow, so it's not a good weapon to use on jittery types like the Berserkers. Tanks are a bit resistant. The explosion is devastating and even causes collateral damage if you miss your target. Very dangerous in close quarters. Tip: *Rocket jumping* is a skill you must develop to truly master the game. You'll remember it from the first *Quake*. To rocket jump, aim your rocket launcher straight down at the ground, then start your jump and fire. The force of the explosion will propel you very high, and knock about 20 points off your health.

Type of ammo:	Rockets
Firing rate:	11 rounds per 1.4 seconds (1 rocket per)
Max clip count:	50
Damage inflicted:	100–120
Effective range:	Long
Most useful against:	Iron Maidens, Gladiators, Brains

Hyperblaster--This is a

kind of energy chaingun without the spin-up delay. It uses the same ammo as your blaster, but the lightening-fast delivery rate makes it a deadly cyborg-cutting device. Eats up ammo, but shreds the medium-sized bad guys. Not the best choice against heavily armored opponents, such as the Tank. One peculiarity: after a long period of fire, the barrel requires a second to spin down, during which time you can't fire.

Type of ammo:	Cells
Firing rate:	about five rounds per second (1 cell per)
Max clip count:	200
Damage inflicted:	10 per round (15 in death match)
Effective range:	Close to Medium
Most useful against:	Berserkers, Gunners

Railgun--

Remember the secret weapon the bad guys were shooting at Arnold Schwarzenegger in the film Eraser? Well, now you've got one of your own. This one fires a depleted uranium slug at a super high velocity. It'll shoot a hole in a rhino—better yet, a Tank or a Gladiator. The reload time is slow, so save it for longer range attacks. Keep in mind that it can be very tough to aim.

Type of ammo:	Slugs
Firing rate:	11 rounds per 2 seconds (1 slug per)
Max clip count:	50
Damage inflicted:	150 (100 in deathmatch)
Effective range:	Medium to Long
Most useful against:	Tanks, Gladiators

BFG10K--The biggest, bad-

dest rod on your gunrack. You might remember it from the *Doom* series. Far and away the most deadly weapon in the game. It takes several seconds after you hit the trigger to cough up a round, but that slow-moving ball of green energy will cause major damage wherever it goes—and sometimes where it doesn't. Rounds fired from the BFG themselves fire additional laser shots at bystanders, and the impact explosion delivers a lot of collateral force. In short, when you shoot this thing, nearly everything in front of you dies. Downsides: *very* slow reload time; yaks up 50 rounds per shot.

Type of ammo:	Cells
Firing rate:	1 round per 3.5 seconds (50 cells per)
Max clip count:	200
Damage inflicted:	up to 500 (500 impact, 1000 detonation)
Effective range:	Medium to Long
Most useful against:	Tanks, Tank Commanders, Gladiators, Iron Maidens, Bosses—hell, everybody

MILITARY SUPPLIES

In addition to your weapons and ammunition, you will be using a wide variety of military supplies and special devices. Some items, such as medkits and armor shards, go into effect the instant you pick them up. Other items, such as the quad damage power-up and the invulnerability device go into your inventory until you activate them.

Armor

Armor takes the sting out of being close—to armed aliens who want to kill you. Specifically, it decreases the amount of damage you take from enemy hits, from falls, and from close proximity to explosions. The hits you take reduce not only your health, but the effectiveness of your armor, so you will want to replenish it whenever possible. Most of them go to work as soon as you pick them up.

Armor Shards--bits of shattered armor that beef up whatever armor protection you currently have in your inventory. Each shard adds 2 points to your armor total.

Flak Jackets--your basic armored vest, adds 25 points to your armor total.

Combat Suit--a more advanced armored tunic, adds 50 points to your armor total.

Body Armor--state-of-the art protection, adds 100 points to your armor total.

Power Shield--high-tech personal force absorption device. Uses cells to dissipate hits from energy weapons. Placed into inventory.

Carrying Equipment

The amount of ammunition you can carry in your inventory is limited. You can increase those limits with two essential pieces of equipment.

Bandolier--increases your carrying capacity for all ammunition except grenades and rockets.

Ammo Pack--increases your capacity to carry all types of ammo. Used immediately and constantly.

Health and Healing

No matter how fast or clever you are, Marine, you're going to take a hit once in a while. Truth be told, you're going to take a lot of them. Fortunately, you will be able to heal yourself and even improve your health with a number of devices. All you have to do is pick them up and they go to work immediately.

 First Aid kit--restores 10 hit points.

 Medkit--restores 25 hit points.

 Stimpacks--provide small boosts to your health (restores 2 hit points). May go over your max health level.

 Adrenaline--jacks up your health points temporarily. May go over your max health level.

 Megahealth--adds 100 points to your health total, but the effect is temporary.

Special Devices

You'll also come across a number of special-purpos devices on Stroggos that will make your life (and your attacks) easier, including

 Invulnerability--similar to the Pentagram of Protection from *Quake*. Makes you completely invincible for 30 seconds. Placed in inventory.

 Quad Damage--quadruples the damage done by any weapon. Two hits with a quadrupled super shotgun will frag just about anything. Placed in inventory.

 Enviro-Suit--similar to the biosuit in *Quake*. Put it on and you can swim in the toxic slime-but only for about 30 seconds. Placed into inventory.

 Rebreather--enables you to breathe underwater. Essential for long swims through sewers and water-filled areas. Begins to fail in about 30 seconds. Placed in inventory.

 Silencer--an underused treasure. Makes your weapons almost inaudible for about a minute. Excellent for sneak attacks and whittling down inattentive groups *a la* Sergeant York. Placed in inventory.

THE ENEMIES

LOOKING AT THE INHABITANTS OF STROGGOS, it's difficult to know whether to refer to this crazy world as a zoo or a used car lot. The Strogg represent no readily definable "race" nor "species." They're more like … appliances. Very mean, very powerful, very hungry appliances. Body piercing has met technology in a big way on Stroggos. Like the man said, "it's a bloody marriage between bone and metal, flesh and machine."

Light Guard--The weakest of your enemies, armed with only a blaster, you can take him out with a couple of blaster shots. Often attacks in packs, finding strength, if not longevity, in numbers. And he will snipe at you from ledges and balconies from a distance that makes him hard to hit.

Weapons:	Blaster
Level of threat:	Low
Damage potential:	10
His health:	20

Shotgun Guard--A better-armed version of the Light Guard, this guy has a "scatter gun prosthetic" and he can do some damage with it. Keep your distance; they like to charge in close with a group and blast you.

Weapons:	Shotgun
Level of threat:	Low
Damage potential:	20
His health:	30

Machine Gun Guard-- Better-armed and a little bigger than his litter mates. He's just as vulnerable, but he can do some serious damage with his machine-gun arm. Also attacks in groups.

Weapons:	Machine Gun
Level of threat:	Low
Damage potential:	30
His health:	40

Enforcer--Big, bald, and burly, this chaingun-armed cyborg tends to charge you when he attacks. There's a limit to the duration of the bursts he can fire. When he gets in close, he'll beat you with his gun arm. He likes groups, and he knows how to duck. When you kill him, watch out for a dying spray of bullets. Also, get out of there fast; the flies are on his corpse like a shot.

Weapons:	Chaingun (also uses it as a club)
Level of threat:	Medium
Damage potential:	3 per round (4-6 if he clubs you with his gun)
His health:	100

Gunner--This is one of the tougher monsters you'll meet early in the game. One arm is a powerful machine gun; the other is a grenade launcher. His attack is smooth and direct, but he's not that tough to kill. Likes to drop grenades on you from balconies. When he launches them directly at you, they scatter, making them very tough to dodge.

Weapons:	Machine Gun and Grenade Launcher
Level of threat:	Medium
Damage potential:	50 per grenade, 3 per round
His health:	175

Part 1: Quake II Basics

Berserker--Whatever this guy is worked up about, the consequences of his marauding rage are not good for you. He can't shoot you, but he doesn't mind taking a few hits on his way to spike and club you to death. Watch out for that hammer, he can extend it farther than you'd expect. And if he connects with it, you will be leaving the ground. He's vigorous, but not unstoppable, so keep your distance and keep firing.

Weapons:	Hammer and metal spike
Level of threat:	Medium
Damage potential:	10-20 per hit, depending on how close he gets
His health:	240

Iron Maiden--She's as tough as a Gunner and twice as mean. With her arm-mounted rocket launcher, and her slashing claws, she gives new meaning to the term femme fatale. She often attacks with a sister cyborg, announcing her arrival with a moan and a screech. The good news is, because she has no medium-range weapons, she's fairly easy to kill. Her rockets are as slow as yours, so you can usually dodge them. Keep your distance from her claws.

Weapons:	Rocket Launcher and claws
Level of threat:	Medium
Damage potential:	10-15 per claw, 50 per rocket
Her health:	175

Gladiator--Now here's a big, tough monkey. Two hydraulic machine legs. Shoulder-mounted railgun. A huge clamping claw. He's vigorous and difficult to kill, and he's a dead shot with that railgun. Up close, he'll switch to his claw. Give this one a wide berth. Use a run-and-gun tactic and a super shotgun (usually three shots up close), or an all-out attack with a chaingun. If you can get him onto some stairs, he's off balance and vulnerable on those weird legs.

Weapons:	Railgun and clamp-grip claw arm
Level of threat:	Medium/High
Damage potential:	50 per railgun hit, 20-25 per claw hit
His health:	400

Parasite--It's not a dog, but it seems to think it is. It's got four legs, a human face, and a proboscis mounted on its back. This little beastie will jump at you from out of nowhere and attack with that proboscis like a canine mosquito. The longer the tube stays attached to you, the more life it sucks away. Needless to say, shoot it from a distance.

Weapons:	Life-sucking probe
Level of threat:	Medium
Damage potential:	about 25 per attack
Its health:	175

Quake II

17

Medic--This is a vigorous bugger, tough to kill with a lot of health points, but his blaster isn't that deadly. The greatest threat from this monster is his ministrations to other monsters. If he comes on the scene, and your newly dispatched adversary isn't lying there in pieces, this cyborg will revive him to fight another day—or right then and there.

Weapons: Rapid-fire laser blaster
Level of threat: Medium
Damage potential: 2 per blaster hit
His health: 300

Barracuda Shark-- These monsters can be hard to kill despite their low health numbers, basically because you have to fight them underwater. In that environment, they move fast and strike hard, and they usually attack in packs. Good candidates for a super shotgun lobotomy. You can sometimes shoot them from shore. This is the only indigenous creature in the waters of Stroggos.

Weapons: Teeth and spiked tail
Level of threat: Medium
Damage potential: 5 per bite
Its health: 50

Brains--Welcome to the night-of-the-living-dead octopus. On the very weird world of Stroggos, this creature stands apart as one of the weirdest. He's very slow, walking with a crippled shuffle, but he's tough to bring down because he sports a green force shield. He's also a croucher. When he gets close to you, he flails his tentacle arms until he's close enough, then he rips open his chest and reaches out with a spray of life draining extra tentacles. Weird. Give him a wide berth.

Weapons: Tentacle arms and
                 life-sucking tentacles in
                 his chest cavity.
Level of threat: Medium
Damage potential: 15-20 per arm tentacle
                 hit; 10-15 per chest
                 tentacles hit
His health: 300

Technician--These floating fire hydrants are almost totally machine. There's an organic brain inside somewhere, floating in a red preserving fluid and controlling the show. Though their movements are slow, they're heavily armed with a shocking prod, a flesh-ripping claw, and a laser blaster. They're easy to hit, but vigorous and not easy to kill before they inflict a lot of damage.

Weapons: Rapid-fire blaster,
                 shocking prod, claw
Level of threat: Medium
Damage potential: 1 per blaster hit, 5-10
                 per claw or prod strike
Its health: 200

Quake II

Part 1: Quake II Basics

Mutant--Now here's a monster nature made … sort of. A product of Stroggos' polluted ecosystem, this once docile animal has mutated into a raging beast. It can't shoot you, but its close attacks are fast and deadly. And it can jump. You'll need plenty of room to take this one down with a super shotgun, chaingun, or hyberblaster.

Weapons: Claws and teeth
Level of threat: Medium/High
Damage potential: 10-15 per claw,
                    approx. 40 per jump
Its health: 300

Flyer--The least of the flying Strogg, this one almost looks cute from a distance. It even chirps to announce it's presence. Then it starts firing its blasters. If it gets up close, it will swing its razor wings and do it's best to shred your face. The blaster doesn't do much damage, but they often attack in swarms and do a pretty good job of dodging fire from the ground.

Weapons: 2 blasters, 2 wing-
                    mounted blades
Level of threat: Medium/High
Damage potential: 1 per blaster hit, 5 per
                    blade strike
Its health: 50

Icarus--Using two huge jet packs to keep himself aloft, this monster attacks with laser blasters mounted into his shoulders. He likes to sneak up and drop down low behind you. He's fairly vigorous, much tougher to take down than the flyers. His armor can absorb quite a bit of punishment. But when he's alone, he's not that tough to kill. He is often accompanied by other Icaruses, and Flyers. Whenever you have the chance, shoot this one from a distance.

Weapons: Rapid-fire blaster
Level of threat: Medium/High
Damage potential: 1 per blaster hit
His health: 240

Tank--He's big and he's bad. Luckily he's slow, too. One of the baddest boys on the block, he carries an arm-mounted machine gun, an arm-mounted laser blaster, and a shoulder-mounted rocket launcher—and literally tons of body armor. (No wonder he's slow!) He can fire any of these weapons at random and do a lot of damage. He's powerfully resistant to most attacks, but launching grenades directly at him often breaks him down significantly. Best advice: stay out of his way.

Weapons: Triple blaster,
                    machine gun, triple
                    rocket launcher
Level of threat: High
Damage potential: 50 per rocket, 30 per
                    blaster hit, 20 per
                    machine gun round
His health: 750

Quake II

Tank Commander-- Another big, bad boy— very big, and very bad! More heavily armored than his cousin, this is one tough mutha. With health points of 1,000, he will be difficult to kill. Quad damage power-ups were made for these monsters. When you do have to fight him, hit him with everything you've got and he will go down. His damage potential is no greater, he's just much harder to kill.

Weapons:	Triple rocket launcher, triple blaster, chaingun
Level of threat:	High
Damage potential:	50 per rocket, 30 per blaster hit, 20 per chaingun round
His health:	1000

The Bosses-- Two of the most powerful creatures in the Stroggos army. One is a Tank creature raised up on actual tank treads; the other is the granddaddy of all flying Strogg. Both are heavily armored, heavily armed with rockets and guns, and extremely hard to kill. Only the heaviest artillery in your inventory will bring down either of these huge beasts.

Weapons:	Rocket launcher, railgun
Level of threat:	Very high
Damage potential:	Huge
Their health:	1000+

The Makron-- Your ultimate target, he's actually two monsters in one. His "mount," called Jorg, is a massive killing machine with dual chainguns and an endless supply of ammo. To kill him, you'll need your BFG and a quad damage power-up. When you do waste him, a new monster will emerge from the rubble. The smaller Makron is actually deadlier than the bigger version. He's quicker and he fires a cutting blaster stream, BFG blasts, and railgun slugs!

Weapons:	Chainguns, BFG, Railgun
Level of threat:	Very high
Damage potential:	Huge
His health:	1000+

Part 2
WALKTHROUGH

WELCOME TO STROGGOS. It's a lovely, warm, and happening place, where the art of body piercing meets technology in a big way. Unfortunately for you, it's also a human flesh-craving society that looks at Earth as its own private meat locker. You and your fellow Marines came a long way to tell our intergalactic neighbors to keep their claws to themselves. But you've been separated from your unit, and the others on your team have been captured or killed. This detailed Walkthrough should help you make the best of your situation. Stuffed with custom maps, secret locations, and strategies and tips, it will be your ultimate guide to the lair of the super-Strogg, the Makron.

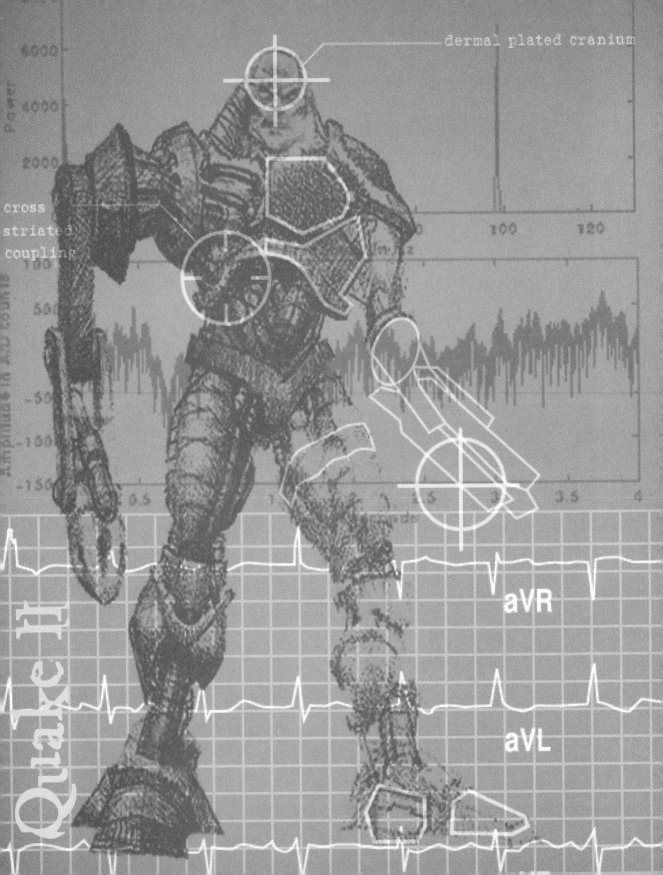

Mission 1
LOCATE THE BASE INSTALLATION ELEVATOR AND ESTABLISH A COMMUNICATIONS LINK TO THE COMMAND SHIP

If you are reading this, your Mark 9A drop pod has successfully penetrated the Stroggos planetary perimeter defenses and you have survived planetfall intact. Your initial objective is to establish a communications link to the command ship. To accomplish your mission you must locate the base installation elevator, use it to access the base sewer system, and make your way to the Comm Center. Command intel reports the existence of a Lost Station, at which local you may have an opportunity to renew or enhance your supplies and armaments. To complete the mission, you must enter the Comm Center, setup the communications link, and exit the facilities.

Mission 1 by Unit Locations

1. Outer Base
2. Installation
3. Comm Center
4. Lost Station (Secret Level)
5. Comm Center
6. Installation

dermal plated cranium

OUTER BASE

Exit
(to Installation)

Secret
(lower
level)

14   13   12

Secret

Window

10   11

Secret
(under stairs)

4

9

2

1

5

8

3

Start   7

to Ⓐ
(upper room)

7a

Upper Room

6 Ⓐ

To 7

Intel Brief

Primary Objective:	Establish a communications link to the command ship
Secondary Objective:	Locate the base installation elevator
Unit Location:	Outer Base
Potential Kills:	19
Goals:	1
Secrets:	3
Enemies:	Light Guards, Machine Gun Guards, Enforcers
Weapons:	Blaster, Shotgun

24

Objective 1
LOCATE THE BASE INSTALLATION ELEVATOR

HEADS UP, MARINE, IT'S PARTY TIME! You've been dumped into Hell and it's time to rock 'n' roll. Your first mission is to establish a com link to the command ship. This part of your mission familiarizes you with a good deal of the structural systems and less hazardous aspects of the Strogg environment. Technically it's a cakewalk, but don't get cocky. Explore every nook and cranny. Search for secret areas stocked with supplies and ordinance. And whatever you do, don't underestimate these cyborg bastards or you're one dead Gyrene.

Objective Summary

1. Start; explosive barrels
2. Entry to lower level
3. Adrenaline
4. Secret Area: Armor Shards, Grenades
5. Crack in ceiling (entry point to upper room)
6. Machine Gun Guards, Shotgun, Shells, First Aid, Stimpacks
7. Light Guard, Jacket Armor
8. Stimpacks
9. First Aid, Armor Shards, Light Guard
10. Machine Gun Guards, First Aid
11. Machine Gun Guards, Shells, First Aid, Secret Area: Silencer
12. Stimpacks (jump through window), Machine Gun Guard
13. Light Guard, Enforcers, Shells, Medkits, Secret Area: Medkits, Grenades
14. Enforcers, Shells, Exit (to Installation)

Mission 1

Quake II

Field Report

1   This is it, Marine. Operation Alien Overlord has started. After climbing out of your pod, pull up your field computer (press F1) to check your primary and secondary objectives, the number of potential kills and goals to accomplish, and the number of secret areas to explore in this god-forsaken Outer Base area. Ahead and to your right you'll notice two explosive barrels. Blast them. The explosion takes out a glass pane at the far end of the room.

2   You now have three options to proceed. You could turn left at the end of the hall, and explore either area behind the blown-out wall (on the left) or the broken door (straight ahead), or you could check out what's in store for you behind the broken window. For now, jump through the window, turn right, and follow the narrow passage to a hole in the floor.

3   Drop through the hole and collect the **Adrenaline** in the corner to your right. Then crawl through the narrow opening on your left. Follow the passage straight through a large, dark area with evenly spaced-out red tiles along the walls until you reach the water.

4   Dive in and turn right, following the wall on your right as far as you can (careful you don't run out of air), then surface to reach **Secret Area #1**—three **Armor Shards** and five **Grenades**. Jump back into the water and swim straight across to the other side. You'll come to a low opening that leads you back into the dark crawl-space.

5   Crawl through the opening and head for the dimly lit area in the far left corner straight ahead. As you approach the corner, you'll notice a crack in the ceiling. Raise your Blaster and shoot at it. The resulting explosion creates a nice big hole through which you can climb into another two-story room of the Outer Base. Careful, there's a Machine Gun Guard waiting for you, trying to shoot you in the back.

6   Turn around and take him out from below, then jump out of the hole and follow the passage between the wall and crates. Turn right, and right again to collect a **Shotgun** and some **Shells**. Straight ahead and to your left is another Machine Gun Guard hiding behind some crates. Surprise him with your newly acquired fire power. Run around the crates and collect the two **First Aid** kits in the corner. Turn left and head up the stairs. As soon as you reach the top of the stairs, turn around and take out the Machine Gun Guard on the upper level of this room, then head up the ramp and collect another two **First Aid** kits, two **Stimpacks**, and some **Shells**.

7   Leave through the blown-out wall. Careful, there's a Light Guard hiding in an alcove to your right. Make sure he gets his before continuing on your way through the narrow passage. Put on the **Jacket Armor**, then crouch down and crawl to the area beyond.

8   Collect the two **Stimpacks** in the corner to your left, then walk through the broken door.

9 Take out the Light Guard at the end of the passage. This area contains another **First Aid** kit and some **Armor Shards**.

10 Ready your shotgun. There's a welcoming party of machine gun-wielding guards ready to fry your ass. Show them how much you appreciate their hospitality. Take out the Machine Gun Guard hiding behind the crates, then collect the two **First Aid** kits in front of them.

11 Walk through the door to the right of the crates, head down the stairs, and kill any remaining guards. Carefully walk down one of the ramps and take out the Machine Gun Guard to your left.

note On the other side of the water, up on a ledge, you'll notice three Stimpacks underneath the banners—you can get them later. Following the water to the right would take you back to the secret area you discovered earlier.

Collect the **Shells** hidden behind the crates and the two **First Aid** kits to the right of the stairs, then crawl underneath the stairs to collect **Secret #2**— the Silencer. Crawl back out and head up the stairs and turn right (left takes you back to the start point).

12 Cautiously walk down the hallway. A Machine Gun Guard is waiting for you around the corner. Take him out and approach the door ahead. As it opens, you'll be greeted by another Light Guard. Kill him, but don't rush in, or you'll be butchered by a committee of Enforcers.

note If you need more health, you can jump through the window on your right as you walk down the hallway and collect the three Stimpacks underneath the banners, then slide down one of the ramps and go back up the stairs.

13 Lure the Enforcers out of their hiding places by entering and leaving the area beyond the door a couple of times. Then take them out, using the door and the crates beyond as cover. As you collect the **Shells** and **Medkits** in this area, watch out for the Enforcers hiding out on the upper deck. Go back around the stairs and shoot the glowing tile in the ceiling to get to **Secret #3**—two **Medkits** and five **Grenades** hidden behind the wall. Crawl in to collect the goodies, then head up the stairs.

14 Upstairs, two more Enforcers are anxious to avenge their dead buddies. Show them who's the boss, then head for your goal. The entrance to the base installation elevator is located around the corner, overlooking the space below. The door to the elevator opens as you approach it. Don't forget to collect the **Shells** at the far end of the upper level before you exit through the elevator.

Mission 1

27

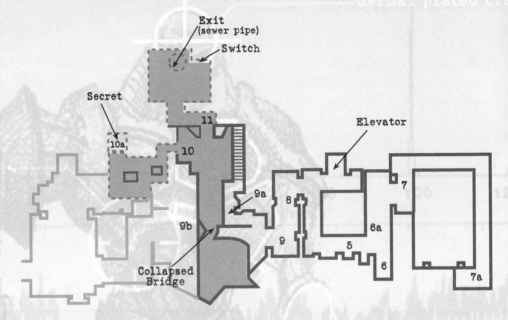

INSTALLATION

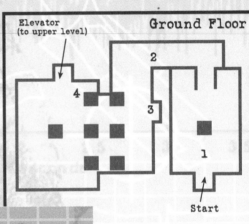

Intel Brief

Primary Objective:	Establish a communication link to the command ship
Secondary Objective:	Use sewer tunnels to gain access to the Comm Center
Unit Location:	Installation
Potential Kills:	35/50
Goals:	1/3
Secrets:	1/2
Enemies:	Light Guards, Machine Gun Guards, Enforcers
Weapons:	Blaster, Shotgun, Machine Gun

Objective 2
USE SEWER TUNNELS TO GAIN ACCESS TO THE COMM CENTER

THIS IS PART ONE OF A TWO-PARTER. You will temporarily abandon this mission objective about two-thirds of the way through to pursue some other important goals. But don't worry. You'll be getting back to the sewers soon enough. Your goal now is to locate the sewer tunnel that grants you access to the Comm Center.

———Objective Summary

1. Start; Light Guards, Machine Gun Guards, First Aid, Armor Shards, Shells, Medkit
2. Enforcer, Machine Gun Guards, Medkit
3. Machine Gun, Bullets, Enforcers, Machine Gun Guards
4. Enforcer, Bullets, Medkits, Elevator (to upper level)
5. Light Guards
6. Light Guards, Jacket Armor, First Aid
7. Light Guards, Bullets, Armor Shards
8. Enforcers, Light Guard, Stimpacks
9. Light Guards
10. Secret Area: Shotgun
11. Light Guards, First Aid, Switch (open sewer pipe), Exit (to Comm Center)

Mission 1

V4

V2

V5

Part 2

29

Field Report

1 The elevator takes you to a large, heavily guarded storage room. As soon as you open the doors, you'll see only one Light Guard. After you take him out, four more appear from behind the crates. Take them out, using the crates and pillar for cover. Stay clear of the left-hand side of the room, or you'll take some serious hits from the Guards on the upper level. When you're done, collect the **First Aid** kits (to the left), **Armor Shards** (on the left-hand ledge at the far end of the room), and **Shells** (right-hand ledge at the far end). You can reach the **Medkit** on the crate on the right by jumping from the ramp (or using the explosive barrels as steps).

2 Advance into the hallway—with caution. An Enforcer is waiting for you at the far end on the right. Using the crates to your left as cover, take out the three Machine Gun Guards around the corner, then collect the **Medkit** across from you.

3 Run to the barred alcove, and hit the access panel to the right to get the **Machine Gun** and **Bullets** behind the bars—but watch your back. You'll have company from two Enforcers and a Machine Gun Guard approaching you from behind. Turn around and take them out.

4 Advance to the room with the pillars. An Enforcer is hiding out in an alcove around the right corner (next to the elevator)—surprise him. Grab the **Bullets** and **Medkits** in the room, then take the elevator to the upper level.

5 Ignore the door to your right for now and follow the walkway instead. A Light Guard is waiting for you around the corner to the left, and two more are hiding in an alcove around the following corner.

6 As you round the corner, the wall behind you slides up, revealing two Light Guards and some **Jacket Armor.** Kill the Guards, put on the armor, and continue down the hallwa, collecting the **First Aid** kits to your left (6a).

7 Make sure you've got all three Light Guards on the upper level of the storage room (the room in which you started), collect the **Bullets** (to the left of the door) and the **Armor Shards** and **Bullets** in the far corner (7a).

8 Go back toward the elevator and take the door to your left. Surprise the Enforcer hanging out around the corner. Approach the door at the far end and prepare to fight off another Enforcer and a Light Guard. Collect the **Stimpacks** at the end of the corridor.

9 As you pass the door, the bridge outside explodes. Take out the two Light Guards hiding around the corner to your right (9a), then head for the water.

note You could jump across the collapsed bridge and clear the area of some Enforcers and Machine Gun Guards, but there's nothing you can do there yet, except get a glimpse of the inaccessible Comm Center and collect some Bullets and Shells (9b). Don't worry, you'll get there soon enough. For now head for the sewers.

10 Enter the water at the bottom of the stairs and wade across to the small opening. Keeping to the right-hand wall, follow the passage and you'll come to a crack in the wall (10a). Shoot it to get to **Secret Area #1**—a **Shotgun**. Go back to where you came from and take the entrance to the sewer tunnel to your left.

11 Follow the tunnel to a room guarded by three Light Guards. Take them out and collect the **First Aid** kit. Hit the switch to the right of the closed sewer pipe entrance to gain access to the pipe. There's nothing else you can do here for the moment, Marine, so drop down the pipe to advance to the next level. And don't worry—you'll be back soon enough.

Mission 1

31

dermal plated cranium

Exit
(to Secret Level)

Secret

5

Start

1

2

Secret

4

3

2a

COMM CENTER

Intel Brief

Primary Objective:	Establish a communication link to the command ship
Secondary Objective:	Locate the Communication Center
Unit Location:	Comm Center
Potential Kills:	4/48
Goals:	0/2
Secrets:	0/2
Enemies:	Light Guards, Machine Gun Guards, Enforcers
Weapons:	Blaster, Shotgun, Machine Gun

Objective 3
LOCATE THE COMMUNICATION CENTER

THIS SECTION WILL HELP YOU LOCATE THE ENTRANCE TO Quake II's first secret level: the Lost Station. We're taking this detour so you can stock up on supplies and ordinance before resuming your mission.

Objective Summary

1. Start; First Aid, Light Guard
2. Enforcer, Light Guards, Armor Shards, Bullets, Rebreather, Shells, Shotgun
3. Hole (underwater)
4. Secret Area: Bullets, Medkit
5. Secret Area: Elevator (to Secret Level)

Mission 1

Field Report

1 Exit the sewer pipe and collect the two **First Aid** kits at the top of the stairs. A curious Light Guard is on to you—relieve him of his miserable life as you turn around the left corner of the door, then continue down the hall.

2 The room beyond is patrolled by two Light Guards (around the corner to the right) and an Enforcer. Ready your Shotgun and take out the Enforcer in the far back of the chamber. Then, using the corner as cover, take a peek and finish off the two Light Guards. Collect the three **Armor Shards** along the wall, and the **Bullets** and the **Rebreather** across the room. There are also some **Shells** and a **Shotgun** at the end of the walkway (2a).

3 Ignore the closed door for the moment. Instead, put on your Rebreather and dive into the water. At the far end of the stairs, you'll find a hole in the floor. Dive into it.

4 Swim along the wall into the nearby underwater passageway which will take you to **Secret Area #1**—**Bullets**, a **Medkit**.

5 Step through the blown-out wall and follow the passage until you come to **Secret Area #2**—an elevator that leads you to this unit's secret level, the Lost Station.

> **note**
> You have two options now. You can either return to the room with the closed door and proceed toward your mission goal, or you can explore the secret level where you can stock up for the missions ahead. Given that you're low on supplies, we recommend you suspend your current mission and find out what the Lost Station holds in store for you.

Quake II

33

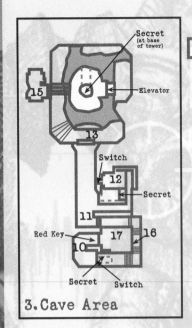

1. Start Area

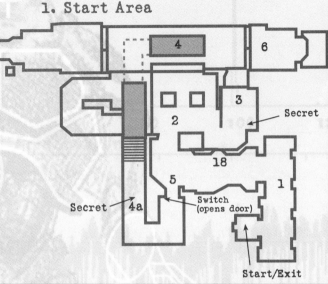

LOST STATION

2. Secret Area

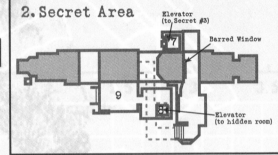

aVR Intel Brief

Primary Objective:	Establish a communication link to the command ship
Secondary Objective:	Locate a Powerful Weapon
Unit Location:	Lost Station
Potential Kills:	65
Goals:	2
Secrets:	6
Enemies:	Light Guards, Machine Gun Guards, Enforcers, Flyers, Parasites, Barracuda Sharks
Weapons:	Blaster, Shotgun, Machine Gun, Super Shotgun

Secret Level
LOST STATION

LOCK AND LOAD, MARINE. Time for some recreational target practice. This level is packed with belligerent Strogg forces out to separate you from your vital organs. There's also a fair amount of ammo, some great power-ups, and a super weapon here. So don't be bashful. Now's the time to load up on the goodies. As long as you stay alert and save your game often, you'll make your squad leader proud.

Secret Level Summary

1. Start; Armor Shards, Shells, Machine Gun Guards, Shotgun
2. Enforcers, Bullets
3. Machine Gun, **Secret Area:** Silencer
4. **Secret Area:** Armor Shards, Rebreather, Stimpacks, Shells, Bullets, Switch (opens locked door)
5. Parasite
6. Doors (to secret area)
7. Barracuda Sharks, **Secret Area:** Light Guard, Parasite, First Aid, Enforcer, Bullets
8. Barracuda Shark, First Aid, Grenades, Bullets
9. Machine Gun Guards, First Aid
10. Light Guards, Switch (raises ramp), Machine Gun Guard, Red Keycard, Armor Shards, First Aid
11. Stimpacks, Enforcer, Machine Gun Guards
12. Switch (lowers wall), **Secret Area:** Adrenaline; First Aid, Armor Shards
13. Enforcer, Light Guard, Flyers
14. Enforcers, Light Guards, Stimpacks, Bullets
15. Enforcers, Super Shotgun, Shells, Medkit, Flyers, Sliding Stone (base of tower), Barracuda Sharks, **Secret Area:** Shells, Medkits, Jacket Armor, Invulnerability
16. Flyers, Switch (raises ramp), **Secret Area:** Medkit; Switch (to exit secret chamber)
17. Enforcers, Machine Gun Guards
18. Enforcers, Flyers, Exit (to Comm Center)

Mission 1

Quake II

dermal plated cranium

Field Report

1 Step out of the lift and grab the **Armor Shards** and **Shells**. Run up to the corner and take out the two Machine Gun Guards that come running toward you. Next, jump up on the crates and grab the Shotgun and Shells.

2 Walk down the hall and approach the door to your right (the door to your left is inaccessible from this side). Open the door and follow the wall to your right. Two Enforcers are hanging out in the sideroom off this tram station. Kill them, using the corner as cover.

3 Walk around the corner of the sideroom and collect the **Machine Gun**. Climb the boxes to your left and jump over and to the right, and climb the small boxes there to collect **Secret #1**— a **Silencer**. Climb back down and return to the landing area. Climb the first crate, then jump across to the second one to collect the **Bullets**.

4 Step up to the ledge of the platform, wait for the tram to pass, then dive into the water pool. Turn left, and follow the passage around to **Secret Area #2**—a narrow passage stocked with **Armor Shards**, a **Rebreather**, **Stimpacks**, **Shells**, and **Bullets** (4a).

5 Hit the access switch to your left to leave the passage through the locked door. Be careful as you exit—a Parasite is lurking behind the door as it opens. Run to the right, turn around, and finish off the critter from a distance.

6 Return to the tram station and jump to the right of the platform, near the doors through which the tram leaves. Wait for the tram to pass and the doors to open, then dash through and jump into the water far below (and don't forget to put on your Rebreather).

Quake II

aVL

7   Fight off the four lurking Barracuda Sharks and swim to the far end of the canal. Step over the small platform on the right and ride it all the way to the top to reach **Secret Area #3**—a narrow room with a Light Guard and a fierce Parasite. Collect the two **First Aid** kits as you carefully walk down to the end of the corridor. There's an Enforcer around the corner to the right with his back to you. Walk up to him and let him have it in the back. Collect the **Bullets** and leave through the water.

8   Follow the underwater passage to a small platform to your right. Kill the Barracuda Shark that's hanging out here and take the platform lift up to a small hidden room above the second tram station where you'll find a **First Aid** kit, **Grenades**, and **Bullets**.

9   Collect the goodies, then cautiously step up to the opening in the wall. Across from you, you can see a Red Keycard guarded by three Machine Gun Guards. Take them out. Then jump down on the crate of the platform, collect the **First Aid** kit, and leave the station through the door.

10 Follow the passage around the corner and up the ramp and stairs. Four Guards are waiting for you near the first landing. After killing them, turn around and shoot the redish-glowing square tile (with your Blaster, don't waste your valuable shells or bullets) to raise a ramp that will enable you to access the room with the Red Keycard. Walk up the ramp and take out the Machine Gun Guard that is lurking around the corner. Next, grab the **Red Keycard**, the **Armor Shards**, and the **First Aid** kit and continue up the stairs.

Mission 1

Quake II

37

dermal plated cranium

11 Collect the **Stimpacks** at the top of the stairs and continue through the two doors. Behind the second door, you'll be greeted by an Enforcer and three Machine Gun Guards. You know what to do. Two more Enforcers are patrolling a narrow balcony immediately to the right. Take them out, then follow the balcony and look to the left.

12 Aim at the impact switch to cause a wall below to rise up. Wait until the wall cannons have finished spitting energy blasts, then drop down and move into the open space below. Drop into the water-filled cave and swim to the far end to reach **Secret Area #4**—an energizing **Adrenaline** power-up. Ride the elevator back up, collect the **First Aid** kit and **Armor Shards**, and continue toward the entrance to the cavern that harbors the Super Shotgun.

13 Cautiously approach the entrance. Behind the door and to the right is an Enforcer anxious to blow your guts out. He's not alone. A Light Guard and two Flyers come to his rescue. Better save and ready your Machine Gun before you enter.

14 Head for the stairs to your left. You'll see a cavern with a moat and a tower in its center. Using the corner as cover, take out the two Enforcers on top of the tower and the two Light Guards patrolling the walkway at the far end of the cavern. When you're finished with them, collect the **Stimpacks** and **Bullets** in the area and underneath the water, and ride up the elevator up to the tower.

15 Open the red door, take out the two Enforcers inside, and collect the **Super Shotgun**, some **Shells**, and a **Medkit**. Proceed with caution when exiting this chamber. Three Flyers have invaded the cavern, trying to avenge their dead Strogg brethren. Try to bring them down from inside the chamber, rather than fighting them in the cavern—you stand a much better chance of survival.

aVR

aVL

note

Before leaving the cavern, drop into the water on the far side of the tower. Shoot the ill-fitting stone door in the tower's base. As it drops, blast away at the Barracuda Sharks that come at you. Then crawl into the space and submerge to find **Secret Area #5— Shells**, two **Medkits**, a **Jacket Armor**, and an **Invulnerability** power-up. Now you can leave the cavern for good. But watch yourself. On your way out, you'll encounter another Enforcer and four Light Guards.

tip

Before you leave, walk up to the lower ledge of the moving ramp that lead you to the Red Keycard earlier and shoot the impact switch above. However, instead of riding the ramp up, jump forward (off the ramp) and turn around to discover **Secret Area #6**—a hidden chamber with a refreshing **Medkit** inside. Hit the red access switch to raise the ramp again and leave this secret chamber.

16 Back in the stairway that lead up to the cavern entrance area you can hear the ominous hissing sound of Flyers. Approach the window halfway down the stairs and take out the Flyers that are swarming above the second tram station. Then head for the station.

17 Head through the door on your right to the second platform and wait for the next tram to catch a ride back to the first tram station. As you arrive, be prepared to fight off a welcoming committee of Enforcers and Machine Gun Guards.

18 When you leave the station, there are two more Enforcers and Flyers anxious to put an end to your mission. Once they're gone you can safely head back through the elevator to resume your original mission.

39

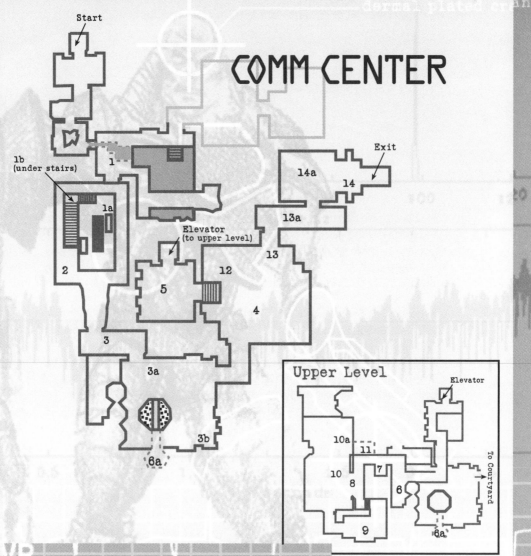

COMM CENTER

Start

1b (under stairs)

1a

1

2

Elevator (to upper level)

12

5

4

3

3a

3b

6a

14a

14

Exit

13a

13

Upper Level

Elevator

10a

11

10

8

7

6

9

6a

To Courtyard

Intel Brief

Primary Objective:	Establish a communication link to the command ship
Secondary Objective:	Locate the Communication Center
Unit Location:	Comm Center
Potential Kills:	44/48
Goals:	2/2
Secrets:	2/2
Enemies:	Light Guards, Machine Gun Guards, Enforcers, Flyers, Parasites, Gunners
Weapons:	Blaster, Shotgun, Machine Gun, Super Shotgun

Quake II

Objective 3 (continued)
LOCATE THE COMMUNICATION CENTER

THIS PART OF THE MISSION CONTINUES where you left off to explore the game's secret level. Before you finish this level you'll be meeting a new type of enemy: the Gunner, a vicious, gun-wielding and grenade-throwing social misfit, who eats mutants for breakfast. Don't come too close to these guys—they can throw a grenade (or two or four) and splatter you into wall art.

Objective Summary

1. Start; Parasites, Shells, First Aid, Enforcer
2. Light Guards, Stimpacks, Machine Gun, Quad Damage
3. Enforcers, Light Guards, First Aid, Bullets
4. Machine Gun Guards, Shells, Bullets, Armor Shards, Medkit
5. Light Guard, Enforcer, Shells, First Aid
6. Stimpacks, Light Guards, Machine Gun Guard, Bullets
7. Enforcer, Shells, First Aid
8. Machine Gun Guards, Parasite
9. First Aid
10. Gunners, Shells, Medkit, First Aid, Blue Keycard, Stimpacks
11. Parasite
12. Gunner, Flyers
13. Light Guards, Machine Gun Guards, Enforcer
14. Gunner, Grenades, Bullets, First Aid, Stimpacks, Exit (to Installation)

Mission 1

41

Field Report

1 At your entry point, swim out of the secret area and up through the hole in the floor. Climb out of the pool and open the door you ignored earlier. Careful, a Parasite will jump out of the opening in the floor (1a) as soon as you cross the threshold of the door. Have your Super Shotgun ready to take out this bug—three well-placed shots should do it. Go through the door and to the right. Crawl underneath the stairs to collect the **Shells** and **First Aid** kit (1b). Be careful around the second opening in the floor—it's the lair of another Parasite. Also, there's an Enforcer hiding out behind the crates.

2 Head up the stairs and finish off the two Light Guards on the upper level. (The Parasite can't follow you up the stairs, but you can take it out from above.) Collect the **Stimpacks**, **Machine Gun** and **Quad Damage** power-up (you can reach it by jumping from the crates across, or by climbing the explosive barrels next it, if you haven't shot them during your match with the guards), then proceed through the corridor up to another area of this complex.

3 As you reach the top of the ramp, two Enforcers are trying to give you a hard time. Take them out, then head for the room to the left and finish off the Enforcer and Light Guards in here (3a). Careful, there are guards on the upper level who have you in their crosshairs— so watch your back and your front. Once you've taken care of these freaks, collect the **First Aid** kits and **Bullets** in the far corner of the room (3b) and proceed through the door at the other end.

4 Around the corner, in the open area, there are four more Machine Gun Guards, some **Shells** (in an alcove to your right), **Bullets** (to the left of the stairs on your left), **Armor Shards** (along the wall), and a **Medkit** (to the right of the stairs). Snag 'em—you'll need 'em— then proceed carefully through the open door into the room to the left.

5 A Light Guard is firing at you from the upper level, and an Enforcer is hiding behind the crates in the far left corner. Watch out for the explosive barrels near the entrance inside as you take them out. Collect the **Shells** and **First Aid** kit in this room, then ride the elevator to the upper level.

6 Follow the ledge to the next room, grabbing the **Stimpacks** on your way. Three Light Guards and one Machine Gun Guard are hanging out in the small room to the left at the end of the walkway. Kill them, grab the **Bullets**, and proceed left through the passage.

note

If you're desperate for another energy boost, jump over the ledge you came from and grab the Enviro-Suit on top of the crates. Then jump on the walkway in the pit to collect an **Adrenaline** boost in the small room (6a). On your way out, put on your Enviro-Suit and hit the switch on the wall. When the slime rises far enough, jump out and return to the upper level of the room.

7 Around the corner, in an alcove, an Enforcer is guarding some **Shells** and a precious **First Aid** kit. Do what you have to do to get the goodies and proceed around the corner to the left.

8 You'll notice a glass pane straight ahead and to your right, and two Machine Gun Guards coming at you. Finish off the Guards. As you step forward a vicious Parasite dashes around the corner at the far end. Don't let it come anywhere near you.

9 Run down the hallway and enter the small room to the left. Collect the two **First Aid** kits and approach the closed door at the far end and to the right. Before opening the door, get out your Grenades and prepare for a serious encounter with the two gunners behind the closed door.

note If you'd rather take them on with your Machine Gun or Shotgun, keep in mind that you can shoot the grenades they throw at you.

10 Once you've taken out the Gunners collect the **Shells** (to the left) and the **Medkit** and **First Aid** kit (below the window). Next, approach the control unit at the far end of the room. When you're close enough, a platform to the right rises, revealing a Blue Keycard (10a). Before you can snag the card, two more Gunners open fire on you from the ledge of the window. Using the installations in the room for cover, take them out, then grab the Blue Keycard—you'll need it to access the alien bunker installation—and head back for the courtyard.

11 On your way out, you'll have to fight off another annoying Parasite. Don't forget to grab the two **Stimpacks** in the small room behind the exploded wall—the former lair of the Parasite.

12 Before dashing into the courtyard, you'll have to face another Gunner and three more Flyers. Use the doorway and crates for cover—your Super Shotgun should take care of them.

13 Head for the closed door across the courtyard and open it with your Blue Keycard. Your new goal is to locate the unit exit and retire all resistance. Fight your way past the Light Guards, Machine Gun Guards, and Enforcer inside (13a).

14 There's also another Gunner hiding on the upper level to the right in the exit room. Shoot from behind the entrance, then grab the **Grenades** from the pipe on your left as you enter the room, collect the **Bullets** and two **First Aid** kits (14a), and ride the elevator to the top. Collect the **Stimpacks** in the alcove to the left and return to the Installation through the door.

Mission 1

Quake II

dermal plated cranium

INSTALLATION

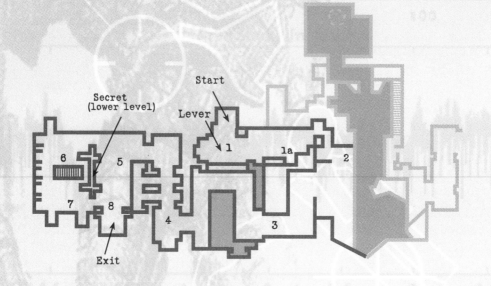

Quake II

R Intel Brief

Primary Objective:	Establish a communication link to the command ship
Secondary Objective:	Locate unit exit and kill all resistance
Unit Location:	Installation
Potential Kills:	15/50
Goals:	2/3
Secrets:	1/2
Enemies:	Light Guards, Machine Gun Guards, Enforcers, Flyers, Gunners
Weapons:	Blaster, Shotgun, Machine Gun, Super Shotgun

Objective 4
LOCATE UNIT EXIT AND KILL ALL RESISTANCE

YOU'RE ALMOST THERE, MARINE. This part of your mission is actually a continuation of your second objective which lead you to the sewer tunnels, which, in turn, enabled you to gain access to the Comm Center. Here you'll fight your way to the unit exit, which is guarded by three Gunners. At this point, you should be an old hand at dealing with these freaks. Your entry point is the Comm Center.

───────Objective Summary

1. Start; Lever (lowers bridge), Bullets, Light Guard, First Aid
2. Enforcer, Flyers, Medkit
3. Enforcers, Machine Gun Guards, Shells, Stimpack
4. Machine Gun Guards, Bullets, Stimpack
5. Gunners, Shells
6. Stimpacks, Secret Area: Super Shotgun, Shells; Light Guards
7. Quad Damage
8. Light Guard, Exit

Mission 1

Quake II

dermal plated cranium

Field Report

1 At your entry point, immediately push the lever straight ahead to lower a bridge that will enable you to reach the unit exit, then collect the **Bullets** along the wall to your right. Proceed through the door at the far end of the center. As you approach the door, a Light Guard dashes out from an alcove on the right (1a). Take him out (but watch out— you're next to an explosive barrel!) and collect the two **First Aid** kits to your left.

2 Follow the corridor until you reach an open-air area. You're now on the other side of the collapsed bridge, where you'll have to fight off an Enforcer (hiding out in an alcove to your right) and three Flyers. Collect the **Medkit** in the alcove to your right and proceed through the corridor to your right.

3 Fight off the Enforcers and Machine Gun Guards who are trying to give you a hard time as you're approaching the final room in this mission. When they're history grab the **Shells** and cross the bridge to bag more **Shells** and two **Stimpacks**.

4 Open the door and kill the two Machine Gun Guards in the corridor beyond. Collect the **Bullets** to your right (as you enter) and head down the hallway. Before crossing the door at the end and to your left, there's another **Stimpack** hidden in the darkness of the corner.

5 There are two Gunners in the room to your left. Take out your Grenades and make sure they get theirs, using the door-way as your cover. Straight ahead, at the far end of the room, another Gunner is lurking behind the wall. Apply the same strategy to finish him off, then collect the **Shells** next to his hideout.

6 At the far end of the room, behind the two support columns, you'll notice stairs leading down into an underground area. Grab the two **Stimpacks** at the top of the stairs, drop down, and follow the cramped passageway to the right until you come to the last **Secret Area** in this part of the mission—a **Super Shotgun** and some **Shells.** Take out the four envious Shotgun Guards that come dashing at you, then head back upstairs.

7 Climb the crates on your right to claim the **Quad Damage** power-up.

8 Finish off the Light Guard that crosses your path as you're heading for the exit on your right. Hit the access switch on your right to leave the Installation through the elevator. Congratulations, Marine. Mission accomplished. HOO-hah!

Mission 1

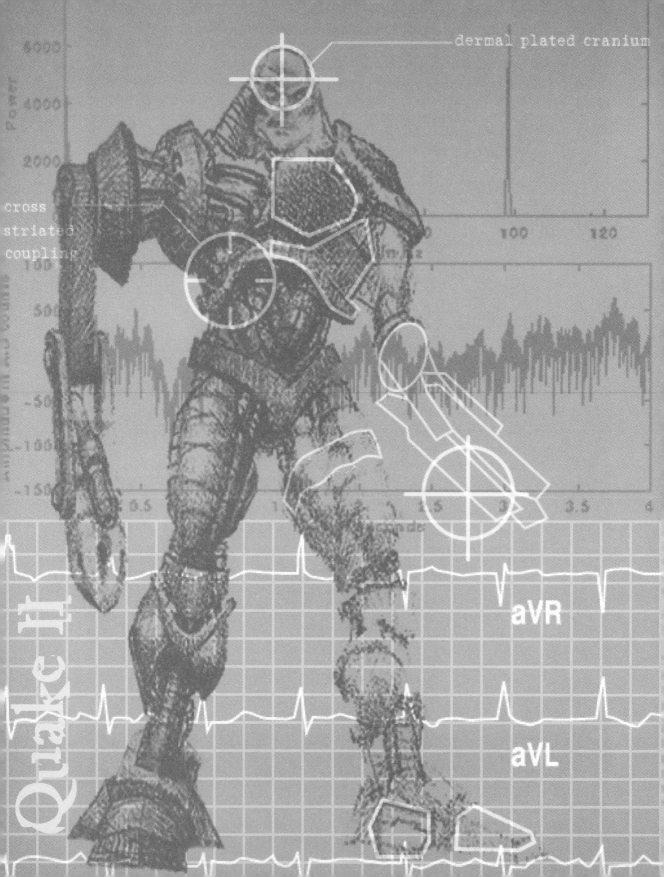

Mission 2
DESTROY THE STROGG LOGISTICAL TRAIN

Your next target is the Strogg transportation system, primarily the logistical train. The Supply Station is your primary target area. Begin at the Ammo Depot, where the entrance to the station is located. Disable the train and inflict as much damage as possible. When you've accomplished your objective, evacuate through the Strogg Warehouse. Intel reports that power is down in these facilities, so you must locate four power cubes to restore power to that area and get out alive.

Mission 2 by Unit Locations

1. Ammo Depot
2. Supply Station
3. Ammo Depot/Warehouse

21

20

19

22

18

23
21 Secret

17a

17 16 24

25

Secret

11 12

10
9

8
Elevator

15

26

A
(to exit area)

14 13

6

Extended
Bridge
7
Elevator
Ladder

7a 5

4

3a

3

2 1

Secret

1a

Start

AMMO DEPOT

Exit

Exit Area

27
A

28
Ladder

Intel Brief

Primary Objective:	Destroy Strogg logistical train
Secondary Objective:	Find entrance to Supply Station
Unit Location:	Ammo Depot
Potential Kills:	68/71
Goals:	0/2
Secrets:	3/3
Enemies:	Light Guards, Machine Gun Guards, Enforcers, Technicians, Berserkers
Weapons:	Blaster, Shotgun, Machine Gun, Super Shotgun, Chaingun

Quake II

Objective 1
FIND THE ENTRANCE TO THE SUPPLY STATION

WHAT ARE WAITING FOR? You've succeeded in hauling your ass deep into Strogg territory, and you've managed to set up a com link, but the job ain't over, Marine. Your next objective is the ammo depot. While you're there snag yourself a chaingun and show the bad guys how a Marine slices and dices. And for cripe's sake, watch out for the Berserkers. They're crazier than a boot camp drill sergeant.

Objective Summary

1. Start; Machine Gun Guards, Super Shotgun, Grenades
2. Secret Area: Quad Damage
3. Enforcers, Shells, First Aid, Grenades, Bullets, Machine Gun Guards, Technician
4. Stimpacks, First Aid
5. Machine Gun Guards, Light Guards
6. First Aid, Light Guard, Machine Gun Guard, Shells, Bullets, Grenades
7. Switch (extends bridge), First Aid
8. Berserker, Shells, Bullets, Stimpacks
9. Light Guards, Machine Gun Guard, Berserker, Technician
10. Enforcer, Berserker, Shells, Bullets, First Aid
11. Enforcer, Switch (crashing pod), Switch (to Secret Area)
12. Secret Area: Bullets, First Aid, Stimpack
13. Machine Gun Guard, First Aid
14. Grenades, Machine Gun Guard, Shells, First Aid
15. Berserkers, Machine Gun Guards
16. Berserkers, Machine Gun Guard, Light Guard
17. Shells, Jacket Armor, Bullets, Medkit
18. Elevator to Berserker
19. Machine Gun Guards, Light Guard, Stimpacks, Bullets
20. Berserker
21. Secret Area: Grenades, First Aid, Elevator to Chaingun
22. Machine Gun Guards, Shells, First Aid
23. First Aid, Barracudas, Light Guards
24. Shells, Switch (to open opposite door)
25. Berserker, Machine Gun Guards
26. Berserker, Shells, First Aid
27. Enforcer, Machine Gun Guard
28. Machine Gun Guards, Switch (to open door)
29. Enforcer, Berserker, Exit (to Supply Station)

Mission 2

Field Report

1 Step out of the elevator and kill the Machine Gun Guard rushing you at one o'clock. Hold on to your Machine Gun and drop over the side of the ledge to the level below. Nail the guard down here. Grab the **Super Shotgun** (1a) in the corner, and collect the Grenades next to the explosive barrel. Hit the switch near the right-hand corner and ride the elevator back up.

2 Approach the door to the next room, turn around, and look up on the ceiling. In the far corner, you'll notice an impact switch. Blast it and grab the **Quad Damage** power-up inside the **Secret Area #1** on your right.

3 Proceed through the door to the next room. As you walk down the stairs to your right, ready to collect the goodies, the wall behind you lowers revealing two Enforcers, some **Shells**, and a **First Aid** kit. Show them how much you appreciate them, then shoot the explosive barrels to find some **Grenades** (3a). Collect the **Bullets** and **Shells** on the floor, then hit the switch behind the crate at the bottom of the stairs to open the door to the next room. Three Machine Gun Guards come rushing toward you. Finish them off, then concentrate on the howling Technician in the next room—four or five well-placed Super Shotgun blasts should take care of him.

4 Ignore the annoying howling of another Technician and collect the row of **Stimpacks** in the next room, as well as the **First Aid** kit behind the crates in the far left corner. Hold on to your Shotgun, then take a deep breath and hit the switch to the right of the next door to open it.

5 Fight off the two Machine Gun Guards beyond the door. From the door, also take out the two Light Guards that are patrolling the upper walkway to your right.

6 When you're done, look down to the right of the door. You'll notice some **First Aid** kits on top of the crates. Drop down and collect them, while fighting off the Light Guard and two Machine Gun Guards that are hiding behind the crates. Search the entire floor for more **Shells**, **Bullets**, and **Grenades** that are hidden between the crates. Before leaving, hit the switch on the wall, then lower the lift in the back by activating the nearby switch.

7 Upstairs, take the elevator at the opposite end of the door to the upper walkway and activate the switch to your left. This will extend the bridge below so you can proceed to the next room. Turn around and jump on the crates below to collect a **First Aid** kit (7a), then cross the bridge and enter the door. Jump down to the bridge and open the door—Super Shotgun in hand.

8 Fight off the Berserker in the corridor beyond. You can reload your guns with the **Shells** and **Bullets** in the alcoves to the left and right of the door, then collect the row of **Stimpacks** as you follow the corridor to the next room.

9 Carefully peek around the corner. There are several Light and Machine Gun Guards, a Berserker, and another Technician ready to cut you into bite-size pieces. You'll also notice two Light Guards patrolling along an upper level area. First take out the forces that come rushing you from the room, then aim your Shotgun at the explosive barrels on the upper level to finish off the Light Guards there.

10 Next, go after the Enforcer and the Berserker who are guarding some **Shells**, **Bullets**, and **First Aid** kits in the small, dark room to your left.

11 When you've stocked up, finish off the Enforcer on the ledge behind the force field, then blast the impact switch on the wall behind him. This will lower the force field, enabling you to climb the stairs and hit the switch that activates the "crashing" cargo pod suspended on the cargo crane.

12 Before leaving the platform, hit the switch to your right to enter **Secret Area #2** on your left (in the corridor) that contains **Bullets**, a **First Aid** kit, and a **Stimpack**.

13 Make sure you cleared the storage chamber (9) of all supplies, then leave through the hole in the wall, watching out for the Machine Gun Guard lurking beyond. Grab the **First Aid** kits, then open the door to your right.

14 Climb the crates on your left and grab the **Grenades** on top. A Machine Gun Guard is lurking behind a crate in front of you. Toss a Grenade in his direction and watch him fly through the room. Load up on the **Shells** and **First Aid** kit and approach the door at the other end of the room.

note The wall behind you slides up when the door opens, revealing a ladder. Ignore it for now—you have more important business to attend to.

15 Fight off the two Berserkers that come for you, then surprise the two Machine Gun Guards lurking behind the crates in the small hallway before opening the next door.

16 Be prepared to take on two more Berserkers that rush you, as well as a Machine Gun Guard to the right and two Light Guards on the upper walkway. More fiends in the storage area below.

Mission 2

53

17 Drop on the first crate next to the door, and use some Grenades and your Super Shotgun to take them out. (Don't worry, the Berserkers can't get to you as long as you squeeze yourself into the corner.) When all is quiet on the western front, collect the goodies and proceed through the lower-level door in the far corner (17a).

18 Follow the howling Berserker sound to the end of the narrow passage. Push the switch on the right to open the door, and take the lift to the upper level. Once on top, step up to the ledge and look below. You'll notice two noisy Berserkers standing there. Look up again, and you'll notice two crates that happen to be placed right above them. Hit the switch in the center to drop the crates and shut them up. Now drop through the floor, and collect the **Shells**, **Grenades**, and **First Aid** kits. Drop through the floor again and take the lift back up. Walk across the room and take the other lift down (you have to push the nearby button first).

19 Blast the Machine Gun Guard that greets you at the bottom and proceed through the next door to a room with two Machine Gun Guards (one on each side of the door) and a Light Guard on an upper-level walkway. Take no prisoners. Collect the **Stimpacks** and head for the **Bullets** at the other end of the room.

20 Before you can reach the supplies, a Berserker will come after you. Turn around and run for the switch to the left of the door. Once you activate it, the walkway will lower and the Berserker will melt in hot lava—provided you were fast enough.

21 Wait for the suspension to rise again, cross the bridge and jump off the platform to your right to enter **Secret Area #3**, which reveals **Grenades**, a **First Aid** kit, and an access way to an elevator that takes you to a hidden **Chaingun** and two more **First Aid** kits.

> **note**
>
> For those of you who enjoy fragging their friends and foes during deathmatches, the switch up here lowers the walkway into the lava.

22 Jump down to the walkway (careful—don't get too close to the wall, or you'll lower the walkway just when you're about to drop) and fight off the Machine Gun Guards that attack you from the corridor ahead. Rummage through the alcoves, and you'll also find some **Shells** and **First Aid** kits.

23 Follow the corridor to the end and around the corner, and you'll be rewarded with more **First Aid** kits. Dive into the water and swim through the broken mechanical door. Barracuda alert! Nail this dentally challenged guppy with your Chaingun, then surface and fight off the guards that have you in their crossfire.

24 Next, climb the floating crates until you reach the small chamber with the **Shells.** Hit the switch to open the door at the other end of the flooded hall, and make your way across, using the crates as stepping stones. Collect the **Grenades** underneath the platform, then use the nearby crates to climb the platform and enter the door.

25 Frag the approaching Berserker with your Chaingun, then pick off the Machine Gun Guards on the upper level at the end of the corridor. Take the lift upstairs.

26 There's another Berserker guarding some **Shells** and a **First Aid** kit in the dark alcove to the left. Snag the items, then proceed through the door opposite the alcove.

27 Watch out for the Enforcer on the bridge and the Machine Gun Guard to your left.

28 Kill any resistance in the next room, and note the top of the ladder you first saw in the small chamber on the floor below. Climb inside and hit the switch on the wall to open the door around it.

note   If you happen to fall below at some point, it will take ages to get back up here any other way.

29 Follow the corridor to the end and open the door. Take out the Enforcer and his Guards, then turn left (you can't do anything in the Warehouse to the right, yet) and proceed through the door down the ramp. Ignore the howling, imprisoned Berserker in the cell on your right for the time being, and exit through the Supply Station doors.

Mission 2

55

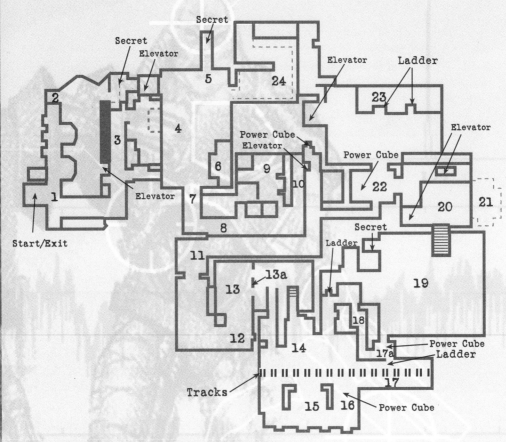

SUPPLY STATION

Intel Brief

Primary Objective:	Destroy Strogg logistical train
Secondary Objective:	Collect the four power cubes to restore power to the warehouse
Unit Location:	Supply Station
Potential Kills:	47
Goals:	5
Secrets:	3
Enemies:	Light Guards, Machine Gun Guards, Enforcers, Gunners, Berserkers
Weapons:	Blaster, Shotgun, Super Shotgun, Chaingun

Objective 2
COLLECT FOUR POWER CUBES

THE POWER IS DOWN IN THE AMMO DEPOT, and you can't complete your mission without the juice. In this case, you'll be squeezing four power cubes, which you must first locate and then deploy. Along the way, you'll also have a chance to execute your primary objective: taking out the Strogg logistical train. Good luck, Marine.

Objective Summary

1. Start; Machine Gun Guards, Gunner, Bullets, First Aid
2. Secret Area: Combat Armor
3. Elevator
4. Gunners, Light Guards
5. Moving crate Secret Area: Quad Damage
6. Switch (open door below)
7. Bullets, First Aid, Machine Gun Guards, Light Guard
8. Berserker, Light Guards
9. Chaingun, Berserkers
10. Machine Gun Guards, Bullets, Switch (activates elevator), Power Cube
11. Shells, Bullets, Gunner, Jacket Armor
12. Switch (causes floor to lower)
13. Switch (rolls crate)
14. Enforcers, Gunner
15. Switch (disables train)
16. Switch (disables tracks), Power Cube
17. Floor Switch (lowers ladder), Power Cube, Armor Shards, Grenades
18. Light Guard, Gunners
19. Enforcers, Machine Gun Guards, Shells, First Aid, Secret Area: Mega-Health
20. Switch, Light Guards, Grenades, First Aid
21. Berserker, Enforcer, Switch (starts elevators), Bullets, Shells
22. Enforcer, Power Cube
23. Light Guards, Gunners, Grenades, Shells, First Aid, Berserker
24. Machine Gun Guards, Berserker, First Aid, Shells, Super Shotgun, Exit (to Ammo Depot)

Mission 2

Strogg

57

Field Report

1 At your entry point, turn left and frag the approaching Machine Gun Guards. Using your inside of your entry point and the crates on the deck as cover, take out the Machine Gun Guards and Gunner on the other side, while trying to avoid his Grenades—Man, this dude can throw!

2 Stock up on your health items and ammo, then step up to the ledge at the far left side of the deck and drop to the ground below. Turn right and head for the wall across from you. Push on the wall to access **Secret Area #1**—and some **Combat Armor**.

3 Grab the armor and take the lift outside and to your left to the top where the Gunner was wreaking havoc. Follow the corridor and enter the room ahead.

4 Lob a few Grenades into the area below to take out the unsuspecting Gunners and Guards there, while covering yourself against the Light Guards that are shooting at you from the upper deck across the room.

5 When they're history, jump onto the moving crate below, crouch, and ride it until it starts to enter the wall in the far left corner. You need to jump into the space ahead to find **Secret Area #2** and a **Quad Damage** power-up.

note

Jumping on the moving crate is tricky. If you miss the crate, hit the switch on the right-hand side of the alcove to activate an elevator that will take you back up to the entry point of this room. Try again. Also, prepare to fight off more Guards when you drop on the floor in the area below.

6 When the crate leaves the space, jump down and head for the stack of crates next to the upper deck where the Light Guards used to patrol. Using the crates, climb to the deck and hit the switch to open the door below on the left.

7 Jump down and collect the **Bullets** and **First Aid** kits below, then proceed through the now open door. Duck the sniper fire straight ahead (he's on top of the crates on the right) and take out the two Machine Gun Guards that rush you.

8 Fight off the Berserker around the corner and take out the Light Guards that are lurking on the platform above and to your right and on the crates at the far end of the room, respectively.

9 Cautiously proceed along the wall— there are some **Bullets** next to the crates to your left. At your next turn, you'll see a **Chaingun**. When you grab it, the wall behind you comes down, releasing two Berserkers. Frag them with your new fire power.

10 Continue around the corner to your left and surprise the Machine Gun Guards hiding there. Replenish your Chaingun with the **Bullets** along the crates. Activate the switch at the far end on the left and ride the lift to the top to collect your first **Power Cube**. Immediately the room will turn dark.

11 Follow the passageway to the next door. Collect the **Shells** and **Bullets** next to the crates and proceed through the door to the room beyond. You'll see a **Jacket Armor** on the crate straight ahead. Don't rush to it. Take out the Gunner hiding behind the crates around the corner first.

12 When he's dead, collect the armor, then push the switch at the end of the room to cause the floor to lower.

13 Push the switch on your left to get a crate to roll toward the double doors on your left. Follow behind it, and activate the switch inside and on the right (13a) of the next room to permanently open one of the doors.

14 Jump on the conveyor belt below and open the door at the end. Turn left and frag the Enforcers patrolling the station outside. Looking to the other side, you'll notice the head of a Gunner peeking out of a Control Room. Take him out with your Super Shotgun, while ducking his Grenades and fire power.

15 When he's history, jump across the tracks—careful, if you slip, you're fried. (The tracks themselves are deadly.) Walk around the corner and hit the switch to complete your Primary Unit Objective— the train is disabled.

Mission 2

59

16 Head for the other part of the room and hit the second switch to retrieve another **Power Cube**, and disable the tracks as well.

17 Walk along the tracks toward the train, and hit the floor switch underneath the train to lower a ladder. Crawl to the other side of the tracks and climb the ladder to collect another **Power Cube** and some **Armor Shards** (17a). Leave this chamber through the slope on your left and follow the narrow passage to some **Grenades** and another room.

18 Crouch and open fire on the Light Guard and two Gunners on the deck above. When they're dead, drop into the room, and climb the ladder to reach the ledge above.

19 The storage room in the back hides a bunch of Enforcers and Machine Gun Guards. Try to keep your cool as you fight them off, collecting the **Shells** and **First Aid** kits as you progress. There's also **Secret Area #3** with a **Mega-Health** power-up inside the crawlspace in the left-hand corner.

20 When you're save, push the switch underneath the hanging crate and walk down the stairs. Take out the two Light Guards patrolling this room, then collect the **Grenades** and **First Aid** kit inside.

21 Next, step onto the lift on your left and ride it down. Ready your Super Shotgun for the lurking Berserker downstairs, then take out the Enforcer firing at you from the room on your right. Climb the ladder and push the switch to your left to start two lifts that will take you back up to the ledge above the stairs. Before you leave the area, collect the **Bullets** and **Shells** by jumping from the ledge with the switch to the crates in the center of the room. Jump from crate to crate until you have all the goodies.

22 Upstairs, jump off the lift and open the door to your right. Frag the Enforcer inside and grab the final **Power Cube**. Immediately the doors on your right will open.

23 Take out the two Light Guards on the upper level and run for the ladder. Upstairs, pull out some Grenades and finish off the Gunners below. Using the crates as stepping stones, collect the **Grenades**, **Shells**, and **First Aid** kits, then hit the switch on the upper ledge to open the other door below. Before leaving, jump on the crates along the wall to grab more **Shells** and **First Aid** kits, then approach the lift behind the door you just opened. Watch your back, a Berserker is trying to cut you off! Shotgun him, then use the lift.

24 Upstairs, take out the two Machine Gun Guards, then continue around the corner and downstairs. Another Berserker is hiding in the narrow passage below. Slice and dice him with your Super Shotgun, then collect the **First Aid** kits along the wall and the **Shells** and **Super Shotgun** in the room beyond. Hit the switch on the right to open the doors. Activate the switch ahead on your left to ride the lift upstairs and return to the Ammo Depot.

Mission 2

Quake II

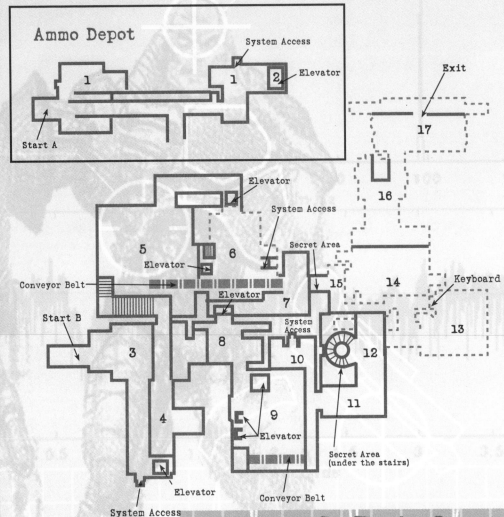

Ammo Depot

Start A

System Access

Elevator

Exit

17

16

Elevator

System Access

Secret Area

Keyboard

5   Elevator   6

Conveyor Belt

Elevator

15   14   13

7

Start B

System Access

3   8   10   12

4   9   11

Elevator

Secret Area
(under the stairs)

Elevator

Conveyor Belt

System Access

WAREHOUSE

Intel Brief

Primary Objective:	Destroy the Strogg Logistical Train (accomplished)
Secondary Objective:	Restore Power to Key Warehouse Components
Unit Location:	Warehouse
Potential Kills:	40
Goals:	3
Secrets:	2
Enemies:	Light Guards, Machine Gun Guards, Enforcers, Gunners, Berserkers, Parasites, Tank
Weapons:	Blaster, Shotgun, Machine Gun, Super Shotgun, Chaingun

Objective 3
RESTORE POWER TO KEY WAREHOUSE COMPONENTS

WITH THE POWER CUBES IN YOUR INVENTORY, you must return to the Warehouse and restore power to four key areas. During this part of your mission, you will encounter your first Tank—a heavily armed cyborg with a whole lot of attitude. The good news is, Tanks are slow; the bad news is, they are very hard to kill. Hammer this sucker with everything you've got, and stay the hell out of his way while you're doing it.

Objective Summary

1. Start; Berserker, Bullets, Shells, First Aid
2. Machine Gun Guard, Berserker, First Aid, Bullets
3. Machine Gun Guards, First Aid, Shells, Bullets, Berserker
4. Machine Gun Guard, Enforcers, Berserker, Bullets, First Aid
5. Enforcers, Light Guards, Machine Gun Guards, Berserkers, Shells, First Aid, Parasites
6. Enforcer, Bullets, First Aid, Armor Shards, Grenades, Berserker
7. Enforcers, Switch (to open nearby door), Switch (to lower nearby lift)
8. Parasites, First Aid, Shells
9. Machine Gun Guard, Grenades, Shells, First Aid, Parasite
10. Gunner, Bullets, Shells
11. Gunner, Bullets, Armor Shard, First Aid
12. Secret Area: Flak Jacket, First Aid, Shells, Bullets, Adrenaline; Parasite, Medkit
13. Tank, Armor Shards, Shells, Bullets, First Aid, Keyboard (to open door)
14. Gunners, Enforcers, Light Guards, Grenades, Parasites
15. Secret Area: Quad Damage
16. Enforcer, First Aid, Grenades
17. First Aid, Exit

Mission 2

Quake

Field Report

1 Back in the Ammo Depot, run through the laser beams to your left into the chamber. Kill the howling Berserker, then grab whatever you can carry—**Bullets**, **Shells**, and **First Aid** kits—and head up the ramp, through the door and across the bridge to the Warehouse entrance. Grab the **Shells** near the entrance, and place one Power Cube in the System Access panel to restore power for this part of the Warehouse. Then hit the switch at the far end of the room to bring down the elevator.

2 Ride the elevator up and be prepared to take on a rookie Machine Gun Guard and, around the corner to your right, a pissed-off Berserker. Collect the **First Aid** kits and **Bullets** in the small room, then head down the ramp and into a new, dark part of the Warehouse.

3 Your first order of business here is to shed some light on the dark areas. From the entrance, turn right and head down the hall to the System Access panel at the far end. Plug in another Power Cube, then return to the now brightly lit entrance area to mop up three Machine Gun Guards and collect some **First Aid** kits, **Shells,** and **Bullets**. Before heading for the lift at the far end of the hallway, sneak back toward your entry point and take aim at the Berserker running back and forth on the upper walkway. When he's history, head around the corner and ride the lift on the left to the next floor.

4 Take out the Machine Gun Guard upstairs and proceed down the walkway—with caution. Two Enforcers and a Berserker will attack you as you pass their hidden alcove on the right. Take careful aim, and don't waste your ammo—you'll need it soon. Once the critters are wasted, enter their alcove to collect the **Bullets** and **First Aid** kits. Next, continue down the walkway and open the door at the end.

5 Don't rush down the stairs. The area below is swarming with Enforcers, Guards, and Berserkers. Drop a few Grenades to do some preliminary cleaning (use the wall and beam to put some English on your bombs and send them to the area underneath your position), then walk sideways down the stairs, shooting at everything that moves. Mop up the survivors with your Machine Gun. Collect the goodies, including **Shells** (underneath the stairs) and **First Aid** kits. As you cross the room, you'll be stalked by a Parasite. A few well-placed Shotgun rounds, and the slimy critter is history. Next, walk up to the ledge and the dead conveyor belt. Take out the Parasites and the Berserker below. If you look to your left you can see another System Access panel.

6 Leave through the door to your left, and surprise the Enforcer waiting for you around the corner. Grab the **Bullets** and run down the hallway and ride the lift to the left down to the lower level (you have to hit the switch first). If you still hear a slashing sound that means you've missed a Berserker. Proceed with caution, while bagging the **First Aid** kits,

Armor Shards, and **Grenades** in this area. If all is clear, insert the third Power Cube in the System Access panel here. Now you can take the lift across from the panel to the next floor.

7 Take the now moving conveyor belt to the next room and frag the Enforcers inside. Continue around the corner, then hit the left-hand switch on the wall to open the door, and the one on the right to lower the lift toward the end of the short walkway.

8 Ride the lift to the chamber above. Take out your Super Shotgun, then run into the room and quickly turn around to take out the two Parasites that are guarding the left and the right sides of the entrance inside. Grab the **First Aid** kits (you probably need them now) and **Shells** and proceed through the door ahead.

Mission 2

Quake II

65

9   Shoot the Machine Gun Guard across the hall (at the end of the conveyor belt), then look over the ledge to recon the area below. Drop a couple of Grenades to soften things up, then jump down and take care of whoever is left. Collect the Shells and **First Aid** kits. Beware of the Parasite hiding behind the crates along the wall to the left! After inserting the last Power Cube in the System Access panel, check your field computer—you've got an incoming message that tells you to proceed to the Detention Center.

10 Take one of the two lifts on the wall to the right to the ledge with the conveyor belt. Follow the conveyor belt to the top and be prepared to take out the Gunner on your right. Collect the **Bullets** and **Shells** near the crates, and then hit the switch at the far left. This will cause a crane set a crate down in front of the locked door. From a safe distance, shoot the crate. It will explode and blow a hole in the door (don't waste precious Shells; use your Blaster).

11 Take on the Gunner in the corridor. After he gets his, collect the **Bullets** and continue to the next room. Snag the **Armor Shard** on top of the crates ahead and the **First Aid** kit below, then push the switch in the donut-shaped alcove on the left to extend a stairway.

12 Follow the stairs to the lower level. Stop at the first window you come to and shoot the glass. Notice the corner of an impact switch behind the crates? Shoot it to extend the stairway below you into **Secret Area #1**, stocked with a **Flak Jacket**, **First Aid** kits, some **Shells**, **Bullets**, and an **Adrenaline** power-up. Fight off the two Enforcers halfway down the stairs, then continue to the secret area to load up, then return to the ground level. A Parasite is lurking in the dark alcove across from the door, guarding a **Medkit**. Blast it, then open the door.

13 Cross the room ahead and walk around the crates to your left to get a glimpse of your first Tank. He's a very bad boy, and the door is locked behind you. Fortunately this ugly S.O.B. is as slow as a snail on Prozac. Using the crates as cover, you can take him out with your Grenades. After you've finished him off, take your pick from the **Armor Shards**, **Shells**, **Bullets**, **First Aid** kits. Push the keyboard behind the crates (where you first saw the Tank) to reopen the door, then hit the switch near the exit to open another door.

14 Take a deep breath, then turn left and fight off the platoon of Gunners, Enforcers, and Light Guards in the next room. Lob a few Grenades into the pit below to take out the Parasites. Jump into the pit, collect the items you need, and take the lift in the corner to return to the ground floor.

15 Next, turn around the corner to the left and activate the switch to get the two platforms moving above the room. Turn around, look up, and shoot the impact switch on the ceiling. Climb the ladder and grab the **Quad Damage** power-up in the **Secret Area #2** above.

16 Using moving platforms, cross the pit to the ledge on the other side of the room. Proceed through the door, killing the Enforcer and grabbing the **First Aid** kit and **Grenades** from the pit in the center of the room. Now hit the switch on the left and leave through the door on the right.

17 Grab the **First Aid** kits in the room beyond the door, then hit the Exit switch on the wall. A part of the wall will lower, making room for you to step out onto the conveyor belt. Mission accomplished!

Mission 2

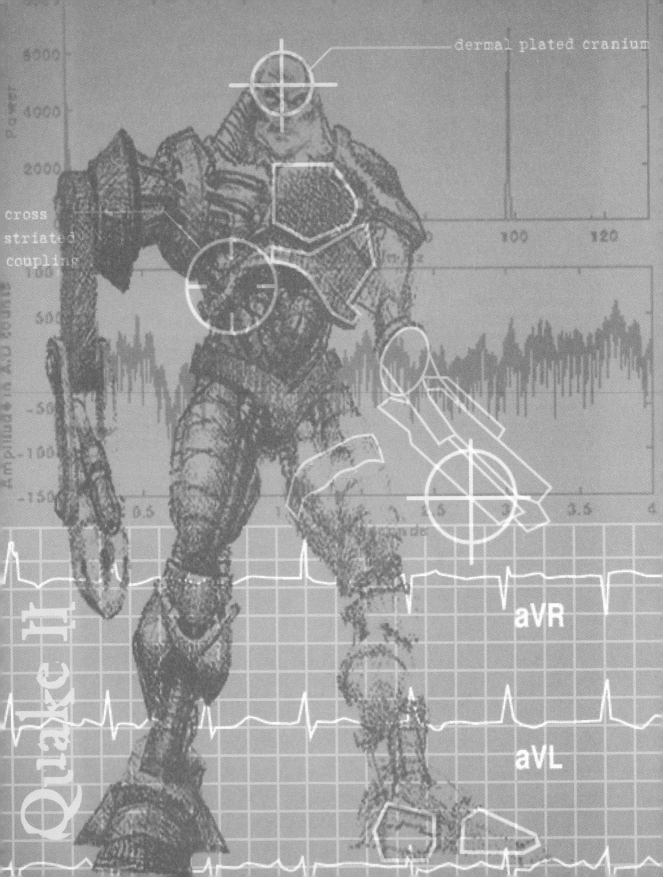

dermal plated cranium

cross
striated
coupling

aVR

aVL

Quake II

Mission 3
DESTROY THE SECURITY GRID PROTECTING THE INDUSTRIAL REGION

Your next mission requires you to penetrate the Strogg prison
facilities. Once inside the Strogg prison, you must locate a Blue
and a Red Keycard. Both devices are required to gain access to the
Detention Center. Intel reports the presence of a laser grid,
which will inhibit your movements. You must deactivate this grid
to reach the Control Pyramid. This access point requires a special
Pyramid key. To pass beyond it to the Security Grid itself, you
will need a Security Pass. Once you have penetrated to the
Security Grid, you must destroy the Grid Control Computer and
exit the complex. Stay focused on your primary objective, but do
not hesitate to exploit as many opportunities as possible to free or
aid prisoners trapped in the Strogg cells and torture chamber.

Mission 3 by Unit Locations

1. Main Gate
2. Detention Center
3. Security Complex
4. Detention Center
5. Security Complex
6. Guard House
7. Security Complex
8. Torture Chambers
9. Grid Control

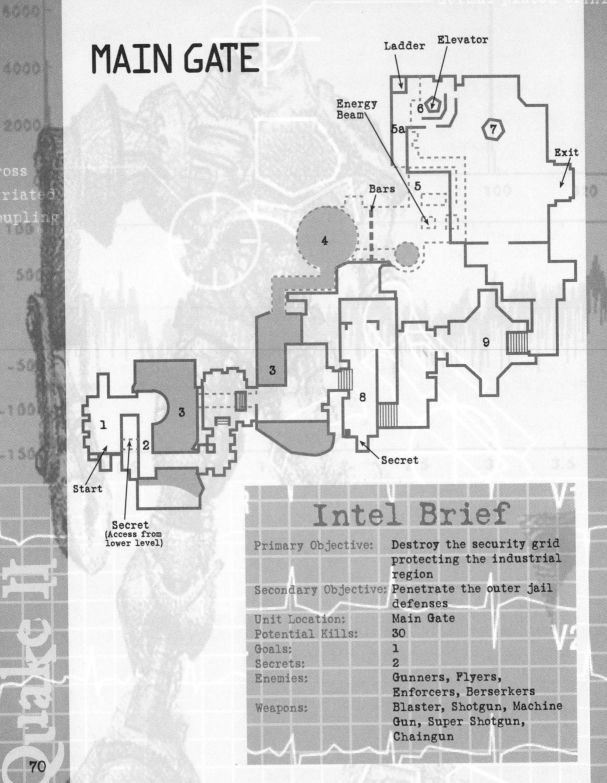

MAIN GATE

Ladder

Elevator

Energy
Beam

Ladder

5a

6

7

Exit

Bars

4

5

1

3

3

2

9

8

Start

Secret

Secret
(Access from
lower level)

Intel Brief

Primary Objective:	Destroy the security grid protecting the industrial region
Secondary Objective:	Penetrate the outer jail defenses
Unit Location:	Main Gate
Potential Kills:	30
Goals:	1
Secrets:	2
Enemies:	Gunners, Flyers, Enforcers, Berserkers
Weapons:	Blaster, Shotgun, Machine Gun, Super Shotgun, Chaingun

Objective 1
PENETRATE THE OUTER JAIL DEFENSES

YOU BEGIN MISSION 3 MUCH DEEPER IN THE STROGGOS COMPLEX. In this region, you've really got to keep your head down and your eyes open. With Gunners, Flyers, and Enforcers patrolling the area, it'll take plenty of luck and Marine know-how to keep from becoming cyborg stew. Your job is to get inside the enemy prison facility, find the key to the Industrial Region's security grid, and kick the damned grid offline—and while you're at it, keep all your body parts intact.

Objective Summary

1. Start; Medkit, Shells, Combat Jacket, Enforcers
2. Shards, Flyers, Gunners, Grenades
3. Secret Area: Rebreather, First Aid; Flyers, Grenades
4. Silencer, Shotgun, Medkit, Gunners
5. Chaingun, Combat Armor, Shards, Machine Gun, Shells, Bullets
6. Gunner, Shells, Floor Switch (opens door to Detention Center)
7. Huge Cannon, Flyers, Exit (to Detention Center)
8. Secret Area: Jacket Armor; Gunners, Enforcers, Flyers, Shells, Fist Aid
9. Enforcers, Floor Laser Beams

Mission 3

Quake II

Field Report

1 As you start this mission, you've got your back against the wall in rather close quarters. Grab the **Shells** on your right and get ready to rumble. As you move toward the **First Aid** kit and the **Combat Jacket**, an Enforcer runs out from behind the crates. Try not to hit the barrel when you shoot him, but hit him quick; you've got no cover. Another Enforcer is waiting in the hallway on the right. Frag 'em both, grab your goodies, and head down the hallway.

2 Open the door at the end of the hallway and turn right. You'll be attacked by a couple of Gunners and Flyers. Again, there's not much cover. Hit the Gunners then retreat back behind the door. The Flyers will hover close outside—you can hear them—and you can open the door and pick them off. Use the Super Shotgun to nail them with a couple of shots. Go back out onto the walkway and pick up the **Shards** on the left, but avoid the obstacle course ahead of you— there's a healthier (and easier) way to proceed. Return to the platform outside the doorway, grab the **Grenades**, and jump over the edge into the water.

3 Swim to the right where you'll discover **Secret Area #1**—a small open alcove with a **Rebreather** and some **First Aid** kits. Next, proceed through the tunnel on your left until you come to an open area. There's a small platform on your right with two **Grenades** on it, but it'll be tough to get to; two Flyers are attacking you from the left. They can hit you under water, so you'll have to use the tunnel as cover and shoot them from the water. (Got a spare Rebreather, Marine?) When you've killed the Flyers, grab the Grenades and head for the tunnel on your left, past where the Flyers were hovering. Follow the tunnel to a wide, lighted shaft, and then surface.

4 Climb out of the water quietly. Collect the **Silencer**, **Shotgun**, and **Medkit**. Notice the Gunner beyond the bars in the next room. You'll also see a circular pool—that's your next destination. To get to it, you have to kill the power that's running a circulating fan deeper down the shaft from which you just emerged. To do that, you have to shoot the red energy beam running through the square, blue power conduits mounted on the wall in the next room. You can see them beyond the Gunner. Your best shot is from the farthest opening on your right. When you blast the beam, the Gunner will notice you, push an alarm button, and start shooting. Worse, another Gunner will burst through the wall on your left. You've got no cover, but you've got to kill him. When he's out of the way, gun the Gunner in the next room. Now dive back into the water and swim down and through the fan blades, and up into the pool in the next room.

5   You've cleared the room, so you can climb out of the pool unhindered. Grab the **Chaingun** and the **Combat Jacket** in the passage ahead. Proceed down the hallway, bearing left. The hallway angles left again. Collect the Shards at the end of the hallway (5a). Take the **Machine Gun**, **Shells**, and **Bullets**. No one should bother you here. Go to the ladder. You'll notice a grate blocking the way. Blast the grate to open the way and climb the ladder.

6   On the next level, a Gunner is on guard duty, but his back is turned so you have a chance to nail him without taking too much damage. Blast him quick, and when he turns, run to the right while you shoot. Grab the **Shells** on the right. The two open hatchways around the corner lead out onto the main courtyard, but the huge cannon in the center of the yard will terminate you almost immediately if you go that way. Instead, take the lift right in front of the ladder.

7   On the next level, you'll find a **First Aid** kit and a **Grenade**. Hit the large floor switch and you'll see the door to the Detention Center opening in the courtyard below. Take out the Guard behind the cannon with a few well-placed Shotgun shots, then jump down and run for the door. Don't waste any more ammo on the Flyers. You can make it. Inside, take the lift down into the Jail.

note

If you feel perky, you can enter the other doorway in the courtyard and take on the enemies in the four rooms you bypassed by taking a dive earlier. But why challenge fate when you've made it this far, Marine? Answer: To find **Secret Area #2** (8). To get there, proceed with caution. You'll have to fight off a fair number of Gunners, Enforcers, and Berserkers, as well as three Flyers, who are hiding in the Secret Area above. When they're history, use the instruments along the wall (to the left of the stairs) as stepping stones to get to **Secret Area #2** and a **Jacket Armor**. On your way back, watch out for the laser beams on the floor in the second room (9). You can shut them off by hitting the switch to the right of the staircase—but you'll take some damage first. Don't worry about wasting ammo or getting hit. There's plenty of ammo and health to scoop up, should you decide to choose this scenic detour before exiting this level. What you should worry about is that you're wasting time while your fellow Marines are being tortured in the Detention Center—your next official stop.

Mission 3

73

thermal plated cranium

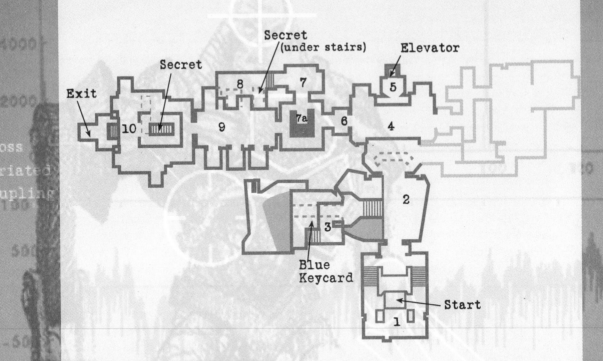

Secret
(under stairs)

Elevator

Secret

Exit

Blue
Keycard

Start

DETENTION
CENTER

cross
striated
coupling

Intel Brief

Primary Objective:	Destroy the security grid protecting the industrial region
Secondary Objective:	Find Blue Keycard and use it to gain access to the Detention Center
Unit Location:	Detention Center
Potential Kills:	31/52
Goals:	1/3
Secrets:	2/2
Enemies:	Gunners, Flyers, Gladiators, Enforcers, Medics, Tank, Medics, Berserkers
Weapons:	Blaster, Shotgun, Machine Gun, Super Shotgun, Chaingun

Objective 2
LOCATE THE BLUE KEYCARD TO ENTER THE DETENTION CENTER

YOU'VE MADE YOUR WAY INSIDE THE JAIL and managed to keep most of your skin. But the job ain't over, hotshot. Now you've got to get into the Detention Center proper. To do that, you need the Blue Keycard. Stay awake in here, Marine. There are some exceptionally bad boys crawling around who don't like Gyrenes—except maybe for spare parts.

Objective Summary

1. Start; Gunners, Shells, Enforcers, First Aid
2. Bullets, Grenades, Tank, Bandolier
3. Enforcer, Flyers, Gladiator, Blue Keycard
4. Berserkers, Shells, First Aid, Gunners
5. First Aid, Gladiator, Bullets
6. Berserker
7. Med Kits, Berserker, Flyers, Grendades, Stimpacks
8. Gunners, Enforcers, Bullets, First Aid, Shells, Impact Switch (raises stairs), **Secret Area:** Combat Armor
9. Quad Damage, Gladiators
10. Enforcer, Tank, Medics, Shells, Grenades, Bullets, First Aid **Secret Area:** Adrenaline, Cells, Power Shield, **Exit** (to Security Complex)

Mission 3

75

Field Report

1 As you move off the lift, grab some wall. There are two Gunners around on either side waiting to nail you. Use the wall for cover and take them out. Pick up the **Shells** on the right and the **First Aid** kits on the left. Continue left and down the stairs. Hang back at the bottom of the stairs; two Enforcers are on their way with an attack from the left. Use the wall for cover and blast them. Be quick, they're moving fast.

2 Go on to the next room. Grab the **Bullets** and **Grenades** on the left. Head to the open area at the right. Hold up at the door. Get ready to throw everything you've got at the Tank on guard at one o'clock. He's slow, but he's very, very tough and heavily armed. You could take him out with a few Grenades, using the doorway and room as cover; or you could try to draw him in after you, slip behind him and grab the **Bandolier**, and then head for the doorway at the bottom of the stairs. (You'll need the Blue Keycard to get into the other door.) He'll follow, but it'll take him a while to get to you.

3 Inside the doorway, take out the Enforcer waiting for you beyond the doorway. The room at the foot of the stairs is where you'll find the **Blue Keycard**. Unfortunately, a Gladiator with a Railgun guards the damned thing. There are also three Flyers in your hair. Time to run and gun. Keep moving, but go for the card immediately. Pounce on it, then put some distance between you and old metalhead, quick!

> **tip**
>
> To get the card and survive, you can apply one of two strategies. You can grab the card and hit the stairs. The Gladiator is awkward enough that you might make it without firing a shot. Or you can jump the wall and hit the water. There's no direct outlet—there's a tunnel underneath the room that connects both water areas—but this move gives you the distance you need to frag the monster and keep your skin intact.

4 With the card in your Inventory, head back up the stairs and turn to the gate on the left—the entrance to the Detention Center. Your Blue Keycard will open it for you. Proceed with caution—two Berserkers are guarding the courtyard beyond the gate. Kill the monsters and collect the **Shells** and **First Aid** kit in front of you. Move inside, but watch for the two Berserkers waiting for you around the corner. Use the center wall as cover and take them out. As you enter the inner courtyard, a Gunner up on the ledge in front of you is lobbing grenades with deadly accuracy. Use the wall as cover and blast him. If you don't, he'll be a problem every time you come back here—and you're coming back here a lot.

5 Cross the courtyard directly to the entryway beneath where the Gunner was firing at you. Take the lift up. Step off the lift into the tiny chamber and collect the **First Aid** kits. A Gladiator guarding the ledge across the way will fire at you, but you can crouch down behind the step for cover while you take him out. (If you don't, he'll dog you.) Go out the window and drop down to the ledge below you. You've already killed the Berserker (if you haven't, get ready to boogie). Grab the **Bullets** stashed there. Now the courtyard is free of snipers.

6 Jump down to the courtyard and head for the door on your right. Hang back; there's another Berserker inside. (If you hang back far enough, you can use the opening and closing door for cover.) If you get too close, he'll come out after you. If he does, keep your distance. Run and gun!

Mission 3

Easy II

V2   V5

7 When you've removed the Berserker, go inside. You'll find a **Medkit** inside the door. You'll also hear the sounds of torture and insanity—the voices of ruined men begging to die. Keep your eyes peeled for another Gladiator and two Flyers that patrol the halls in the area. Move inside, bearing right. You'll see a **Quad Damage** (7a) on your left protected by a red laser grid. Turn into the room on your right, then drop back; a Berserker will follow. Frag him, and then use the doorway as cover while you shoot down the two Flyers inside. A huge grate covers the floor of the room, but you can walk on it without falling through. If you've got the stomach, look down. That's what's in store for all of us if you fail your mission, Marine. Collect the **Grenades** in the right corner and the **Stimpacks** on the left. Hit the switch on the right wall to kill the power to the laser grid blocking the Quad Damage.

8 Climb the stairs on your left. A Gunner and three Enforcers guard the room at the top. Blast the Enforcers and duck behind a crate. There's a Gunner above the stairs behind you, shooting. Blast him, and then shoot the red-orange impact switch on the wall behind him. The stairs you just climbed rise to give you access to that area. Go up and grab the **Bullets** stashed there. The stairs will drop automatically after a few seconds and you can return to the hallway.

To get to **Secret Area #1**, do the following. After blasting the Gunner above the stairs, shoot the impact switch, which causes the stairs to rise. Run to your right, jump down into the cell block, then run to your left (basically circling back to where you started the puzzle). If you're fast enough, you should be able to slide under the stairs and grab the **Combat Armor** before they drop again. Now head back up the stairs and collect the **First Aid** kits and the **Shells** at the back of the room before you go.

note

9 Collect the **Quad Damage** (7a) on your way down the stairs and into the cell block, then head all the way to the end and to the right (away from the entrance). Go right at the door and proceed a short way into the cell block. This will draw out the Gladiator on guard there. Drop back and take him from the doorway. As you enter the cell block another Gladiator will charge out of a cell on the right. Use the same strategy on him. Now stop and look around. It's a scene right out of hell. Nearly every cell holds a bloodied and broken Marine. Most of them have been tortured into insanity. Now's not the time, but later, you'll have time to do the humane thing.

10 Exit the cell block at the far side of the room. Notice the green switch, but don't bother with it right now. Head around to the right. Notice the door on your left leading into the central room. Leave it for now. You'll be attacked by an Enforcer. Blast him and move on. At the end of the hall is a Tank guarding the Exit at the bottom of a short flight of steps. It'll take awhile, but you've got to

kill this oversized food processor. Keep whittling away at him until he falls. (Grenades work well.) When he does, two Medics will come out of nowhere. One will attack you while the other tries to revive the Tank. If you don't stop him, that's just what he'll do. When they're history, collect the nearby **Shells**, **Grenades**, **Bullets**, and **First Aid** kits.

tip

Before you proceed through the Exit door, turn around and hit the green switch on the wall opposite the doorway. The door next to it opens. Go in and hit the green switch on the inside wall. Now go back to the first green switch around to your left. Hit that switch and the door around to your right will open, giving you access to **Secret Area #2**. Enter and collect **Adrenaline**, **Cells**, and a **Power Shield**. To lower the pillars and get back out, you have to hit the green switch to the left of the ramp. Now head back to the door the Tank was guarding to proceed with your mission.

Mission 3

Quake II

V5

79

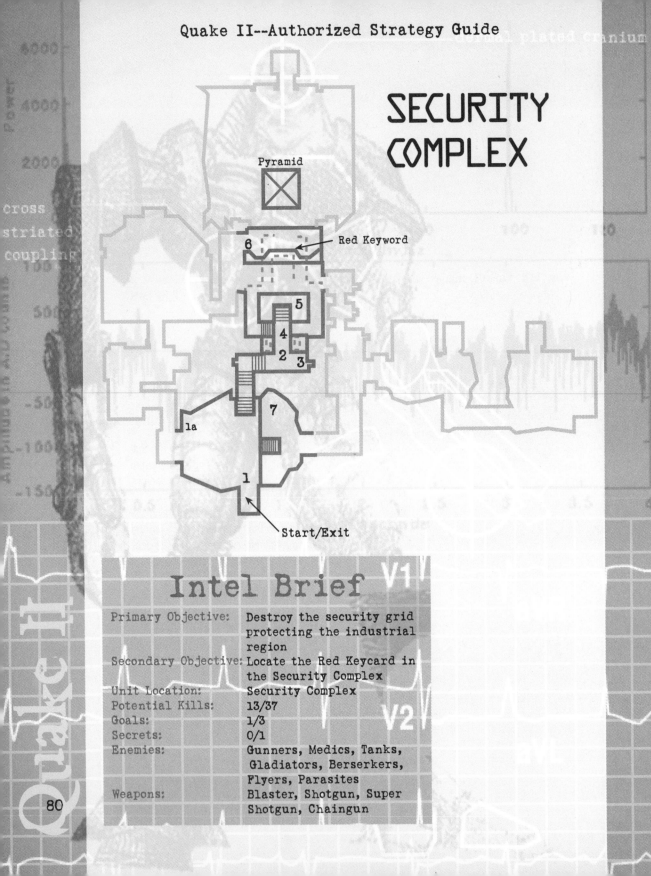

SECURITY COMPLEX

Pyramid

6 — Red Keyword

5

4

2 3

1a

7

1

Start/Exit

Intel Brief V1

Primary Objective:	Destroy the security grid protecting the industrial region
Secondary Objective:	Locate the Red Keycard in the Security Complex
Unit Location:	Security Complex
Potential Kills:	13/37
Goals:	1/3
Secrets:	0/1
Enemies:	Gunners, Medics, Tanks, Gladiators, Berserkers, Flyers, Parasites
Weapons:	Blaster, Shotgun, Super Shotgun, Chaingun

V2

Objective 3
LOCATE THE RED KEYCARD

SECURING THE RED KEYCARD IS A FAIRLY STRAIGHTFORWARD JOB, but it's no cakewalk. There's a crowd of Strogg charm school graduates between you and the card, and they're all set to give you a full-body manicure. Gunners, Flyers, Gladiators, Medics, Parasites, Tanks; just about everybody comes out to play, because that little red card is the key to kicking some serious cyborg butt.

Objective Summary

1. Start; Gunners, Medic, Shells
2. Gladiator, Gunners, Berserkers
3. Shells, Medkits, Gunners
4. Berserkers
5. Bandolier, Quad Damage, Grenades, First Aid, Gunners, Shards, Stimpacks
6. Gladiators, Red Keycard, Chaingun, Bullets, Stimpacks
7. Flyers, Cells

Mission 3

Field Report

1 At your entry point, you'll notice a Gunner standing with his back to you. Look closely and you'll see that he's abusing a prisoner…a fellow Marine…one of the good guys, man! Let the cyborg bastard have it in the back. If you hit him hard and quick, he won't get off a shot. Give your comrade a quick death, then blast the Medic bouncing down the stairs. On your right is a tunnel that leads to a switch protected by a Tank and a laser grid. Even if you destroyed the Tank, the switch, which you must hit to proceed further, would still be inaccessible. On your left a Berserker, two Gunners, and a rabid Enforcer guard the hall beyond the door. Beyond them, another laser grid blocks the way. Your only option is the stairs ahead. Grab the **Shells** by the left door (1a), and climb the stairs ahead.

2 Go down the inner stairs and to your right, but don't go inside. There's a Gladiator, some Berserkers, and a few Gunners in there. Throw a few rounds into the room and lure the Gladiator out. Head back up the stairs and wait for him. He's slow and clumsy on the stairs. You can use that to your advantage. But he's still very tough, and his Railgun is one of the deadliest weapons you'll encounter. Hit him repeatedly with something powerful—say a Super Shotgun or a Chaingun, or some Grenades.

3 With the Gladiator out of the way, grab the **Shells** and **Medkits** at the foot of the stairs. Gunners are shooting at you and dropping Grenades from the ledge above. Hang back and shoot around the corner at them. They'll be tough to hit, but you'll want them out of the way.

4 As you move into the room, two Berserkers will attack. Use the wall for cover and blast them. Remember, if they get within striking distance they'll knock hell out of you. Just back up and keep firing until they're dead.

5 Drop down to the lower level and collect a **Bandolier**, two **Quad Damage** power-ups, some **Grenades**, and **First Aid** kits. Next, dash up the stairs. Even if you nailed the Gunners, more have appeared to rain on your parade. On the upper level, scoop up the **Shards** in front of the large map and go left. Collect the **Stimpacks** while you move down the hall and frag the Gunner at the end.

6 Beyond the next doorway, a second Gladiator guards the **Red Keycard** at the foot of a short staircase. You can either kill him and take the key more or less at your leisure, or dodge him and pounce on the key without wasting ammo on the tough S.O.B. You might try luring him up the stairs, where he's at a disadvantage, and then jumping down and literally pouncing on the key. You might want to snag the **Ammo**, the **Chaingun**, and the extra **Stimpacks** stashed near the key. Also, notice the gray pyramid outside the room. You'll be seeing it again before your mission is over.

7 Return to the courtyard. Three Flyers are waiting for you. Shoot at them from the doorway and take them out. Go down the stairs and straight across to the door leading back to the Detention Center, snagging any **Ammo** the Flyers might have coughed up on the way.

Mission 3

Quake II

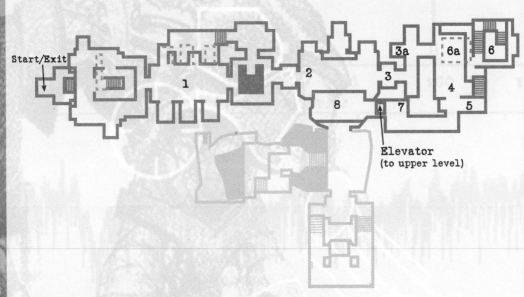

Start/Exit

1

2

3a · 6a · 6

3

4

8 · 7 · 5

Elevator
(to upper level)

DETENTION CENTER

Intel Brief

Primary Objective:	Destroy the security grid protecting the industrial region
Secondary Objective:	Find the yellow laser control console
Unit Location:	Detention Center
Potential Kills:	21/52
Goals:	2/3
Secrets:	0/2
Enemies:	Medics, Parasites, Enforcers, Flyers
Weapons:	Blaster, Shotgun, Super Shotgun, Machine Gun, Chaingun, Grenade Launcher

Objective 4
DEACTIVATE THE LASERS

YOU'VE SECURED THE RED KEYCARD, and now you're heading back through the Detention Center to use the card to deactivate the yellow lasers you spotted earlier. It's the only way to get to the security grid. The good news is, it's known territory; the bad news is, all the critters you croaked before have been replaced. Run and gun, Marine, or the boys in the steel jockey shorts will grind you into jarhead paté.

Objective Summary
1. Start; Medkits, Stimpacks, Shells, Bullets
2. Medics, Stimpacks
3. Medkits, Parasites, Enforcers, Bullets, Combat Jacket
4. Enforcers
5. Parasite, Machine Gun, First Aid
6. Enforcers, Grenade Launcher
7. Enforcers, Parasite, Shards
8. Flyers, Grenade Launcher, Jacket Armor

Mission 3

Quake II

Field Report

1 You've cleared this area before, so you should face no resistance. As you pass through the cell block, this would be a good time to deal with the suffering prisoners. Open the cells by hitting the control panel outside each cell. Quickly and mercifully send your comrades in arms to a better world. Collect the **Stims**, **Medkits**, and **Shells** and **Bullets** they leave behind. Continue on out into the main courtyard.

2 At the entrance to the courtyard, hang back. A Medic is waiting for you out there. Use the doorframe for cover and take him out. Cross the courtyard toward the opposite door. Another Medic will attack from the left alcove. Frag him and collect the two Stims. Go to the door; the keycard in your inventory will get you in.

3 Collect the **Bullets** and **Medkits** inside the door. As you move inside, a Parasite will attack from the right. Dispatch the obnoxious little monster and bear left. Watch yourself! Another Parasite lies waiting in the alcove along the left wall (3a). Kill it and hang back and wait for an Enforcer charging from the right. Now collect the **Shells** and **Combat Jacket**.

4 Go right from where the Enforcer attacked. More Enforcers are waiting, both at ground level and above. (Another huge grate covers the floor in here. A strategically dropped grenade might set some poor bastard free.) Blast your way through the attack and take the door on your right.

5 Hang back a bit and nail the Parasite crouched inside. When you enter, four more Enforcers will attack. All you can do is run and gun. Scoop up the **Ammo** they drop when you frag them and dash up the stairs on your left. Grab the **Machine Gun** and **First Aid** kits you find there.

6 Next, take the second entrance down to the torture chamber. Lob a few Grenades down into the pit to take out the Enforcers, then head for the chamber to collect a **Grenade Launcher** (6a). Behind you, two more Enforcers emerge from a hidden alcove. Introduce them to your newly acquired fire power, then head back to where you entered this area.

7 Continue down the hallway heading left. At the end of the hallway, two more Enforcers and a Parasite will jump you. This is a deadly combination, and a strategic retreat is called for here. Give yourself some room to cream these creeps, then scoop up the **Shards**.

8 Take the lift up to the next level. Be ready to blast the two Flyers hovering right above you when you arrive. There's not much cover here, so move fast. Be careful not to stumble into the laser grid. It'll burn you. Go to the computer terminal. The Red Keycard in your inventory will enable you to disengage the laser grid. Return to the Security Complex.

tip

Before you return to the Security complex, grab the **Grenade Launcher** in the corner. In an alcove above the lift, there's a **Jacket Armor**. Jump across to snag it, then head back all the way to the Security Complex.

Mission 3

V1 V4

V2 V5

87

dermal plated cranium

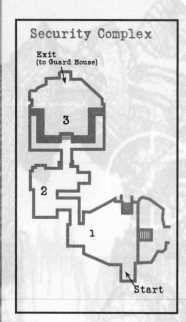

Security Complex

Exit
(to Guard House)

3

2

1

Start

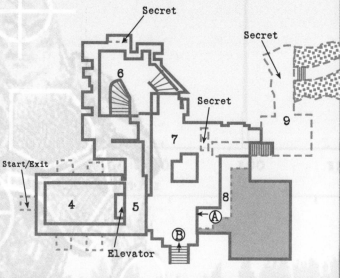

Secret

Secret

Secret

6

7

Start/Exit

4

5

8

9

A

B

Elevator

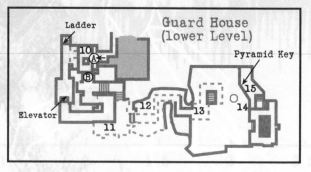

Ladder

Guard House
(lower Level)

Pyramid Key

10

A

B

15

Elevator

12

13

14

11

GUARD HOUSE

Intel Brief

Primary Objective:	Destroy the security grid protecting the industrial region
Secondary Objective:	Open the Control Pyramid and locate the security pass
Unit Location:	Guard House
Potential Kills:	56
Goals:	1
Secrets:	3
Enemies:	Berserkers, Enforcers, Guards, Gunners, Mutants
Weapons:	Blaster, Shotgun, Super Shotgun, Machine Gun, Chaingun, Grenade Launcher, Hyperblaster

V2

Quake II

power

6000

4000

2000

100%

500

-500

-1000

-1500

cross
striated
coupling

Amplitude in A-3 counts

Objective 5
FIND THE KEY TO THE CONTROL PYRAMID

THE YELLOW LASERS ARE OUT OF THE WAY and you're ready to rock 'n' roll, but you've got two more keys to find—or rather, a key and a pass. The key to the Control Pyramid is located in the Guard House complex. To get to it, you'll have to leave the Security Complex and face a swarm of Strogg. Remember: Pain is good; extreme pain is extremely good—especially when you're the one dishing it out. Lock and load!

————Objective Summary

1. Start; Berserker, Gunner
2. Enforcer, Gunner, Combat Armor, Medkits, Grenades
3. Enforcers, Chain Gun, Power Shield, Gunners, Exit (to Guard House)
4. Guards, Gunners, Grenades
5. Gunner, Shards, First Aid, Enforcers, Machine Gun, Bullets
6. Enforcers, Machine Gun Guards, Secret Area: Shells, Ammo Pack, First Aid
7. Secret Area: Adrenaline; First Aid, Stimpacks, Combat Armor, Mutant
8. Mutant, Guards
9. Secret Area: Grenade Launcher, Medkit
10. Hyperblaster, Guards, Bullets
11. Mutants, Guards, Ammo, Stimpacks, Combat Armor
12. Access to water
13. Mutant, Power Armor
14. Enforcers, Tank, Super Shotgun
15. Guards, Control Pyramid Key

Mission 3

Quake II

Field Report

1 From the Security Complex courtyard, take the next door on your left, but hang back or a Berserker will cream you. You know by now to keep your distance from these psycho cyborgs. Drop back and he'll follow you to a space where you can run and gun. A Gunner will back him up, so stay awake and keep moving.

2 When you've finished them off, go through the door and head left. Follow the hallway to a room patrolled by a Gunner and an Enforcer. Blast them, and then put on the **Combat Armor** (you're going to need it), and scoop up the **Medkits** and **Grenades**.

3 As you proceed down the next hallway to the open area, a pair of Enforcers hits from right and left. Drop back and blast away and keep going. Two more Enforcers are waiting out in the courtyard. Nail them and dash to the Marine landing pod across the courtyard on the left. Willits didn't make it, but he left a **Chaingun** and a **Power Shield** he'd want you to have. Gunners are dropping grenades from an upper level, so grab the gear and hustle into the doorway to the right of the pod. You've just entered the Guard House.

4 Inside is a cell block manned by Guards who attack from floor level and above. Gunners drop grenades. You can use the cells for cover, but your best bet is to run and gun. Shoot the Guards as you beat it to the lift at the other end of the room,

collecting the Grenades on your right along the way.

5 On the next floor, get off the lift fast and nail the Gunner on the ledge. Collect **Shards**, **First Aid** kits, and **Stims** scattered around the ledge. Take the hallway left. You'll have to blast through two Enforcers and two Machine Gun Guards as you go. Scoop up the **Bullets** you see along the way.

6 You'll eventually reach the stairs leading down into a dim room. Shoot down at the two barrels you see there. The explosion might take out the two Enforcers shooting up at you. If it doesn't, you'll have to do it the hard way. When you descend the stairs, Machine Gun Guards swarm up into the room from another stairway. They go down easy if you act fast. Notice that the explosion has revealed some Shells, and a small door in the wall behind them—**Secret Area #1**. Enter this secret area and collect an **Ammo Pack** and **First Aid** kit. The pack enables you to carry many more rounds.

7 Proceed down the stairs from which the Guards came. More **First Aid** kits at the bottom. Through the door is an open courtyard. Notice the protruding stone ahead and slightly to your left? Push it and the ramp on the left lowers, revealing **Secret Area #2** with an **Adrenaline** power-up. Grab it and the two **Stims** on your left, and more up the ramp along with a twirling piece of **Combat Armor**. If you go to retrieve the armor, a Mutant will burst through the wall and attack. Get rid of this ugly bugger.

8 Go straight up the ramp in front of you and turn left. Drop down onto the ledge by the water and go to the door to the right. From outside, shoot the raving Mutant inside, and then blast the Guards backing him up.

9 Enter, go down the stairs, and shoot the barrels you find there. The explosion blasts a hole in the door. Crouch down and crawl through the hole into **Secret Area #3**. Grab the **Grenade Launcher** and the **Medkit**. Return to the room above. Collect the **cells** on the left, and then head up the stairs and out onto the ledge.

10 Around the other side is another door. Inside, you'll see a **Hyperblaster** twirling in the air. Collecting that gun could be hazardous to your health. When you grab it, the floor collapses into a spiked pit. (You'll see other Marines impaled there.) If you decide to go for it, you must jump quickly to the wall ahead. Shoot the Guards that attack you next, then take the ladder down into the pit to collect some **Bullets**.

11 Go to the elevator and take it to the upper level. Open the door and then drop down into the lower level. Blast the Mutants and Guards you find there. Scoop up the **Ammo** and **Stimpacks** in the corners, and grab the **Combat Armor**.

12 Go down the stairs and follow the walkway until you find a spot to drop down under it. Try the gaps along the edges as you go; one of them will be wide enough to accommodate you.

13 Shoot the Mutant you encounter, then follow the passage and collect the **Power Armor**. Keep following the passage until you reach the stairs that lead you to another courtyard.

14 The doorway you want is protected by a force field and guarded by Enforcers. Shoot the Enforcers that attack you, then find some cover from which to blast the Tank standing on the high platform. Behind him is the switch that shuts off the force field. It'll take you a while to kill him, but keep chipping away. When he goes down, climb up onto the platform and hit the switch. You now have access to the door. Before you go through it, climb up on the crates in the middle of the courtyard and snag the **Super Shotgun** twirling up there, then scan the area for any equipment or ammo you might have missed.

15 Now, go through the door and head down the passageway. Shoot the Guards you encounter. Take the stairs to the room with the **Control Pyramid Key**. Grab the key and head back to the Security Complex via the courtyard exit.

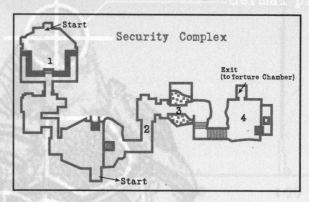

Security Complex

Start

Exit
(to Torture Chamber)

1

2

3

4

Start

TORTURE CHAMBERS

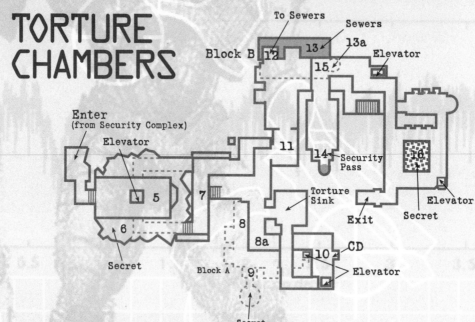

To Sewers

Sewers

Block B   12   13   13a   Elevator

15

Enter
(from Security Complex)

Elevator

11   14   Security
Pass

16

5

7

Torture
Sink

Exit   Elevator

6   8   Secret

Secret   8a   10   CD

Block A   9   Elevator

Secret

Intel Brief

Primary Objective: Destroy the security grid protecting the industrial region

Secondary Objective: Find the security pass

Unit Location: Torture Chambers

Potential Kills: 33

Goals: 2

Secrets: 3

Enemies: Tanks, Icaruses, Enforcers, Gunners, Guards, Berserkers, Parasites

Weapons: Blaster, Shotgun, Super Shotgun, Machine Gun, Chaingun, Hyperblaster

Objective 6
FIND THE SECURITY PASS

THE CONTROL PRYAMID KEY IS ESSENTIAL TO YOUR MISSION, but it's worthless without the Security Pass that gives you access to the security grid control computer. Your mission is nearly completed, but the most gruesome leg of the trip lies just ahead. For some damned reason, the Strogg keep the pass in their favorite playroom: the Torture Chambers. It's probably the last place on Stroggos you want to go, but seeing your hosts' handiwork up close and personal should inspire you to press on.

Objective Summary

1. Start
2. Tank, Cells, Switch (extends bridge)
3. Icaruses, Medkits
4. Enforcers, Gunners, Berserkers, Shells, Bullets
5. Shells, First Aid, Tank, Floor Switch
6. Secret Area: Hyperblaster, Cells
7. Machine Gun Guards
8. Gunners, Guards, Tank
9. Secret Area: Invulnerability
10. Switch (gives access to CD), Data CD, Tank, Gunner
11. Machine Gun Guard
12. Sewer Entrance
13. Parasite, Rebreather
14. Guards, Security Pass, First Aid
15. Shells, Guards, Gunner, Tank
16. Hyperblaster, Secret Area: Shells, First Aid, Bullets, Grenades, Switch (lowers elevator), Exit (to Grid Control Room)

Mission 3

Field Report

1 Backtrack your way to the Security Complex and snag any ammo or supplies you might have had to leave behind earlier. Your field computer is telling you to return to the Control Pyramid, but you'll only discover that you need the Security Pass to get into the grid controls.

2 In the courtyard where the Gunner was abusing the prisoner, take the tunnel to the right as you face the stairs. (You haven't been there yet.) There's a Tank waiting inside. Get out your big gun and blast him down. (You know how to handle these guys by now.) When he goes down, hit the switch behind him to extend the bridge on your right.

3 Before you can cross the bridge, you'll have to shoot down two flying Icaruses. They're a lot tougher than regular Flyers. When you've brought down the bird boys, cross the bridge and go through the door on the other side. Snag the **Medkits** inside and follow the passageway down.

4 The room below is packed with bad guys, so you've got your work cut out for you. Hang back at first and use the strategies you've developed to clean the room. On the upper level, collect the ammo and put the suffering soldier out of his misery. Watch out for the hole—it's a lava pit. Go back down and proceed through the door to the Torture Chamber.

5 Grab the **Shells** and **First Aid** kits inside the door, then head down the passageway. Go down the stairs on your right and you'll see a Tank patrolling the area. Avoid the large floor switch as you blast the Tank. Keep pounding him until he goes down.

6 Beyond the Tank's position, outside and around the structure to the right, you'll find **Secret Area #1** containing a **Hyperblaster** and some **Cells**. (Don't fall into the hole at the far end.) Snag the supplies, then come back and step on the floor switch. Jump on the lift in front of you and ride it down through the floor to the lower level.

7 Follow the hallway to the left of the switch on the wall of the lift shaft. Then continue through the long passageway. It angles left, goes down some stairs, and angles left again, then right to a walkway. Before the walkway you'll see some stairs. Shoot the Machine Gun Guard pestering you and turn to the door on your right. Open the door and enter Cell Block A.

8 Inside, two Gunners and some Guards are on patrol. Take out these sentries, and keep your head down. A Tank patrolling up above (8a) will take pot shots at you. The angle is bad, and he's a ways away, but you can bring him down, too, if you want to take the time.

9 Go to the third cell. Shoot the lowermost center brick to open a door into **Secret Area #2**. Inside you'll find an **Invulnerability** power-up. Come out and go to the end of the cell block.

10 Take the elevator to the upper level. You'll see a CD suspended behind an indestructible windowpane. Hit the switch to the right to remove the pane, and grab the CD. A Gunner will be dogging you (as will the Tank if you didn't get him earlier). Blast the Gunner and avoid the Tank by jumping immediately back on the lift and dropping down to the lower level.

__note__ If you're up for it, ride the elevator to the right of the CD location to the next level. Follow the walkway to another chamber with a torture sink—those sick bastards. You can exit through the second, but you have to fight off more Guards. You're now on the third level of Cell Block A. Exit through the doors (or jump down) and find your way to the entrance of Cell Block B.

11 Go through the door you came and into the passageway. Follow it to its end, where you will find a Machine Gun Guard standing at a locked door. Shoot the Guard, then open the door by pushing the keyboard on your left. Go through the door and into Cell Block B.

12 In the third cell (straight ahead) there is a grate in the floor. Shoot the grate and open a hole into the sewers. (The adjacent cell has the same hole with no blasting necessary.)

13 Jump into the hole and drop down into the sewers below. You'll be greeted by a slavering Parasite. Blast it and then look for a **Rebreather** sitting along the ledge to the right of the round sewer entranceway. Take the Rebreather and go to the entrance. The way will iris open. Put on the Rebreather and jump in (13a).

14 Follow the underwater passage to an ascending pipe, surface quietly, and then quickly swim back out of sight. You'll have to shoot the Light Guards on patrol from the water before you can climb out. This is the room where they've hidden the **Security Pass**. Climb out and you see it twirling in the air on the far side of the huge cross-like apparatus. Grab the pass, and the **First Aid** kits if you need them.

15 Open the door and follow the walkway to the computer terminal. Scoop up the **Shells** you find there, and then shove the keyboard to open the door at your right. Go through the door and blast the two Guards and the Gunner. (Watch him; he ducks!) You can hear the Tank lumbering around the level below. He'll take pot shots at you if you let him see you. Continue down to the walkway past the next door (behind which is a lift) and through the one beyond it.

16 You'll come to a room with a huge cauldron filled with superheated transparent fluid at its center. As you enter, a fellow Marine in a cage is just being lowered into this deadly broth, and when the cage reappears, he's gone, replaced by a **Hyperblaster**. Go to the cage, crawl in, and get the gun. Next, engage your Invulnerability power-up and drop into the cauldron below, then dive down to come to **Secret Area #3**, which harbors substantial rewards, including an **Ammo Pack**, **Shells**, **Grenades**, **Bullets**, **Cells**, and a **Quad Damage** power-up. Now we're talking— if you remember to get back out again before your Invulnerability wears off. Swim back to the surface and climb out of the molten rock. Hit the switch in the corner to bring down the lift (careful you don't get crushed) and ride it up. Look for a sign pointing to the Exit. Go for it. You've got a Tank to deal with here. Blast him and head back to the Security Complex.

Mission 3

95

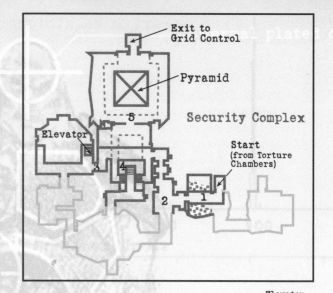

GRID CONTROL ROOM

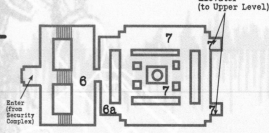

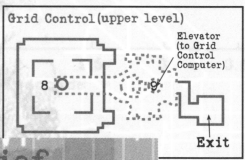

Intel Brief

Primary Objective:	Destroy the security grid protecting the industrial region
Secondary Objective:	Locate and destroy the Grid Control Computer
Unit Location:	Grid Control Room
Potential Kills:	7
Goals:	2
Secrets:	0
Enemies:	Tanks, Gunners, Berserkers, Super Tank
Weapons:	Blaster, Shotgun, Supershotgun, Machine Gun, Chaingun, Grenade Launcher, Hyperblaster

Objective 7
LOCATE AND DESTROY THE GRID CONTROL COMPUTER

THIS IS IT! You're almost there! With the Control Pryamid Key and the Security Pass, you've got everything you need to dissable the security grid. But there are still a few bad guys between you and the successful completion of your mission—including the baddest Tank in the fleet. Now is no time to relax. Heads up, Marine! Time to put a serious hurt on the enemy.

Objective Summary

1. Start; Enforcers, Cells, Medkits
2. Gunners, Medics, Stimpacks, Medkits, Shards, Bullets
3. Tank, Grenades, Bullets, Medkit, Armor Jacket
4. Lower level (jump down)
5. Icarus
6. Combat Armor, Grenade Launcher
7. Elevator
8. Tanks, Gunners, Berserkers, Super Tank
9. Elevator to Grid Control Computer

Mission 3

Quake II

Field Report

1 From the lift, shoot the two Enforcers on guard. Scoop up the **Cells** and **Medkits** on the walkway.

2 Enter the door on the right. Take out the Gunner inside—you should be able to take him by surprise. There's another Gunner further in who doesn't like surprises. Frag him and the Medic with him. Scoop up the **Stims** and **Medkits**. Go right down the hallway. There's another Medic standing there with his back to you, so you might be able to take him out without a fight. Snag the **Shards** and **Bullets** in the corner, and then go left out onto the walkway.

3 Scoop up the **Stims** and go through the entryway. Whittle down the Tank that lumbers toward you (if you haven't done so already). Grab the **Grenades**, **Bullets**, **Medkits**, and **Armor Jacket** on the ledge outside if you need them, then go back inside and jump off the walkway to the lower level.

4 Go down the stairs to the ground floor and follow the hall around to the door in the back.

5 Beyond it is the Control Pyramid. Go through the door and hit the switch to open the Pyramid. An Icarus will fly out. Blast him out of the air. Now go to the shaft he flew out of. It will be closed. Stand on the circle and the lift will lower you down. Jump off the lift quickly or it will take you back up. With the Security Pass in your inventory, the lighted door will open for you. Enter and take the lift to the Grid Control Room.

6 From the lift, walk straight ahead to the stairs. At the top, go left and get the **Combat Armor** in the center of the four, towering blue columns. You have to time it just right and jump in between the pulses or you get burned. Go to the four columns on the other side of the stairs and collect the **Grenade Launcher**. Go to the corridor opposite the columns. Turn right and head toward the red switch (6a). Turn left and go through the lighted doorway. Once you pass through it, a force field engages, blocking your way. A similar force field has fired up in the doorway at the other end of the corridor, so there's no turning back.

7 Proceed forward past the huge central pillar surrounded by pulsing blue light beams. Crouch down and slip under the moving blue lasers blocking your path, keep going until you come to a small lift in the outer wall. Take one of the corner lifts up to the next level. Get ready; the joint is really going to rock.

8 When you hit the upper level, a Tank attacks from the right almost immediately. Another Tank is on his way from the left. Bring out your heaviest artillery to drop these ironbutts as fast as possible. When they go down, an explosion knocks down the walls of the central chamber. Gunners pour out of it, followed by the monstrous Super Tank. He is a very, very tough one to kill—especially with the Gunners and Berserkers dogging you. Luckily he's also super slow. Avoid the Super Tank and take out the Gunners and Berserker with Quad-Damage empowered Super Shotgun fire. Run and gun. Move fast! Use the remains of the walls for cover. When you've cleared out the area, get behind the Super Tank and start firing Grenades up his tail pipes. It'll take a lot of them. When the Super Tank falls, go to the center of the chamber. You can't miss it; there's a big circular space on the floor. There's a ladder, which you can take down into an inner corridor.

9 Follow the corridor bearing left until you come to a circular lift. Take the lift up to the Grid Control Computer. Hit the green switch to raise the protective sheath from around the central power column. Watch out for the beams emanating from the glowing blue inner core; they'll injure you. Use your Super Shotgun to blast the power core and destroy the security grid. Mission accomplished! Head for the doorway outlined in yellow lights. Go down the hallway to the Exit sign. Hit the switch and take the lift down to start your next mission.

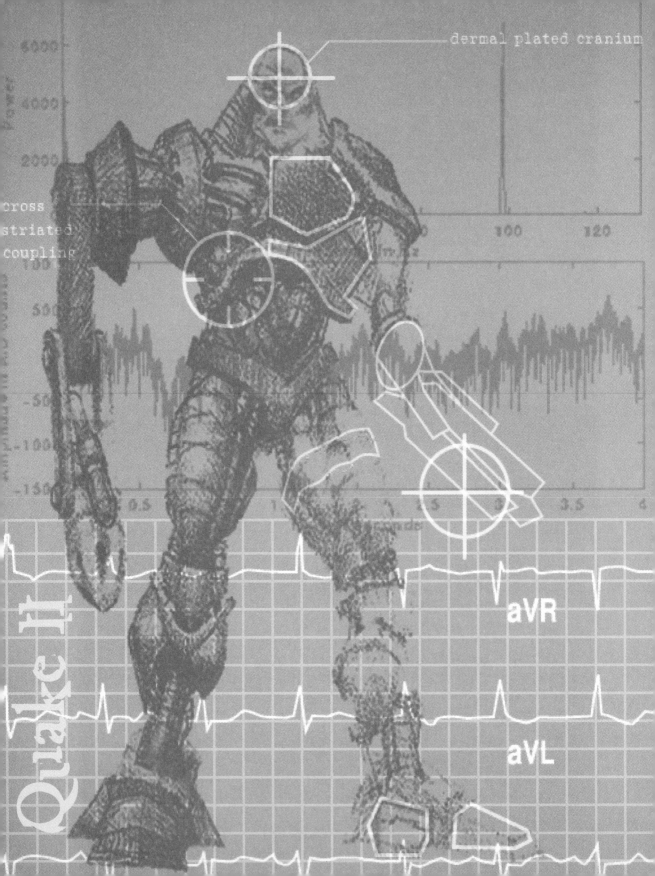

Mission 4
NAVIGATE THE MINES AND FIND THE ENTRANCE TO THE FACTORY

Your next major objective is the Strogg Factory. To reach it, you must make your way through the network of tunnels that make up the planet's mining complex. The Strogg, remember, are not human. Consequently, you are likely to encounter toxic environments within the subterranean complex. When you do, you must find a means to ventilate the area. You must also find a way to activate the mining machinery to connect the passageways to which you must have access. Your final objective here is the Service Elevator. If it is down, you must find a power source, enable the elevator, and use it to enter the Factory.

Mission 4 by Unit Locations

1. Mine Entrance
2. Upper Mines
3. Borehole
4. Drilling Area
5. Borehole
6. Drilling Area
7. Lower Mines
8. Drilling Area

dermal plated cranium

cross
striated
coupling

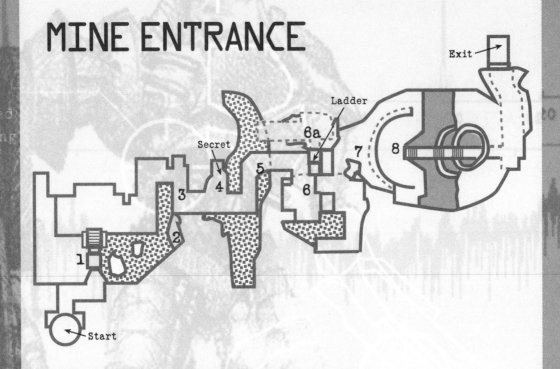

MINE ENTRANCE

Exit

Ladder

6a

Secret

5

7

8

3

4

6

2

1

Start

Intel Brief

Primary Objective:	Navigate Mines. Find entrance to the Factory.
Secondary Objective:	Make your way to the Mine entrance.
Unit Location:	Mine Entrance
Potential Kills:	40
Goals:	1
Secrets:	1
Enemies:	Light Guards, Berserkers, Gunners, Machine Gun Guards, Icaruses, Gladiators
Weapons:	Blaster, Shotgun, Machine Gun, Super Shotgun, Chaingun, Grenade Launcher, Rocket Launcher

V2

Quake II

Objective 1
LOCATE THE MINE ENTRANCE

CONGRATULATIONS, MARINE. Thanks to you, the combat situation on Stroggos is finally shifting in our favor. But now's not the time to slack off. Victory is a ways off, and death and destruction still lurk around every corner. Your next mission takes you to the hellish Stroggos war factory. With the main gate inaccessible, you'll have to make your way there through the mines. Make sure you leave a trail of Strogg blood. Move out!

Objective Summary

1. Start; Shells, Medkit, Light Guards, Berserkers, Stimpacks, Shells, Bullets, Medkits, Hyperblaster, Cells
2. Power Shield, Stimpacks, Flyers
3. Light Guard, Berserkers, Machine Gun
4. Berserker, Secret Area: Rocket Launcher; Flyers, Armor, Shells
5. Light Guards, Berserker
6. Light Guards, Berserkers, Shells, First Aid, Impact Switch (extends stairs), Cells, Medkits
7. Icaruses, Medkits, Cells
8. Icaruses, Berserker, Mutant, Grenade Launcher, Medkit
9. Icaruses
10. Light Guards, Berserkers, Exit (to Upper Mines)

Mission 4

Field Report

1 At your entry point, grab the **Shells** and **Medkit** to your left and right, respectively, and head down the passageway to the first door. In the open area beyond, you'll be welcome by three Light Guards (two to the left, one to the right) and two Berserkers (to the right) patrolling the ledge at the far end. Take out your Hyperblaster and whittle them down from a distance. Grab the **Stimpacks** ahead (to your left) and the **Shells** and **Bullets** (at the far end and to the left). Next, jump to the small rock to your right and grab the **Hyperblaster** and **Cells** next to the dead Marine—don't slip!

2 Take care of the other Berserker rushing you from the ledge, then climb along the wall to the far end to reach a **Power Shield** and some **Stimpacks**. Immediately turn around and shotgun the three Flyers that spotted you. Aim carefully—you have no cover out here. When they're gone, jump back across the lava to the entrance door. You will take some damage, but there are two **Medkits** hidden in the far corner to your left.

3 Grab 'em, then head up the stairs in front of the impassable main factory door and to the left to the next door. Another Light Guard and Berserker rush you—you know what to do. Inside, you'll notice a **Machine Gun** swirling between two electronic units. Grab it, but stay in between the units and wait for the Berserker to come after

you. The corners of the units protect you from his blade arm, and two Super Shotgun shots will take him out at close distance.

4 Cautiously proceed down the walkway. Another Berserker is lurking around the corner. When he's dead, shoot the wall behind him to access a **Secret Area** with a **Rocket Launcher**. As you emerge, two Flyers would like to have a shot at you. Introduce them to your new toy, then grab the **Armor** and **Shells**, while ducking the bullets from two snipers on the far end and below.

5 As you approach the next entrance, two more Light Guards rush you, followed by a not-so-mild-mannered Berserker. If you're fast enough, you can take out the Light Guards with your Shotgun, then lob a Grenade on the lower platform to take care of the snipers, and then shotgun the Berserker. Just don't let this misfit throw you into the lava pit below—there's no way out.

6 Inside, there's more company. Peek around the first corner, and take out the Light Guard on the ledge in the far back. Inside the room, two more Light Guards are on a ledge to the right, and two Berserkers are guarding the entrance. Run and gun, and use the explosive barrels to enhance your firepower. When things are quiet again, look up to the left of the entrance. Shoot the impact switch to extend the stairs that will enable you to continue.

note If you feel like living on the edge, you can get inside via an alternative route (6a). After clearing out the open-air area, take a leap of faith (for God's sake, don't fall into the lava) and jump to the ledge from which the snipers attacked you. Inside, collect some **Cells** and **Medkits** and climb up the ladder on your right. You're now behind the door that has the engraving on it. Step out and surprise the crowd.

7 Proceed through the right-hand door. Ready your Hyperblaster to clip the wings of the two Icaruses hovering outside. These guys are trickier and tougher than the Flyers you're used to. You'll have to hit them with some serious firepower. Collect the goodies behind the tall metal structure and continue to the left.

8 As you proceed around the structure, you'll notice two more Icaruses appearing at the far end. Take 'em down, then proceed cautiously. An extremely agitated Berserker and a foul-smelling Mutant (rushing up the stairs) are waiting for you around the corner. Try to get the Berserker to follow, then you can take him out easily. The Mutant will take three Super Shotgun shots—straight up—before he'll go down. Grab the **Grenade Launcher** and **Medkit** at the far end of the platform.

9 Hyperblaster in hand, continue down the stairs. Watch your left and right—about halfway down, two more Icaruses will come your way. Ruffle their feathers, then continue through the entrance at the bottom of the stairs.

If you're low on health and don't want to face these creatures in the open, **tip** rush back up the stairs and take them out from behind the crates.

10 Around the corner, two Light Guards and two Berserkers are happy to see you. But you don't have time to hang around for any smalltalk—you've got work to do, Marine! Hyperblast them out of your way and head for the Exit to the Upper Mines.

Mission 4

li si ji li 9

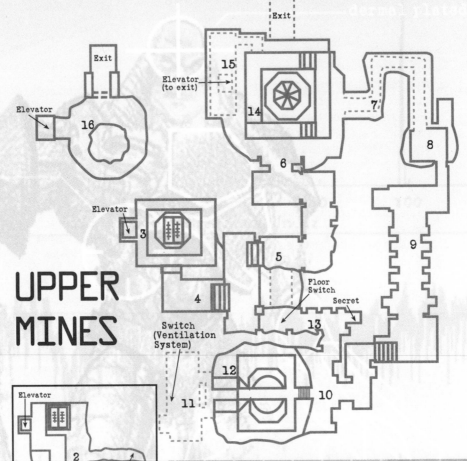

UPPER MINES

Exit

15

Elevator
(to exit)

14

7

8

16

Elevator

Exit

Elevator

6

9

3

Elevator

5

Floor
Switch

Secret

4

13

Switch
(Ventilation
System)

12

11

10

Elevator

2

Rocket Launcher

Start Area

1

Start

Intel Brief

Primary Objective:	Navigate Mines. Find entrance to the Factory.
Secondary Objective:	Toxic conditions found in Lower Mines. Activate ventilation systems.
Unit Location:	Upper Mines
Potential Kills:	64
Goals:	1
Secrets:	2
Enemies:	Light Guards, Shotgun Guards, Machine Gun Guards, Gunners, Icaruses, Berserkers, Gladiators, Mutants
Weapons:	Blaster, Shotgun, Machine Gun, Super Shotgun, Chaingun, Grenade Launcher, Rocket Launcher, Hyperblaster

Objective 2
LOCATE THE MINE ENTRANCE

THINGS JUST HAVE TAKEN A TURN FOR THE WORSE. You were just supposed to find the entrance to the Factory, but now you've been informed that something is wrong with the Mine's ventilation system. Your first order of business now is to keep breathing. You'll need to sweep the joint with a breath of fresh air. It's a delay, but don't whine about it. Marines don't plan, they improvise! While you're improvising, stay out of the sights of those Gladiators!

Objective Summary

1. Start, Armor, Ammo, Shotgun Guards
2. Shotgun Guards, Shells, Bullets, First Aid, Rocket Launcher, Icaruses
3. Shotgun Guards, Gunner, Icarus
4. Shells, Medkits, Gladiator
5. Gunner, Chaingun, Ammo, First Aid, Shotgun Guards, Mutant, Gunners
6. Mutant, Icaruses, Gunner
7. First Aid, Combat Armor
8. Shotgun Guards, Gladiator, Gunner, Shells
9. Shotgun Guards, Rocket Launcher, Gladiator, Gunners, Mutant
10. Light Guards, Shotgun Guards, Shells, Medkits, Stimpacks, Grenades
11. Gladiator, Secret Area: Quad Damage; Switch (activates vent system), First Aid, Shells, Rockets
12. Icaruses
13. Gunner, Floor Switch (extends bridge), Secret Area: Bullets, Medkit
14. Icaruses
15. Gunner, Elevator (to Exit area), Stimpacks, Cells, Bullets
16. Guards, Mutant, Medkits, Rockets, Exit (to Borehole)

Mission 4

Field Report

1. After you enter the mine, go for the **Armor** and **Ammo** straight in front of you, then turn around and take out the two Shotgun Guards in the corridor ahead.

2. In the room at the end of the corridor, you'll find five more Shotgun Guards hanging out. After Berserkers and Icaruses, these guys are easy. Collect the goodies they drop, then jump off the walkway and crawl underneath. Collect the **Bullets** and **First Aid** kits and head to the right and up the ramp. Collect a **Rocket Launcher**. The moment you grab it, two Icaruses will come after you. Rush back down the ramp to take care of them (in this small alcove, you'll only get hammered). To continue on your way, you will have to jump on the rim of the grinding machine and across to the walkway. Try not to slip or you're hamburger.

3. Upstairs, Strogg forces are preparing for your arrival. Shotgun Guards, a Gunner (near the elevator), an Icarus, and a Gladiator (around the corner in the other room) are determined not to let you advance further into the mines. Show them the error of their ways. Ready your Chaingun, fire up a Quad Damage, and ride the lift to the upper level. Try to take out the Gunner and Icarus first, then pick off the rest of the bunch and continue through the door around the corner.

4. Carefully walk around the pit, collect the **Shells** and **Medkits**, and then proceed through the door. Throw some Grenades at the Gladiator around the corner to lure him after you. When he stumbles down the stairs, finish him off with your Hyperblaster.

5. Sneak up the set of stairs in the next room (the one that contains the Chaingun). A Gunner around the left corner and above has the entrance covered. Duck and cover, and take your best shot at him. Snag the **Chaingun**, **Ammo**, and **First Aid** kits in the passage and continue up the stairs on your right. A couple of Shotgun Guards are hiding out in the dark at the far end. Blast 'em. As you pass through the room, the wall to your right will crumble and a Mutant will jump out. Nail this slimeball, then take out the Gunners in the room across the chasm.

6. Follow the passage to an open area and plug the Mutant you find there. You'll also have to take out five Icaruses hovering over the large fan in the center. Continue through the tunnel to your right. At the bottom of the ramp, a Gunner will give you a hard time. Thankfully he's not too good at throwing Grenades uphill. Duck his gunshots and take him out.

7. Follow the howling around the corner to the right and grab the **First Aid** kit and **Combat Armor** ahead.

8. Rush the Guards, Gladiator, and Gunner at the other end of the tunnel to your right. Don't wait too long; speed is of the essence. You'll have an opportunity to learn to live with pain.

9 Continue through the narrow corridor to your right and be prepared to take out three Shotgun Guards in the room beyond. The next few yards of your mission will not be as easy. If you're low on Health, you better retrace your steps and scoop up whatever you were unable to carry earlier. Then activate your Quad Damage power-up, get your Hyperblaster ready, and rush across the hall to the left to get the **Rocket Launcher**. The moment you grab it, the structure starts to shake and a Gladiator will block your access to the next room. Try to get past him and into the next room without taking too much damage. Run up the ramp. Take out as many monsters as you can, but for God's sake don't stop! Ignore the other Gladiator and Gunners until you find some decent cover. If you're lucky, most of the Strogg will take each other out in the ensuing crossfire. Pick and choose your battles with whoever's left.

10 When things have calmed down, enter the next cave. Blast the Light and Shotgun Guards who are patrolling inside the structure as you collect the **Shells**, **Medkits**, **Stimpacks**, and **Grenades** around the outer ledges.

11 Run down the stairs and toward the next entrance. If you're fast enough, you'll get the Gladiator inside the doorway with three or four Super Shotgun blasts at close range. Proceed to the switch in the center on the back wall— but don't hit it, yet. Go to the two main frame units to the left of the switch. Step back and hit the left one with a powerful shot to gain access to **Secret Area #1** and a **Quad Damage**. Hit the switch to activate the ventilation systems. On your way out, scoop up the **First Aid** kits, **Shells**, and **Rockets** in the room.

12 Outside you'll be greeted by three Icaruses. Bring them down, then proceed up the stairs and to the left. Take out the Gunner hiding out around the corner.

13 Continue to the left and hit the floor switch to extend a bridge across the chasm. Before crossing the bridge, turn around and shoot against the wall (close to the corner) to reveal **Secret Area #2** stocked with **Bullets** and a **Medkit**.

14 Cross the bridge and head for the courtyard with the huge vent at its center. Before rushing into the open, pick the Icaruses out of the sky, then proceed down the stairs and into the tunnel in the far left corner.

15 Follow the passage around the corner and surprise the Gunner next to the elevator. Collect the **Stimpacks**, **Cells**, and **Bullets** in the room, then ride the Lift down. (Face the switch as you ride down.)

16 Kill the Guards and Mutant waiting for you down here. Collect the **Medkits** and the **Rockets** (in the water) and head for the Exit to your next objective.

Mission 4

Quake II

109

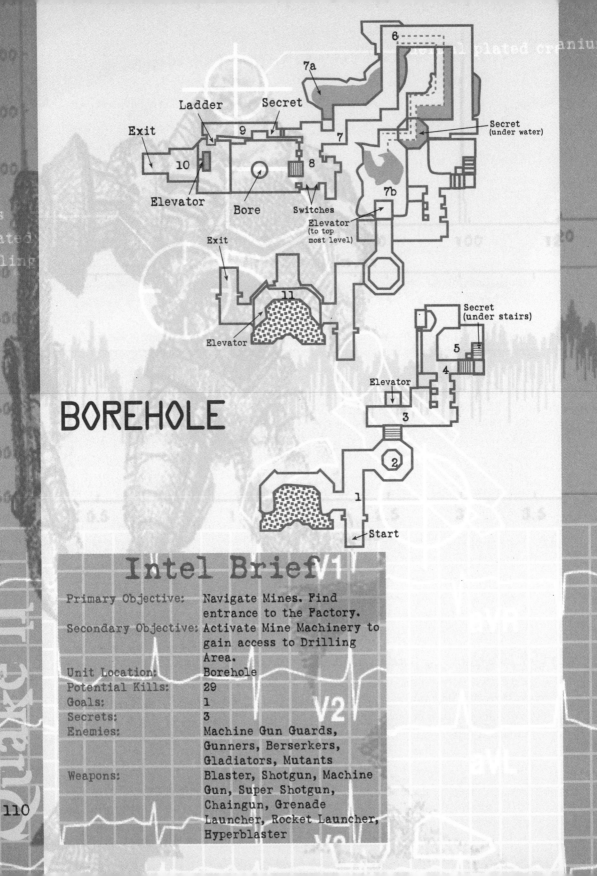

6

7a

Ladder   Secret

Exit   9   7   Secret
                 (under water)
10   8
        7b
Elevator   Bore   Switches
                    Elevator
                    (to top
                    most level)

Exit

11

Secret
(under stairs)

Elevator   5

4

Elevator

3

2

1

Start

BOREHOLE

Intel Brief

Primary Objective: Navigate Mines. Find entrance to the Factory.
Secondary Objective: Activate Mine Machinery to gain access to Drilling Area.
Unit Location: Borehole
Potential Kills: 29
Goals: 1
Secrets: 3
Enemies: Machine Gun Guards, Gunners, Berserkers, Gladiators, Mutants
Weapons: Blaster, Shotgun, Machine Gun, Super Shotgun, Chaingun, Grenade Launcher, Rocket Launcher, Hyperblaster

Quake II

Objective 3
GAIN ACCESS TO DRILLING AREA

PREPARE FOR A SHORT, BUT WILD RIDE, MARINE. As you fight your way closer to your final destination, you'll come face-to-face with more Gladiators and Gunners that have nothing better to do than rain on your parade. Keeping enemies off your back while activating the Mine Machinery (and proceeding to the Lower Mines) may very well prove to be one of the toughest battles you've fought so far.

Objective Summary

1. Start, Grenade Launcher, First Aid, Gladiator, Gunners
2. Gladiator, Gunner
3. Machine Gun Guards, Medkit, Shells, Grenades, First Aid
4. Gladiator, Stimpacks, Berserkers, Guards, Medkit, Shells
5. **Secret Area:** Combat Armor, Rockets; Cells, Hyperblaster
6. Stimpacks, Machine Gun, Gladiator, Cells, Bullets
7. Berserkers, **Secret Area:** Adrenaline
8. Bullets, Stimpacks, Medkit, Switches (to activate machinery), Gunners, Grenades
9. Medkits, **Secret Area:** Armor Shards, Stimpack, Ladder
10. Elevator, Cells, Shells, Medkits, Exit (to Drilling Area)
11. Elevator (to alternative Exits)

Mission 4

Quake II

dermal plated cranium

Field Report

1 Grab the **Grenade Launcher** and **First Aid** kit in front of you and walk straight ahead. (The switch in the room to your left will not work, yet—Mine Machinery inoperable.) Around the corner, you'll be facing a Gladiator and two Gunners (on the ledge above).

2 Take a deep breath, then run around the corner—Kamikaze-style—and shotgun the Gladiator (remember, he won't use his railgun at close range, and it will take you only three Super Shotgun shots to take him out). Turn left and take out the Gunner at the bottom of the stairs, using the walls as cover.

3 Cautiously proceed down the stairs. There's a Machine Gun Guard to your left. Kill him, collect the **Medkit, Shells**, and **Grenades**. Then proceed down the hall. Just past the stairs, there's another Guard at nine o'clock. Surprise him and grab the **First Aid** kit in the right corner of the alcove.

4 Continue down the hall to the left—but not too far. A Gladiator will rush you from the other room. Run back around the corner and wait for him to appear. Then blast him—no reason to take unnecessary risks. As you proceed to the next room, collect the **Stimpacks** to your left and right. Hear that sound?

Those are Berserkers sharpening their blade arms. Lob some Grenades into the area below to kill those twisted creeps, and some Guards, too. Collect the **Medkit** and **Shells** at the far end and proceed to the lower level.

5 Crawl underneath the stairs to come to **Secret Area #1** with a **Combat Armor** and some **Rockets**. Run for the **Cells** and **Hyperblaster** across the room. Leave through the walkway to the left.

6 Three Guards and a Gladiator will rush you from the far end of the walkway. Send a few Rockets their way, then shotgun the two snipers to your left and below. Down the walkway and around the corner are some **Stimpacks** and a **Machine Gun**. Collect them, then rush around the corner. When you see the Gladiator approaching, rush back. Take him out as you did the earlier one, by shooting him as he turns the corner. Collect the **Cells** and **Bullets** as you continue your advance.

7 Two Berserkers are lurking around the corner near the end of the walkway. Knock sense into them with your Chaingun.

Quake II

tip Time is pressing, but there is another Secret Area slightly out of your way that is worth checking out. To get there, jump off the ledge behind you. Take out the two **Mutants**, then collect the **Medkit**, **Rockets**, and **Cells** behind you (7a). Head for the tunnel in the corner to your left. Before entering, crawl underneath the walkway to get to a **Quad Damage** power-up. Come back out again and kill the Guard who is rushing you from inside the tunnel. As you wend your way through the corroded pipe, stop in the water-filled cylindrical chamber before going onward. Take out the Guard inside the pipe to your right, then jump into the water to your left. Dive down to come to **Secret Area #2** and collect the **Adrenaline**. Surface and follow the pipe to the next room (7b). Take out the two Berserkers who are rushing you, as well as the Gunner inside and to the left. Collect the **Grenades**, **Shells**, and **Medkits** in this area, then ride the lift up to the topmost level to take out two Gunners above the room where you took out the first Gladiator (2). (For your best chance to take them by surprise, face away from the wall as you ride the lift.) Collect the **First Aid** kit and the **Bullets**, jump off the ledge, and retrace your steps until you come to the switch room again. (Don't forget to pick up any goodies you couldn't carry earlier.)

8   After you've taken care of business, enter the switch room. Before you hit the two switches to your left, collect the **Bullets** and **Stimpacks** in this area, as well as the **Medkit** in the cave with the drill. Now hit the two switches to start the drill. Immediately turn around and

fight off the Gunner that comes out from behind the wall to your right, and the other two that come from behind the wall at the far end to your left. Grab the **Grenades** in the alcove to your right, then head across the room to the other alcove.

9   Shoot the round structure above the **Medkit** to gain access to the final **Secret Area** on this level. On your way in, grab the Medkit, then follow the narrow passage to some **Armor Shards**, a **Stimpack**, and a Ladder (to your left).

10 Climb down the ladder and jump on the lift that comes out from behind the wall. Ride it to the next room. When you're inside, jump off. Grab the **Cells**, **Shells**, and **Medkits** you see, then head for the Exit to the Drilling Area.

note   Instead of exiting through the Secret Area, you could have also retraced your steps to your entry point to this level and entered the room to your right. The switch on the wall is now active, and you could have taken the U-shaped platform elevator (11) to two alternative Exits (and entry points) to the Drilling Area. However, you would still have to come back and take the first exit in order to be able to accomplish all goals in that level.

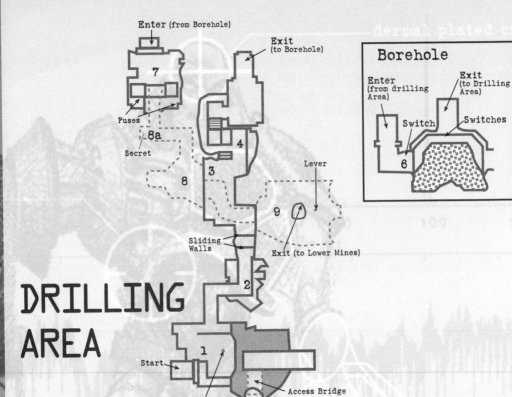

Enter (from Borehole)

Exit (to Borehole)

7

Fuses

8a

Secret

4

3

8

Lever

9

Sliding Walls

Exit (to Lower Mines)

2

DRILLING AREA

1

Start

Lever (lower Bridge)

Access Bridge

Borehole

Enter (from drilling Area)

Exit (to Drilling Area)

Switch

Switches

6

Intel Brief

Primary Objective:	Navigate Mines. Find entrance to the Factory.
Secondary Objective:	Lower access bridge. Find service elevator to the Factory.
Unit Location:	Drilling Area
Potential Kills:	26
Goals:	3
Secrets:	2
Enemies:	Gunners, Gladiators, Machine Gun Guards, Mutants
Weapons:	Blaster, Shotgun, Machine Gun, Super Shotgun, Chaingun, Grenade Launcher, Rocket Launcher, Hyperblaster

V2

V3

Quake II

Objective 4
FIND THE ENTRANCE TO THE LOWER MINES

COMPARED TO WHAT YOU'VE BEEN THROUGH SO FAR, making it through the Drilling Area is a cakewalk. That doesn't mean you should drop your guard—there are plenty of Gladiators and Gunners here who have a taste for deep-fried Marine. If you entered this part of your mission through the exit behind the secret area in the Borehole, you'll be in and out of here in no time.

Objective Summary

1. Start, Silencer, Gladiator, Gunners, Lever (lowers access bridge), Rockets, Grenades, Medkits
2. Gunners, Guards, Rockets, Bullets, Stims, Shells, Sliding Walls, Super Shotgun
3. Guard, Gladiator, Gunners
4. Guards, Gunners
5. Shells, Grenades, Medkits, Exit (to Borehole)
6. Switches (to lower Elevator), Exit (to Drilling Area)
7. Gunners, Rocket Launcher, Shards, Bullets, Shells, Medkits, Stims, Energy Beam Fuses (shoot to lower ramp)
8. Secret Area: Invulnerability; Mutants, Shells, Armor
9. Laser Beam, Lever (to activate laser beam), Medkits, Bullets, Exit (to Lower Mines)

Mission 4

Field Report

1 As you step from the start tunnel onto a dark ledge, grab the **Silencer** on your right. Next lob a few Grenades into the room to take out the Gladiator and Gunners below. Once the area is cleared, drop down and push the blinking Lever to lower the access bridge. Collect the **Rockets** and **Grenades**, and proceed through the corridor on your right. (If you need more Health, there are two **Medkits** to the left on your way out.)

2 Take out the Gunner who's lurking around the corner, and the two Guards around the next corner. The room in front of the sliding walls has two more Gunners with their backs to you. A few well-aimed shots and they're history. Grab the **Rockets**, **Bullets**, **Stims**, and **Shells** in the room, then crouch in front of the sliding walls and take out the Guards at the other end.

3 Cautiously crawl underneath the sliding walls (collecting the Super Shotgun and Shells on your way) and follow the walkway to the left. With your Super Shotgun in hand, rush the Guard, Gladiator, and two Gunners waiting around the corner.

4 More Guards and Gunners around the next corner can't wait to make your acquaintance. Take out the Guards first, then, using the pillar ahead and to your right as cover, take care of the two Gunners near the bottom of the stairs.

5 Follow the stairs to the next room. (If you want, peek over the edge when you reach the top of the stairs. Looks like some Grenades and Armor are waiting for you. We'll come back to them later.) Grab the **Shells**, **Grenades**, and **Medkits** (behind the explosive barrels) and exit back to the Borehole.

6 You're now facing the lava pit (and one of the alternative Borehole exits, had you chosen that route during the previous part of your mission). Push the switch on your left to lower the platform elevator. Step out onto the elevator and head for the two switches in the center. Press the left one to lower the lift, then exit through the tunnel to another section of the Drilling Area.

7 Be prepared to take some damage as soon as the door opens. Two Gunners are making your life hard. Retire them immediately, then collect the **Rocket Launcher**, **Shards**, **Bullets**, **Shells**, **Medkits**, and **Stims** in the room. Next, shoot the two energy beams at the end of the stairs to the left and right to lower a ramp ahead of you.

8 Proceed through the tunnel. At the first turn, shoot the wall to your right to open a **Secret Area** with an **Invulnerability** power-up. Grab it and continue around the next corner (8a). Take out the two foul-smelling Mutants around the next corner, then snag the **Shells** and **Armor** to your right (you saw these items earlier when peeking over the ledge, remember?).

9 Follow the tunnel to the end. You'll see a huge structure with a laser beam in its center. Walk around the structure. Behind it, you'll notice two **Medkits**, some **Bullets**, and a lever. Push the lever and the laser beam will cut a hole into the ground. Jump in to access the Lower Mines.

note

Don't worry if you haven't killed all the Strogg forces or found all the Secrets on this level, yet. You'll be back soon to finish the job.

Mission 4

Quake II

dermal plated cranium

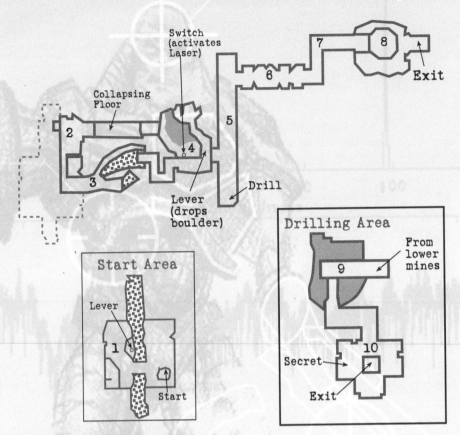

Switch
(activates
Laser)

Collapsing
Floor

7

8

Exit

6

5

2

4

3

Drill

Lever
(drops
boulder)

Drilling Area

From
lower
mines

9

Start Area

Lever

1

Start

Secret

10

Exit

LOWER MINES

Intel Brief

Primary Objective:	Navigate Mines. Find entrance to the Factory
Secondary Objective:	Enable the service elevator to the Factory
Unit Location:	Lower Mines
Potential Kills:	18
Goals:	2
Secrets:	0
Enemies:	Gunners, Light Guards, Machine Gun Guards, Gladiators, Technicians, Tanks
Weapons:	Blaster, Shotgun, Machine Gun, Super Shotgun, Chaingun, Grenade Launcher, Rocket Launcher, Hyperblaster

Quake II

Objective 5
ACTIVATE THE SERVICE ELEVATOR TO THE FACTORY

YOU'RE NOT RUNNING OUT OF STEAM, ARE YOU, MARINE? What's that? I ... can't ... HEAR ... you! That's better! During this final stretch of your mission, you must find the switch that activates the Service Elevator to the Factory, then make a mad dash for the exit where two clunky Tanks are waiting for you. Hint: Save some Rockets for the final showdown. Now quit stalling and move out!

Objective Summary

1. Chaingun, Medkit, First Aid, Technicians, Stimpacks, Lever (activates platforms)
2. Technicians, Gunner, Grenades
3. Technicians, Gunner, Medkit, Grenade Launcher
4. Gunner, Gladiator, Lever (drops boulder), Shells, Medkit, Quad Damage, Bullets, Switch (activates laser)
5. Rocket Launcher, Grinder
6. Technicians, Cells
7. Gunners, Technician
8. Gunners, Stimpacks, Medkit, Grenades, Exit (to Drilling Area)
9. Stims, Cells
10. Tanks, Guards, Cells, Medkits, Secret Area: Adrenaline; Exit (elevator to Factory)

Mission 4

Quake II

dermal plated cranium

Field Report

1 After you land, grab the **Chaingun** and **Medkit** on your right and the First Aid kit on your left, then cross the lava pit. As soon as you start crossing the bridge, two Technicians will come after you from above. Bring them down. Collect the two **Stimpacks** in the left corner on the other side and push the lever to activate two moving metal platforms. Jump across and ride one of the platforms to the room above.

2 Upstairs, you'll be greeted by more Technicians in the tunnel ahead, and a Gunner and yet another Technician in the passage to your right. Kill the bastards, then follow the passage to your right. (Don't forget to pick up the **Grenades** and **First Aid** kits near your entry hole.

note If you go through the tunnel ahead, you will only end up one level below—the floor collapses as soon as you cross it! There's a more elegant way to the lower level.

3 Around the corner, two more Technicians come hovering your way. (Where do they find room to hide these things?) Time for the Rocket Launcher treatment. When the floating dehumidifiers are history, proceed to the end of the passage. Using the pillar in front of you as cover, take out the Gunner on the platform below. Go to the far end of the small ledge, replenish your strength with the **Medkit** there, and jump down to his final resting place. Grab the **Grenade Launcher** and follow the tunnel to a cave.

4 Inside, there's a Gunner to your right and a Gladiator below. First surprise the Gunner, then take out the Gladiator by lobbing a few Grenades down on his head. Push the lever to drop a boulder (and gain access to a laser), then jump down. (Don't forget to grab the **Shells** and **Medkit** behind the lever before you do.) Downstairs, grab the **Quad Damage** and some **Bullets**. Then hit the switch behind the laser to burn a hole into the rock.

aVR

aVL

Quake II

5 After the laser is off again, step through the hole and grab the **Rocket Launcher** on your right. Instantly bolt back out again. If you're too slow by a hair, the grinding tip of a massive drill will come through from your right and drag you down the tunnel and squash you against the next wall. Did the Stroggs really think a Marine would fall for this kind of trap? Follow the drill and take the passage on the right.

6 Launch a few Rockets toward the Technicians hovering in the hallway. When they're dead, grab the **Cells** on the floor and head down the walkway to another tunnel. (Don't let it worry you that the earth starts shaking as soon as you reach the tunnel.)

7 As you wend your way through the tunnel, you'll come across two Gunners and another Technician, so keep your Rocket Launcher handy.

8 Step on the platform at the end of the tunnel. It will take you upstairs, where two more Gunners are waiting for you. Hyperblast them to smithereens. Collect the **Stimpacks**, **Medkit**, and **Grenades**, then head for the exit and back to the Drilling Area.

9 You're now in the section of the Drilling Area that contains the bridge you lowered earlier. Check your field computer. You'll be informed that the Service Elevator is now accessible. Pick up the **Stims** and **Cells** on the walkway in front of you. Cross the bridge and follow the tunnel to the Exit room.

10 Don't enter yet, or you'll be blown away by the two Tanks that are guarding the Exit. Take out your Rocket Launcher and whittle away at them from behind the corner in the tunnel (you'll also have to take out the two rookie Light Guards who are rushing you). When the air has cleared, enter the room and turn to your right. Use the explosive barrel in the corner as a stepping stone to the crates in front of you. From the crates, jump across to the ledge to reach **Secret Area #2** and some **Adrenaline**. Well done, Marine. Now grab the **Cells** and **Medkits** in the room and take the elevator to the Factory.

Mission 4

121

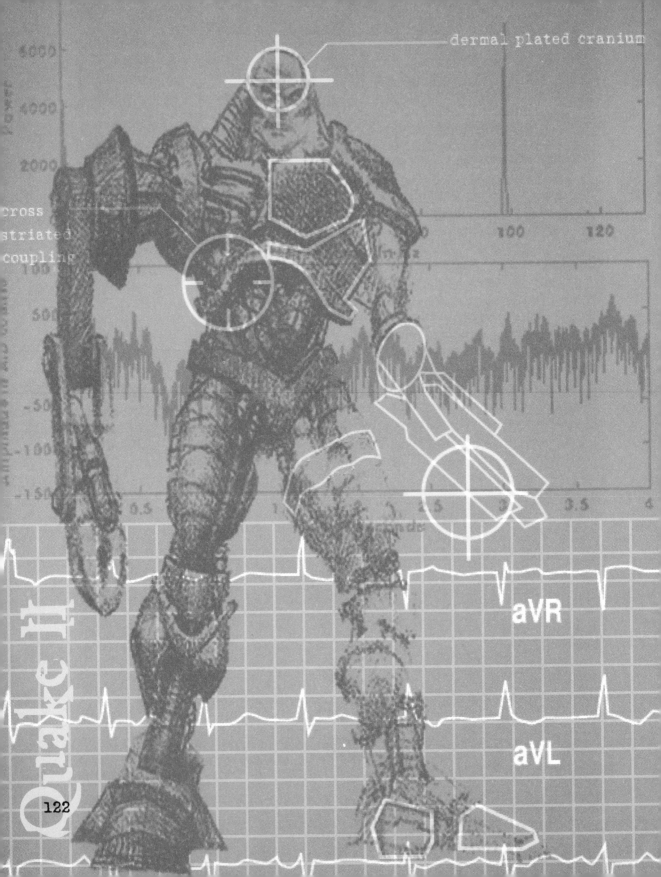

dermal plated cranium

cross
striated
coupling

aVR

aVL

Quake II

122

Mission 5
SHUT DOWN THE STROGG PROCESSING PLANT

Your next mission takes you into the notorious Strogg Processing Plant. Your first objective is the entrance to the plant. Once inside, you must find the five machines that make up the facility and disable them. Along the way, take advantage of the secret level that presents itself. Usually, this provides an opportunity to acquire more supplies and ammunition.

Mission 5 by Unit Locations

1. Receiving Center
2. Secret Level
3. Processing Plant
4. Receiving Center

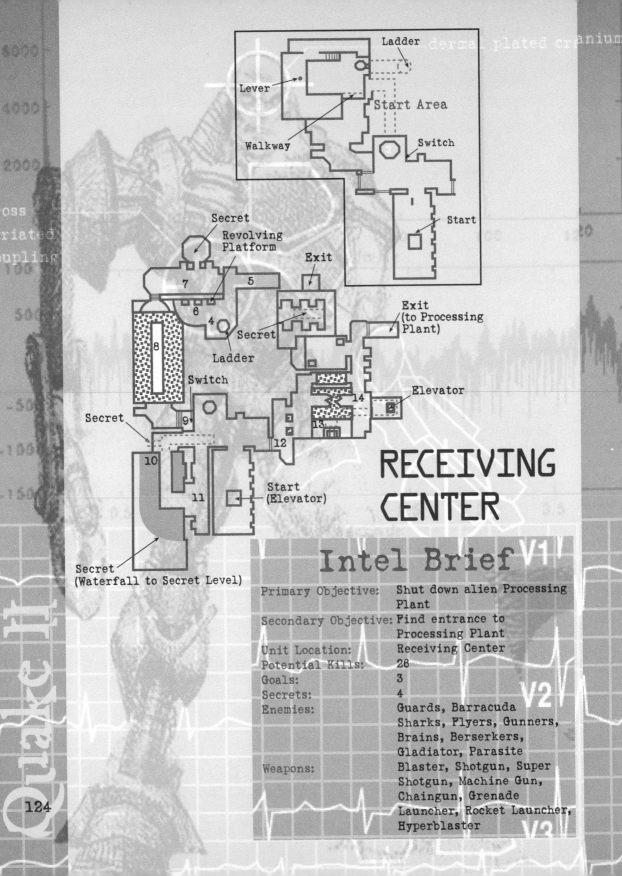

dermal plated cranium

Ladder

Lever

Walkway

Start Area

Switch

Start

Secret

Revolving
Platform

Exit

Exit
(to Processing
Plant)

7

5

6

4

Secret

Ladder

8

Switch

Secret

9

Elevator

14

13

12

Start
(Elevator)

10

11

RECEIVING
CENTER

Secret
(Waterfall to Secret Level)

Objective 1
FIND THE ENTRANCE TO THE PROCESSING PLANT

YOU'RE INSIDE THE SLOGGO WAR FACTORY. This is where the planet's primary military production takes place, and it's up to you to shut the joint down. Your first objective is the entrance to the Processing Plant. Watch yourself, the area is crawling with cyborgs, including a few you haven't seen before. This level also gives you access to the game's second secret level, Sudden Death.

Objective Summary

1. Start; Shells, Bullets, Medkits, Guards
2. Barracuda Sharks, Flyer
3. Guard, Gunners, Lever (to drain lava)
4. Brains
5. Gladiator, Shells, Bullets, Switch (to activate elevators)
6. Shells, First Aid, Bullets, Jacket Armor
7. Rockets, Grenade, Cells, Shells, and Medkits, Secret Area: Armor, Bullets, Rockets
8. Berserkers, Bullets
9. Rockets, Shards
10. Secret Area: First Aid, Grenades, Railgun; Parasite
11. Berserkers, Grenades, Stimpacks, Secret Area: Access to Sudden Death (Secret Level)
12. Gunner, Bullets
13. Stimpacks, Bullets, Shells
14. Gladiator, Quad Damage, Medkits

Mission 5

dermal plated cranium

Field Report

1 From your entry point, come off the elevator. Get the **Shells** and **Bullets** (on the left) and the Medkit (on the right). Around behind the Elevator is another **Medkit**. In the next room, Machine Gun Guards are waiting to jump you. Use the door for cover and take them out. Inside, grab the **Shells**, **Bullets** and **Medkits** you see. The way left is blocked by a laser grid, but don't bother with the door on the right just now. Instead, head toward the lasers and go to the hatchway on the right. Hit the switch to open the shaft, and jump in.

2 You'll drop down into a water-filled chamber, where three Barracuda Sharks attack immediately. Blast them into cat food, then jump to one of the square platforms beside the tunnel entrance to avoid being shot by a Flyer. He'll come into the room and you can shoot him from solid ground.

3 Enter the tunnel and follow it to the end, where you'll find a large lava pool. Look down and drop a Grenade on the lonely Guard below. When he's history, jump down and hit the switch on your left to lower a walkway. Get ready to shoot, then run down the walkway toward the back wall, and turn left at the corner to fire at the Gunner who is waiting around the corner at the end of the walkway. There's no cover so you may take some hits. Go to the lever on the other side of the lava pool. Another Gunner will appear at the doorway on your left, and you'll have to duck and fire. When he's history, pull the lever. The lava pool will drain, revealing a switch on the far wall. Go down the stairs on your left and hit the switch. Another tunnel hatch will open above you. Hurry, go up the stairs and around to your right and step on the small platform elevator, then hop out onto the open hatch and enter the tunnel.

Quake II

aVL

4 Climb the ladder and quickly jump out onto the next level. Behind you, two of the horrific creatures known as Brains are coming toward you. Their green force fields are powerful protection, and they're smart enough to duck and cover, but they're very, very slow. To penetrate the fields, you'll have to get fairly close. If you get too close, the monsters will open their chests and flail you with internal tentacles. It's a little like dancing with them—just be sure you're leading.

5 When the Brains are down, move down the corridor. There's a Gladiator waiting around the corner. When he sees you, he'll come running. Drop back and snipe at him from around the corner with your Chaingun. When he's dead, scoop up the **Shells** in the corner and the **Bullets** at the other end of the hall.

6 Hit the switch at the far end of the wall to activate three short lifts in the chamber where you faced down the Brains. Return to the chamber, grab the **Shells**, **First Aid** kit, and **Bullets** you ignored earlier, and catch a lift upstairs. You can jump on any of them to get over the wall into the next room, but the center one will give you some **Jacket Armor**.

7 Snag the armor and drop down into the next room. Collect the **Rockets**, **Grenade**, **Cells**, **Shells**, and **Medkits** you find there, then walk up to the center bay. The panel will retract, revealing **Secret Area #1** stocked with **Armor**, **Bullets**, and **Rockets**. Snag 'em and head for the door to the left.

Mission 5

127

8 Enter and climb the stairs to a walkway traversing another lava pit. You can hear at least one Berserker howling out there, so you know he's coming. As it happens, he's got a friend, and he'll be charging you from behind. If you're not careful, the two monsters will trap you on the walkway and knock you into the lava. To increase your chances of survival, start down the walkway, then dash back through the door. If you turn fast enough, you'll see the other Berserker rise up through a trapdoor—he would have been right behind you—while the one across the walkway makes a mad dash for your body parts. Dispatch the nearest creep, then blast his backup. This move enables you to take them out one at a time, but you have to work fast.

9 Proceed down the walkway. On the way, grab the **Bullets** the Stroggs have dropped. In the room at the other end, turn right and get the **Rockets** in the alcove, then scoop up the row of **Shards** in front of you. Go up the short stair and hit the green switch. The door on your right will open, and you'll be able to see the laser grid that had blocked the hallway shut down.

10 Go through the door and right, then left. Quickly drop off the edge of the open walkway and crawl back underneath to **Secret Area #2**. You'll find **First Aid** kits, a **Grenade** and … Holy crap! A **Railgun**! Now you can use those Slugs you've been collecting. When you grab the gun, a ramp will drop down in front of you. It leads back up to the hallway, only now there's a Parasite waiting for you. If you wait too long, he'll come down the ramp and give you a big, life-force-sucking kiss. So go up and try your new gun on it.

11 When the ramp closes, go back down the hallway and out to the walkway. A Berserker will rush you from your left. Keep back and blast him. Collect the **Grenades** and **Stimpacks**, and head back the way you came.

note Before you move on, check out **Secret Area #3** behind the waterfall. In fact, it's a Secret Level called Sudden Death that can be reached by jumping from the open walkway to the top of the waterfall. This is a particularly tricky jump. You have to run from the far end of the walkway and hit the edge just right—and you have to jump again as you hit the slippery crest of the water-fall. For a map and details, turn to the next chapter. After blazing through this Secret Level, come back to resume your objective here. Tip: Better save your game before jumping.

12 Go to the door at the other end of the hall, enter, and head right. The Gunner standing on the left behind the pillars with his back turned won't notice you. Shoot him before he does.

13 Grab the **Stims** and then go out to the lava pit. The bridge has collapsed. Next to it is a large grate, which you can use to get to a lower level, and cross under the lava. (Don't dawdle or a Gladiator will come along and put a hole in you.) Drop down through the grate and collect the **Bullets** and **Shells** you find, then proceed to the end of the tunnel.

14 Take the lift up into a small chamber. You're now on the other side of the lava. Shoot the crates in front of you and the explosion will blast away the bars, enabling you to exit this hideout. Don't rush out, yet. There's a Gladiator waiting for you to your right. Hang back and wait until he's near the entrance, then introduce him to your new firepower. Jump out of your hole and collect the **Quad Damage** power-up to your left. Continue to the end of the hall. You'll pass a room on the left in which a grid of lasers covers the floor. There's nothing you can do here right now. It will have to wait for later. Scoop up the **Medkits** in the hall and take the door on your right to exit to the Processing Plant.

Mission 5

Quake II

5a

Floor
Switch

5

3   3

6

Elevator

4

2

1a

Window   Floor
                                Switch

1
Start

Secret Level
SUDDEN DEATH

THIS LEVEL IS TECHNICALLY A SECRET AREA OF THE RECEIVING CENTER. To reach this level, jump from the open walkway in the Receiving Area to the top of the waterfall. This is a particularly tricky jump, so better save your game first. When you succeed, you'll be able to replenish your supplies and equipment on this area's Secret Level. You won't have much time, and you'll only have one crack at the goodies, so you've got to hustle from the instant you arrive.

Objective Summary

1. Start; Chaingun, Floor Switch (fills chamber with lava), Stimpacks
2. Stimpacks
3. Bullets, Grenades, Power Shield, Cells, Stimpacks
4. Quad Damage
5. Floor Switch (lowers pedestal), Railgun
6. Grenades, Shells, Adrenaline (upstairs)

Field Report

1 Jump from the open walkway to the top of the waterfall. This is a particularly tricky jump. You have to run from the far end of the walkway and hit the edge just right— and you have to jump again as you hit the slippery crest of the waterfall. Once over the crest you will fall into a deep pool on the other side. Swim down and you will be transported to a secret chamber. You only have seconds to run through the tunnels and chambers grabbing equipment and supplies. Wherever you go (you won't get far) you'll see timers high on the walls, counting down. When your time is up, you'll be tossed back to the walkway. Although you will be able to jump over the waterfall again, you won't get to the Secret Level a second time. The item immediately in front of you is a **Chaingun**. Grab it and start moving up the walkway, snagging **Stimpacks** as you go. Avoid the floor switch (1a) dead ahead; hitting it fills the chamber on the other side of the window with lava. Go either left or right (it makes little difference), and hit the doors.

2 Scoop up the **Stimpacks** as you run down the tunnels to the next set of doors.

3 In the next chamber you'll find a **Power Shield**, **Bullets**, **Grenades**, **Cells**, and more **Stimpacks**.

4 Take a hard right (or left, depending on how you came in) to score a **Quad Damage** inside the central chamber. Keep moving through the opposite door an down the stairs.

5 In the lower chamber you'll find **Shells**, more **Stimpacks**, and a **Railgun** on a pedestal above the lava. You have to hit the floor switch to lower the pedestal and gain access to the gun (5a).

6 You access the upper walkway with the lift in the room you just came from. Chances are you'll never make it before your time runs out; if you do, you'd find **Grenades**, **Shells**, and some **Adrenaline**.

note

Since you only have seconds until you're being tossed back to the Receiving Area, you may not be able to collect all the goodies on this level. Once you're back in the Receiving Area, go to Point 12 of the previous walkthrough to resume your mission.

Mission 5

QUAKE II

131

dermal plated cranium

PROCESSING PLANT

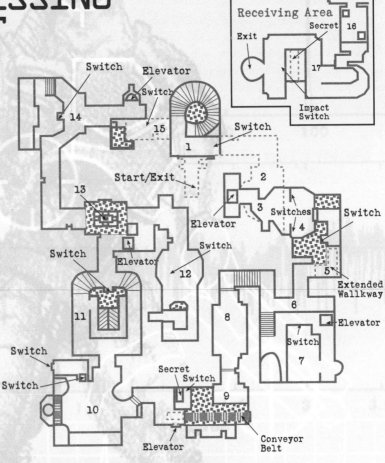

Receiving Area

Enter
(from
Processing
Plant)

Exit

Secret   16

17

Impact
Switch

Switch

Elevator

Switch

14

15

Switch

1

Start/Exit

2

3

Switches

4

Switch

13

Elevator

Switch

Switch

5

Extended
Wallyway

12

Switch

11

Elevator

6

8

Elevator

Switch

7

Switch

Switch

Secret
Switch

9

10

Conveyor
Belt

Elevator

Intel Brief

Primary Objective:	Shut down alien Processing Plant
Secondary Objective:	Shut down all machines
Unit Location:	Processing Plant
Potential Kills:	50
Goals:	5
Secrets:	3
Enemies:	Flyers, Gunners, Guards, Brains, Berserkers, Gladiator, Parasite
Weapons:	Blaster, Shotgun, Super Shotgun, Machine Gun, Chaingun, Grenade Launcher, Rocket Launcher, Hyperblaster, Railgun

Objective 2
SHUT DOWN ALL FIVE MACHINES IN THE PLANT

YOU'VE MADE IT TO THE PROCESSING PLANT. An abattoir by any other name would be every bit as gruesome as this unholy place. Before your objective is achieved, you'll witness horrors undreamed: your fellow Marines, good men all, being mangled and mutilated, ground up like meat and squashed like bugs for some unknown—probably unknowable—alien objective. Your objective is a simple one: Shut this hellhole down! (And keep your barf bag handy.)

Objective Summary

1. Machine Gun Guards, Medkits, Bullets, Stimpacks, Gunners, Jacket Armor, Switch (deactivates laser grid)
2. Shells, First Aid, Gunners, Tank, Guards, Rockets, Grenades
3. Lift, Gunner
4. Shells, Slugs, Medkits, Switches (open door)
5. Guards, Switch (stops Organic Matter Liquifier), Gladiator, First Aid, Grenades
6. Guards, Parasite, Slugs, Bullets, Combat Jacket, Grenades
7. Rockets, Switch (deactivates Bio-Assimilation Tank), Gunner
8. Gunner, Shells, Parasites, Flyers, First Aid
9. Light Guards, Gladiator, Combat Jacket, First Aid, Switch (deactivates Bio-Processing Control Unit) **Secret Area:** Power Shield
10. Parasite, Flyers, Gunner, Shards, Switch (deactivates Ionization Catalyst Chamber), Cells, Shells, Enforcer
11. Enforcers, Switch (deactivates Emulsifying Flesh Press Unit)
12. Light Guards, Medkits, Ammo, Switch (deactivates Bio-Compression Chamber)
13. Gunner, Shards, Grenades
14. Gunners, Machine Gun Guards, Switch (deactivates Enemy Processing Unit)
15. Stimpacks, Switch (opens door)
16. Enforcer, Laser Grid
17. Machine Gun Guard, Shells, First Aid, Cells, Icaruses, Flyer, Switch (opens secret area), **Secret Area:** First Aid, Shells; Exit (to Power Plant)

Field Report

1 From your entry point, two Machine Gun Guards attack from either side. Step back and blast them. Snag the **Medkits** and **Bullets** on your left. The door there won't open. Notice the laser grid blocking the hallway on your right. Take the stairs, scooping up **Stims** as you go. Move fast, Gunners are shooting and dropping grenades. They'll do a lot of damage if you're not moving—and even if you are. Take out the Gunners and grab the **Jacket Armor** you'll find on the upper level. Hit the red switch to deactivate the laser grid.

2 Go back down the stairs and collect the **Shells** and **First Aid** kit in the passageway. Two Gunners will attack from the right, from around the corner. Frag them and move to the next room. Before you enter, get your new Railgun ready. You've got a Tank to kill. The minute you enter the room, he rises out of the floor in the center of the room on a platform. Blast him! You'll have to retreat some, but with your newly acquired firepower he should go down fairly quickly. About four shots should

do it. Turn your attention to the Guards shooting at you from above. Knock them out with a lesser weapon in your arsenal, then scoop up the **Rockets** and **Grenades** the Tank dropped when he expired.

3 To the right of the entry, is a disgusting sight; an auto-lift rising out of an acid bath pulpy with gore and laces with recognizable body parts. Watch the lift careful and time your step—the acid will fry your ass. Also, be ready to jump off as you pass the upper floor. If you don't, you'll be crushed against the spiked ceiling. A Gunner attacks you immediately from across the room. Blast him quickly, but notice that the clever bastard can duck. This is a different breed! Whenever these monsters duck, you'll have to crouch to hit them.

4 After you've killed the tricky Gunner, head for the room at your right. Grab the **Shells**, **Slugs**, and **Medkits** scattered around the area as you go. You'll find two switches on the inside of the doorway. Hit them both, in any order, to open the door.

5 Go out onto the landing and shoot the Guard at the foot of the ramp on your right. Walk down his position and you'll be greeted by a mind-rending sight: live soldiers being dropped screaming into a meat grinder euphemistically known as the Organic Matter Liquifier. Hit the switch to stop the machine and raise a walkway. Blast the Gladiator that comes calling when you do. He'll cough up some slugs you can use in your new gun. Proceed down the walkway. Grab the **First Aid** kits and **Grenade** on your way to the door.

6 About half a dozen Machine Gun and Light Guards are waiting for you on the other side of the door. They're of the ducking breed also. A Parasite backs them up. Go to the door, crouch and shoot fast, and you'll get most of them before they can do much damage. Grab the **Slugs** on the left and take the stairs on the right. Go down into the next chamber, where two Machine Gun Guards will shoot at you from the left of the stairs. Take them out quickly, and then collect the **Bullets** and **Combat Jacket** in the two alcoves in which the bastards were hiding. (Don't miss the **Grenades** across from the foot of the stairs.)

7 Continue into the chamber past the alcoves on the right. You'll find some **Rockets** in a low alcove on the left and behind the panel on the right. Enter the control room and hit the green switch to deactivate the Strogg Bio-Assimilation Tank. Exit the room and duck—Gunner at 11 o'clock. Blast him and take the lift in the corner back up to the level from which you entered.

8 The doors at the other end of the ledge are now open. Enter and blast the Gunner. Go down the stairs. Grab the **Shells** at the foot of the stairs, and then turn left to open the door. Hang back; a Parasite is waiting. Use the doors for cover and take him out. Inside, two Flyers rise out of a door in the floor. Blast them down and grab the **Bullets** and **First Aid** kits you see.

Mission 5

Part 2

135

dermal plated cranium

9 Beyond the next door, three Light Guards fire at you from across the conveyor belt, and a Gladiator fires slugs at you from the far right upper ledge. The Guards are hard to hit because they can duck (bad trend developing among Stroggos cyborgs), but you've got to frag 'em. Hang back and shoot them down with light arms, then switch to your Rocket Launcher. Use it to take out the Gladiator. The machinery is still grinding away in here. Jump over the moving conveyor belt to the alcoves previously occupied by the Guards. Pick up the **Combat Jacket** and **First Aid** kits and continue all the way to the end of the walkway. Then jump across the belt again—don't slip!—and hit the green switch, deactivating the so-called Bio-Processing Control Unit. Now that the conveyor belt is off, you can go back around to your right and crawl into **Secret Area #1** at the start of the belt. Grab the **Power Shield** hidden there.

10 Take the lift up to the ledge above, where the Gladiator was stationed. Find the doors around the corner. Behind them, a nasty Parasite, a Gunner, and two Flyers await. Blast them using the doorway as cover. Collect the **Shards** on the right and left by the windows, and the **Cell** on the right. Jump across the conveyor belt for some **Shells**. Take the

lift up and hit the green switch. This deactivates the Ionization Catalyst Chamber. An Enforcer will fire at you from below. Pick him off. Two more Enforcers attack from the entryway to the left. Kill them, and then enter.

11 Inside, two more Enforcers are waiting, as it turns out if you're lucky, to die at your hands. Blast them and go down the stairs to the green switch. Hit it to deactivate the Emulsifying Flesh Press Unit. Pick up any supplies you missed and proceed down the corridor, bearing right until you come to a lift.

12 Take the lift up and blast the Enforcer waiting for you. Follow the corridor, bearing right, until you come to a door. Inside, three Light Guards work at an especially hideous machine known as the Bio-Compression Chamber. Shoot the Guards and hit the switch to shut it down. Pick up all the **Shards**, **Medkits** and **Ammo** you find.

13 Go back out through the door. There is a Gunner waiting. Blast him and grab the **Shards** ahead of you. Continue left to the large chamber in which Marines are dropping from high shafts into the stew. Jump out on the grid in the center of the room—careful, don't jump too far or you'll join the other marines—and climb out on the other side.

14 Kill the Gunners waiting for you beyond the next door, as well as the three Machine Gun Guards backing them up. Down the corridor you'll find the Enemy Processing Unit. Deactivate this monstrous machine by hitting the green switch. Take out the Guards who come after you.

15 Your primary mission is complete! But you still have to get out of here in one piece. To do that, go down the corridor to the right. Take the elevator on the left. Snag the **Stims**. Go to the door, around a corner (left). Hit the green button to open and enter. You are leaving the Processing Plant and returning to the Receiving Area, where your mission started. (This is the door that wouldn't open when you first entered.) Take the door on your right and head back.

16 Go into the corridor to the left, then look into the opening on the right. In the chamber with the floor laser grid you'll see that two pedestal platforms are moving around the room. Shoot the Enforcer, then look down. You'll see the tracks they are running on: two squares side-by-side. To get across to the other side—which you must do to continue your mission— hop from platform to platform. This is trickier than it looks, so watch the pattern of their movement and time it so you can get across quickly.

17 Once you get to the other side, shoot the Machine Gun Guard who attacks you, grab the **Shells** and **First Aid** kits you see, and get ready to go through the doors. You'll want to get ready because on the other side are two Icaruses. Aim up slightly, go through the door, and clip their wings. Go down the stairs (don't miss the **Cells**) and follow the corridor. Take out the Flyer that's lurking around the corner. Continue around the next corner. Look inside the fourth pinkish buttress structure to your left (just past the Exit, which is on your right). You'll see an impact switch. Shoot it and then go back around the corner. A **Secret Area** will now be open to you. Go in and grab the **First Aid** kits and **Shells**, then head for the Exit and continue to your next mission.

Mission 5

137

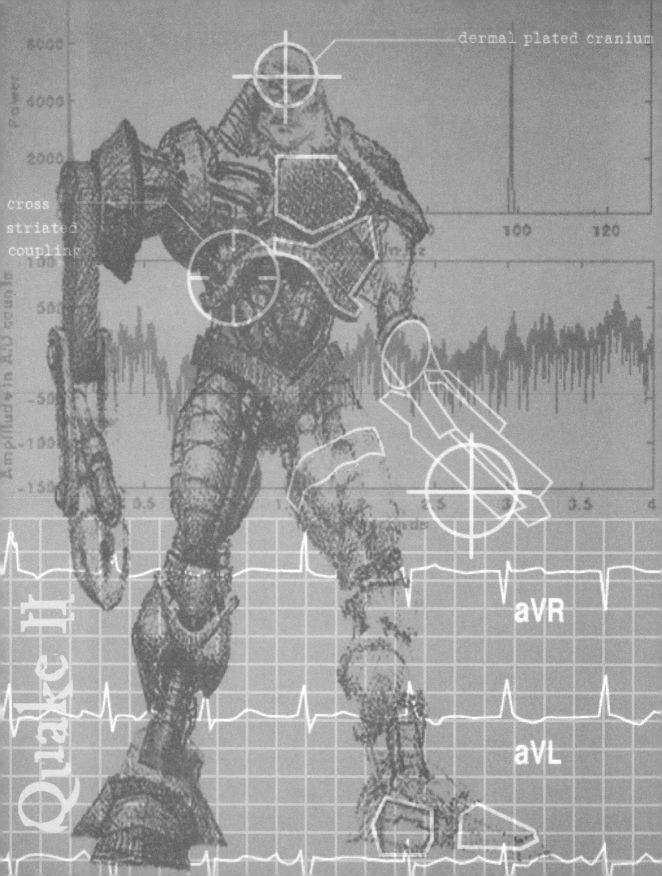

Mission 6

FIND THE REACTOR AND EXPOSE THE REACTOR CORE

Your next mission takes you deep into the Strogg power plant, where, if you are successful, you will strike our most powerful blow against the enemy. You must find and disable the Strogg main power source--the central reactor--by exposing the core and locking open its protective sleeve. Once the reactor is exposed, drain the reactor coolant to begin a chain reaction that will lead to a meltdown. By activating the two pumping stations located in the Toxic Waste dump you will accelerate the destruction by flooding the area with toxic waste. With the reactor disabled, you will have an opportunity to destroy the Strogg's most powerful weapon--the Big Gun.

Mission 6 by Unit Location

1. Power Plant
2. Reactor
3. Cooling Facility
4. Reactor
5. Toxic Waste Dump
6. Pumping Station 1
7. Pumping Station 2
8. Toxic Waste Dump
9. Reactor
10. Big Gun Facilities

dermal plated cranium

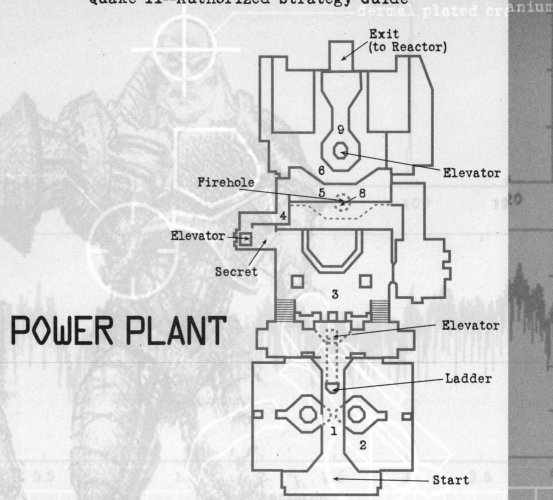

Exit
(to Reactor)

9

Elevator

6

Firehole

5   8

4

Elevator

Secret

3

POWER PLANT

Elevator

Ladder

1

2

Start

cross

striated

coupling

Intel Brief

Primary Objective: Infiltrate and destroy
                         the Strogg main reactor.
Secondary Objective: Find the Reactor. Expose
                         reactor core.
Unit Location: Power Plant
Potential Kills: 24
Goals: 2
Secrets: 2
Enemies: Super Tank, Iron Maidens,
                         Berserkers, Icaruses,
                         Flyers, Gladiators
Weapons: Blaster, Shotgun, Super
                         Shotgun, Machine Gun,
                         Chaingun, Grenade
                         Launcher, Rocket
                         Launcher, Hyperblaster,
                         Railgun, BFG

Objective 1
GAIN ACCESS TO THE STROGG REACTOR

YOU'VE HIT THE STROGG PRETTY HARD, but the damage you've inflicted so far is small stuff compared to your next mission. Right now you're deep enough into the guts of this stinkhole of a planet that you're in position to put a real hurt on Cyborg Central: the Strogg Reactor. If what you've waded through to get here is the guts of the enemy, what you're headed for is their heart—and you're going to drive a stake right through the middle of it. But first, you have to survive a trip through the Strogg Power Plant.

Objective Summary

1. Start; Grenades, Rockets
2. Super Tank, Red Keycard, Ladder, Stimpacks
3. Body Armor, Iron Maidens, **Secret Area**, Berserker, Shells, Rockets, First Aid, Stimpacks, Shells
4. Elevator, Berserker
5. Gladiator, Icarus, BFG, Cells, Flyers
6. Berserkers, Icarus, Cells, Shells, Grenades
7. Chaingun, Cells, Bullets, Iron Maidens
8. Firehole, Gladiator, Berserker, Stimpacks, Bullets
9. Icaruses, First Aid, Exit (to Reactor)

Mission 6

Quake II

Field Report

1 Before you is the Strogg Power Plant. Don't be too impressed; a single Marine is going to bring it crashing down. Grab the **Grenades** to the left of your entry point, and the **Rockets** to the right. Go toward the door ahead of you and two Berserkers will charge. Place yourself between the two smoke stacks and shoot them down. (If they hit you, the stacks will keep you on the walkway.) Go through the doorway and lure the other two Berserkers out for a shellacking.

2 Now get ready to drop down to the level below and grab the **Red Keycard** stashed just under the walkway in front of you. The good news is there's only one Strogg guarding it; the bad news is it's a Super Tank. You remember the half-track batters you fought in Mission 4? His brother is rolling back and forth in front of the key. If you position yourself on the far left (or right) of your entry point, you'll be able to spot the key and the Tank. Take a Quad Damage, then take out your Hyperblaster and send this cyborg critter to the junkyard. When he's a goner, jump down. Grab the key and continue around the central structure to a hole in the floor. Use the ladder to climb down. At the bottom, grab the two **Stimpacks** in the corners and take the elevator at the end of the short tunnel.

3 At the top of the elevator shaft, grab the **Body Armor**, then go into the large chamber through the opening at the right of the bright light. (This chamber is where you would have ended up if you had gone in through the front door.) You'll encounter some brand new

major bad guys (gals, actually) in here, so get your rocket launcher ready. As you enter the room, two Iron Maidens will rise up through the floor on either side of you. Don't let their seductive moaning fool you; these cyborg chicks are here to hurt you. And they've got the firepower to break more than your heart. Now you've got two of them to deal with. Shoot at the barrels behind the one on the right. The explosion will knock a hole in the wall, opening a very important **Secret Area**, and releasing a Berserker. If the timing is right, he will attack the Maiden on the right, giving you a chance to frag the one on the left. Rockets are the babe killer of choice here. By the time you've dispatched one, the other will have terminated the Berserker. Hang back and hit her quick with your rockets. Before you enter the secret area, scan the area for supplies. You'll find **Shells** (next to the staircase on the right), **Rockets** (dropped by a Maiden), **First Aid** kits (next to the staircase on the left), and **Stimpacks** on the main floor. Up the stairs behind you, you'll find more **Shells** in an alcove at the end of the hallway.

4 Enter the breach in the wall and take the elevator up to the second floor. Follow the corridor, but watch out. There's another Berserker around the corner. Hit him fast while you're retreating; you don't have much room to move in here. So you'll be very lucky not to take a hit.

5 Continue down the corridor to a kind of covered balcony area. There's a Gladiator on patrol here, but if you come in slowly, you can start shooting at him before he sees you. Use the corner for cover and retreat and fire if you have to until you bring him down. If you take too long to subdue the Gladiator, an Icarus will buzz by the window and start shooting at you. (He'll come eventually.) Collect the **Shells** and **First Aid** kits by the door, and then hurry past the windows to the other end of the room, grabbing the **Ammo** the Gladiator dropped on your way. It's time to collect your first **BFG** and some **Cells**. This is a big gun, and it'll do some major damage. (You'll love shooting this thing.) But it uses up ammo fast, and aiming it takes some practice. Fortunately, three Flyers will drop by the window to give some targets to warm up on. If you hit them when they're close together, you'll vaporize the lot with one shot. (You really shouldn't waste your BFG ammo on these gnats, though.) Jump on the center window sill and look out. Below you'll see a platform leading to a walkway into the building ahead. That's the door to the Reactor Room. You'll be going that way soon enough, but for now, your best move is to drop down to the level below the platform.

6 Behind you there's a hole belching fire and two Berserkers will attack, so be ready to move and groove. Blast the monsters, and then shoot the Icarus that backs them up. Collect the **Cells**, **Shells**, and **Grenades** in the far corners to the left and right.

7 Enter the corridor and follow it to a high-ceilinged room. You are now behind that red door you saw in the main chamber where you met your first Iron Maidens. Snag the **Chaingun** on your left, then stand back and shoot the crates. The explosion will reveal a cache of **Cells** and **Bullets**. Grab them quickly and head back the way you came or two more Iron Maidens will come through the door to say hi (and die).

8 Back in the big room, go to the hole in the center—the one belching fire. You've got a tricky jump to make here. The fire will damage you, so you've got to time it just right. Go to the edge—but don't get too close or you'll get burned—and slip down the hole between belches. At the bottom you've got to move fast, both to get out of the way of the next gout of fire and to keep from being blasted by a Gladiator. Keep moving while you shoot; a Berserker is on the way. Dispatch the howling cyborg, and then scan the room for supplies—**Cells**, **Stimpacks**, and **Bullets** (behind the elevator). Now you can head for the Reactor knowing you've grabbed all the goodies in the Power Plant.

9 Go to the elevator and ride up to the platform you saw out the window earlier. Get ready to shoot up; two Icaruses will dog you almost immediately. Knock them out of the sky, then head down the walkway, grab the two **First Aid** kits, and enter the door to the Reactor.

Mission 6

Quake II

143

dermal plated cranium

REACTOR

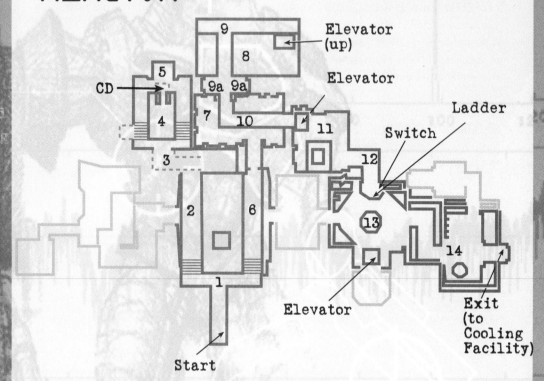

9

8

Elevator (up)

5

CD →

9a 9a

Elevator

4

7

10

Ladder

3

11

Switch

12

2

6

13

Start

1

14

Elevator

Exit (to Cooling Facility)

Intel Brief

Primary Objective:	Infiltrate and destroy the Strogg main reactor.
Secondary Objective:	Find reactor. Expose reactor core.
Unit Location:	Reactor
Potential Kills:	46/57
Goals:	2/3
Secrets:	0/1
Enemies:	Berserkers, Gladiators, Iron Maidens, Flyers, Gunners, Icaruses
Weapons:	Blaster, Shotgun, Super Shotgun, Machine Gun, Chaingun, Grenade Launcher, Rocket Launcher, Hyperblaster, Railgun, BFG

Quake II

Objective 2
FIND AND EXPOSE THE REACTOR CORE

YOU'RE STILL HEADING FOR THE REACTOR, but the enemy is amping up to stop you. No doubt they've figured out your intentions. They will be throwing everything at you but the kitchen sink. (Notice the number of potential kills in your Intel Brief.) So keep your head down and stay in motion! Take special care to collect ammunition and health kits wherever you find them. You're going to need them both.

Objective Summary

1. Start; Berserkers, Bullets, Grenades
2. Medkit, Gladiator, Slugs, Super Shotgun, Shells
3. Berserkers
4. Rockets, Medkit, Iron Maidens, Berserker, CD, Gunners, Gladiator, Medkits, Stimpacks, Grenades, Rockets, Cells, Slugs, Hyperblaster
5. Body Armor, Stims, Grenades
6. Gladiators, Slugs
7. Berserker, Gladiators, Quad Damage, Flyers, Railgun, Stimpacks, Medkit, Laser Grid
8. Berserkers, Gunners, Gladiators
9. Medkits, Stimpacks, Flyers, Berserker, Iron Maidens, Shards, Bullets, Grenades
10. Machine Gun, Gladiator
11. Medkit, Bullets, Berserker, Gladiator, Stimpacks, Shells, Slugs
12. Gunner
13. Reactor
14. Gunners, Stimpacks, Exit (to Cooling Facility)

Mission 6

145

Field Report

1 Look down the corridor ahead and you'll see two Gunners marching back and forth. Take careful aim, and when their paths cross, spray them with a Chaingun or Hyperblaster. You'll drop them both before they know what hit them. Snag the **Bullets** and **Grenade** they left behind and then head down the hallway to the left.

2 Grab the **Medkit** in the corner. Careful, though, there's a Gladiator guarding the narrow walkway to the right. When he comes after you, shoot him down using the corner for cover. Take the **Slugs** he drops and hustle down the walkway to the red door. Grab the **Super Shotgun** and **Shells** as you go, but move fast or the two Gladiators on the parallel walk- way on your right will shoot at you.

3 On the other side of the door you'll have to fight through a total of five Berserkers to get to the end of the cor- ridor. Run and gun or they'll cream you. Hear that feminine moaning? Sounds like there's at least one heavy metal babe in your future.

4 When you get to the ledge, collect the **Rockets** in the right corner and the **Medkit** on the left and then head down the stairs, Rocket Launcher in hand. Cautiously approach the lower landing. Down on the floor of the chamber, an Iron Maiden will be ready to strike with a rocket or two. Hit her first from a protected position on the ledge, and then nail the second one when she comes to check on her cyborg sister. You shouldn't have to change your aim much for the second monster. Beware, however, of the Berserker who charges up to get you. Switch to a spraying weapon, such as a Hyperblaster or Chaingun, and jump down. An alcove has opened up in the space beneath where you were standing, inside of which is a **CD** you'll need to complete your mission. But don't even bother looking at it, yet. Instead, go directly to the open doorway ahead and start blasting left. Two Gunners are hiding in a recess in the wall out in the hallway. They would have ambushed you when you went for the CD. Now grab the CD. Turn immediately and begin firing at the right wall. Taking the disk triggers an explosion that releases a Gladiator from a cubbyhole inside the wall. Run to the doorway as you fire and duck around the corner. Two more Iron Maidens will appear on the ledge where you entered. They won't be happy about what you did to their sisters. Finish off the Gladiator first, then get out your Rocket Launcher for the Maidens. (If you've used up your rockets, use your Railgun.) Work fast; they're on their way down. When all is quiet, rummage around and gather up some supplies, including some **Medkits** and **Stimpacks** (which you will probably need pretty badly), **Grenades**, **Rockets**, **Cells**, **Slugs**, and a **Hyperblaster**. Don't miss the **Stims** in the dark corner, and don't take too long or another Iron Maiden will shoot at you from a doorway on a ledge above and behind you. (If she does, stop and pop a couple of rockets her way.)

5 Go back up to the ledge above the CD alcove. You'll find that some **Body Armor**, **Stims**, and **Grenades** have appeared, which you can add to your inventory.

6 Take the stairs on your right and return to the upper level. Go back through the red door, run down the walkway, then go left toward the start of the other walkway. Two Gladiators guard this one. The first one will come at you when you fire. You should have plenty of room to nail him. The other one will hang back by the door. You'll need a long-range weapon to take him down. Use the **Slugs** you just picked up to give him a taste of his own medicine.

Mission 6

7 Go to the door (the CD in our inventory will let you walk right in), but watch out: there's a Berserker and another Gladiator inside. Use the doorway for cover and take them down (the Gladiator coughs up a **Quad Damage**). If you take too long, three Flyers will attack from behind, so work fast. Kill them, and another Gladiator charges you. Above you, more baddies are shooting, including a Gladiator. Use the far corner of the room as cover, and take them out—this will ease your advance in a few minutes. When they're history, collect the **Railgun**, **Stimpacks**, and **Medkit** in the far-left corner, then go to the hallways blocked by a blue laser grid.

8 The room beyond is packed with monsters. Before you continue, try tossing in a few Grenades to soften things up. Next get out a spraying weapon with plenty of ammo, and queue up the QD in your inventory. Now notice the rhythm with which the lasers change position. Crouch and crawl under the grid. As soon as you're through, fight off whoever's made it through your Grenade assault. The Quad Damage power-up you just collected is essential—hit it the instant you reach the next room. You'll have Berserkers, Gunners, and Gladiators coming at you all at once. (You could use the BFG to clear the room fast, but it takes so long to charge when you hit the trigger, that you'll actually take more damage than you will with the QD and a spraying weapon.)

9 When you've cleared the room (don't miss the **Medkits** in the corner), it's time to play "Follow the Moaning Cyborg." Go to the other side of the room and take the elevator to the upper level. When you go for the **Stimpacks** and **Medkit** at the end of the walkway, Flyers and a Berserker attack from behind. Turn around and take them out. Get your Rockets or Railgun ready and turn right. (You might be out of rockets, but you should have the slugs you collected from the fallen Gladiator.) The Iron Maidens you've been hearing will come at you from both sides of the door (9a). Blow them away and then gather the supplies stashed around the room: **Shards**, **Bullets**, **Grenades**, and a **Medkit**.

10 On the walkway in the other room, you'll see a **Machine Gun**. Don't rush out to get it or a Gladiator standing on the far left will put a hole in you (unless you managed to take him out earlier). Shoot him down from the corner of the doorway, and then take the gun.

11 Proceed down the walkway past the dead Gladiator and take the elevator down to a lower level. (Grab the **Medkit** and **Bullets** in the corners before you go.) A Berserker and another Gladiator are waiting at the bottom, so stay facing the green switch as the elevator descends and be ready to shoot. If you stay on the elevator while you blast the monsters, it'll take you back up out of harms way automatically, creating some badly needed cover. (You have to hit the switch again to go back down.) When you've killed the monsters, grab the **Stimpacks** along the left wall, the **Shells** in the right corner, and the **Slugs** the Gladiator dropped. Take the corridor on your left and follow it to a red door.

12 A Gunner is waiting directly behind the door. Open it and backup, fast. He won't come through, so you can use the door as cover while you waste him. (Crouch and fire under the door as it rises and he won't get off a shot.)

13 Enter the room. That tall pillar in front of you is the Reactor you've been looking for. Turn left and hit the green switch to release the Reactor core lock, exposing the radioactive core. (Can you say "radiation induced sterility"?) Your field computer will be directing you to find the Cooling Facility, which you will need to sabotage to blow this thing.

14 To get there, climb down the ladder and take the tunnel on your right. Follow the tunnel. You'll have to fight your way through two Gunners in the middle of the tunnel and one at the door near the end. Grab the **Stimpacks** in the corner on your right, and then go through the door into the Cooling Facility.

Mission 6

149

derma_plated cranium

13a 13

Switch

Secret

Exit
(to Reactor)

3

Ladder

4

5

2

1

12

6

Start Elevator
(up)

12a

Crates

11

7

9

Secret

Switch

10

8

Valve

COOLING
FACILITY

Intel Brief

Primary Objective:	Infiltrate and destroy the Strogg main reactor
Secondary Objective:	Activate cooling pump to lower coolant around the Reactor
Unit Location:	Cooling Facility
Potential Kills:	39
Goals:	2
Secrets:	3
Enemies:	Gladiators, Gunners, Technicians, Iron Maidens, Berserkers, Icaruses
Weapons:	Blaster, Shotgun, Super Shotgun, Machine Gun, Chaingun, Grenade Launcher, Rocket Launcher, Hyperblaster, Railgun, BFG

Quake II

Objective 3
ACTIVATE THE COOLING PUMP TO LOWER COOLANT AROUND THE REACTOR

NICE GOING, MARINE. You've locked open the Reactor's protective sheath and left it vulnerable. But even though the core is exposed, you can't just blast something like that. What you need is a chain reaction that will lead to a meltdown. Lowering the Reactor's coolant level should get the ball rolling. As your field computer advised, the best place to start this process is, you guessed, the Cooling Facility.

── Objective Summary

1. Start; Shells, Stimpacks, Medkits, Rockets
2. Grenades, Gladiator, Gunners, Chaingun, Switch (to access underground water system)
3. Technicians
4. Shards, Stimpacks, Rockets, Grenade,
5. Ladder, **Secret Area:** First Aid, Bullets, Grenades, Adrenaline
6. Iron Maidens, Hyperblaster
7. Berserkers, Gunners, Rockets, **Secret Area:** Megahealth
8. Gunners, Shards, Slugs, Grenades
9. Gunner, Iron Maiden, Rocket Launcher, Shells, First Aid, Valve (activates pump)
10. Iron Maidens, Switch (completes pump cycle), Rockets, **Secret Area:** Railgun, Body Armor, Quad Damage
11. Ammo, Gladiator, Icarus, First Aid, Bullets, Shells, Grenades, Medkit
12. Gladiator, Gunner, Icaruses, Armor Shards, Medkits, Bullets, Shells, Grenades
13. Gunners, Gladiator, Iron Maiden, Bullets, Shells, Hole (to exit), Exit (to Reactor)

Mission 6

Field Report

1 The room you enter is cyborg free. Grab the **Shells**, **Stimpacks**, **Medkits**, and **Rockets** stashed here. Don't worry about falling through the wide-spaced grating in the floor. Go to the mouth of the shaft and jump in.

2 Follow the tunnel to the open courtyard. Blast the Gladiator and two Gunners on guard here. Collect a **Grenade**, two **First Aid** kits, and the **Ammo** the monsters drop. Don't miss the **Chaingun** twirling above the crates. Behind the Chaingun is a red switch. Hit the switch and a long section of floor at the foot of the ramp will open.

3 Get ready to get wet, and jump into the hole. You'll land in a chamber bisected by a water-filled channel. Three hovering Technicians will attack immediately. Blast them and jump into the moving water.

4 Use the curb to the right into a room full of supplies: **Shards**, **Stimpacks**, **Rockets**, and **Grenades**.

5 Slip back into the water and let it pull you along. Stick close to the left side of the channel. At the point where the channel veers left and down, jump out onto the curb. Make your way to the left and down to a ladder, and climb down. This sloped room is **Secret Area #1**. Enter the open tunnel and collect a secret stash of **First Aid** kits, **Bullets**, **Grenades**, and **Adrenaline**. Before you climb back up the ladder, get your Rocket Launcher or Railgun ready. You shouldn't have to use either one, but better safe than sorry.

6 At the top of the ladder, jump back into the water, but instead of riding the current passively, swim hard with it. You'll be able to move very fast down the slope and through the next room past the three Iron Maidens ready to ambush you there. You'll have to leave behind a **Hyperblaster**, but it's a small price to pay to avoid the damage you would take climbing out to get it.

7 The water will take you down another slope into a large pool. Two lifts are in operation here, cycling up out of the water. Take either one to the upper walkway. Face the wall as you ride up and get ready to fire. Three Berserkers and a Gunner will be waiting for you. Dispatch the monsters and go get the **Rockets** in the bay around the far side of the walkway. There's also **Secret Area #2** located below the walkway. Follow the walkway until it ends, then drop down onto the ledge below. Walk around the ledge counter-clockwise, jump over the stream below, and keep following the ledge to find a **Megahealth**. Jump into the water below, and ride an elevator up again.

8 Go through the door at the top and kill the Gunners on the other side. Collect the **Shards** and **Slugs**. Follow the corridor around, bearing left, past the water on your right. (There are **Grenades** in the water if you need them.)

9 The room beyond the door you come to is guarded by a Gunner and an Iron Maiden—a deadly combination. Hopefully, you have some Rockets left, but if you don't, you just picked up some slugs for your Railgun. Enter the room and turn left immediately and fire at the

Iron Maiden down by the crates at the end of the room. She's far enough away that you should be able to take her out without taking any hits. When you go for the **Rocket Launcher** on your right, the Gunner will come out from behind the big pumping on your left. Turn and shoot him down. Go around the room and collect the **Shells** and **First Aid** kits. Stop at the massive valve where the Gunner came at you. Turn the valve to activate the pump.

10 Now, climb up on the crates. When the huge central pump piston pauses at the bottom of its cycle, step onto it and ride up to a narrow ledge. Jump off to your right onto the ledge—watch out, it's very narrow. On the platform to your left, two Iron Maidens will attack from behind the crates. Hit your QD and blast them. One shot each should do it, and the armor should keep your injuries to a minimum. Sticking close to the left, make your way onto the platform. Snag the **Rockets** the cyborg sisters dropped, and hit the switch on your right to complete the pump sequence and start up the two mushroom-shaped pistons to your left.

note Your field computer will advise you to return to the Reactor, but before you do, notice that hitting the second switch has opened up **Secret Area #3** in the wall down by the crates. Jump down and grab the **Railgun**, **Body Armor**, and **Quad Damage** power-up hidden there, then climb back up to the ledge.

Now, use the crates in front of you to hop to the first piston and then to the second piston until you make your way

up to the walkway high on the back wall. (Careful, don't jump too far or you end up back down in the Valve chamber again.) It's a bit of a challenge unless you're a very accurate jumper.

11 Follow the walkway up the ramp and grab the **Ammo** in the hallway. You'll have to dispatch another Gladiator and an Icarus on your way out. (Don't forget the **First Aid** kits at the other end.) Follow the hallway to an elevator. Grab the **Bullets**, **Shells**, **Grenades**, and **Medkit**, then step into the elevator.

12 The elevator takes you up to an open courtyard guarded by a Gladiator, an Icarus, and a Gunner. You have virtually no cover here, so you'll have to run and gun. Make a mad dash for the water channel in front of you and swim with the current to get your speed up.

note If you want a quick adrenaline rush, go around the elevator to the right. Blast the explosive barrels in front of you and follow the narrow walkway around the corner to some Armor Shards (12a). On your way back, the previous baddies have been joined by three more Icaruses ready to split your bones. If you're brave, try taking them out while collecting the **Bullets**, **Shells**, **Medkits**, and **Grenades** in the courtyard.

13 You'll go around a corner, down a slope, and past several Gunners, a Gladiator, and an Iron Maiden until the stream dumps you out at the end. Be sure you get dumped left. Run and gun while heading for the stairs and drop down the hole at the bottom (13a). Collect the **Bullets** and **Shells** and head for the Exit back to the Reactor.

dermal plated cranium

REACTOR

Start

4

3

2

6

5

1

Secret

Exit
(to Toxic
Waste Dump)

Intel Brief

Primary Objective:	Infiltrate and Destroy the Strogg main reactor
Secondary Objective:	Go to Toxic Waste Dump. Activate Pumping Stations
Unit Location:	Reactor
Potential Kills:	11/57
Goals:	1/3
Secrets:	1/1
Enemies:	Berserker, Gladiators, Iron Maidens, Flyers
Weapons:	Blaster, Shotgun, Super Shotgun, Machine Gun, Chaingun, Grenade Launcher, Rocket Launcher, Hyperblaster, Railgun, BFG

V2

V2

Quake II

Objective 4
GO TO THE TOXIC WASTE DUMP

YOU'VE GOT A NICE CHAIN REACTION STARTED, MARINE, but you should help it along. You don't want the Strogg stopping the show before the climax. Your field computer has advised you to go to the Toxic Waste Dump and activate the pumps there to help lower the coolant levels by filling up the place with toxic slime. The operative word here is "toxic." What the hell, you needed to work on your tan anyway. This leg of your mission takes you back through the reactor section, so you've got to hustle. Move out, Marine. You've got some radioactive slime to distribute!

Objective Summary

1. Start; Chaingun, Medkits
2. Reactor
3. Berserker, **Secret Area:** Adrenaline, Shards
4. Gladiator, Iron Maiden
5. Iron Maidens, Flyers, BFG, Rockets, Cells, Ammo
6. Stimpacks, Exit (to Toxic Waste Dump)

Mission 6

Quake II

155

derbal plated cranium

Field Report

1 Go through the door, grab the **Chaingun** and **Medkits**, and follow the tunnel to the shaft.

2 Jump down the shaft to a familiar room, then go through the lighted doorway. Follow the tunnel back to the Reactor room.

3 Take the next lighted entryway. Go right at the wall map and blast the Berserker that attacks you. On the other side of the central structure, opposite the open doorway, is a **Secret Area**. Shoot the wall and a ladder is revealed. Climb the ladder and grab some **Adrenaline**, and a few handy **Shards**. Don't go through the secret upper panel, you'll just be backtracking. Go back down the ladder (you have to shoot to open the door), jump out and go to the red door.

4 Open the door and blast the Gladiator sentry. Continue past the second red door and shoot the next Gladiator coming toward you. Enter the corridor. Get your heavy artillery ready and go down the stairway. An Iron Maiden will greet you there. Blow her away fast and keep moving.

5   As you round the corner, her sister cyborg will come after you from under the stairs on your right. A third Iron Maiden will attack from below on your left. Dispatch these antisocial females and climb the stairs. At the top of the stairs is another BFG, giving you some much needed extra firepower. Use the gun to clear the air when half a dozen Flyers attack in a swarm. The BFG will make short work of them. Grab the Cells they drop and scoop up the Rockets dropped by the Iron Maidens. (There's more Ammo in the corners and under the stairs.)

6   Go down to the tunnel and follow it into a low-ceiling chamber. Scoop up the row of Stimpacks. In the center of the room is another shaft. Jump down this shaft to exit to Toxic Waste Dump.

Mission 6

PAYBACK

TOXIC WASTE DUMP

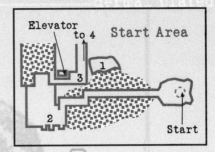

Elevator to 4   Start Area

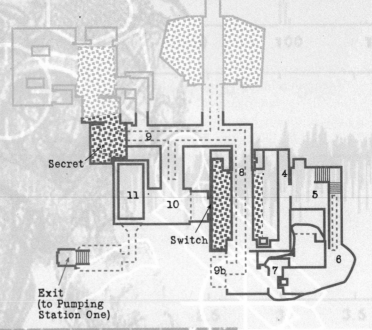

9

Secret

11   10   8   4   5

Switch

9b   7   6

Exit
(to Pumping
Station One)

Intel Brief

Primary Objective:	Infiltrate and destroy the Strogg main reactor
Secondary Objective:	Gain access to Pumping Station One
Unit Location:	Toxic Waste Dump
Potential Kills:	43/61
Goals:	1/2
Secrets:	2/2
Enemies:	Gladiators, Gunners, Berserkers, Iron Maidens, Icaruses
Weapons:	Blaster, Shotgun, Super Shotgun, Machine Gun, Chaingun, Grenade Launcher, Rocket Launcher, Hyperblaster, Railgun, BFG

Objective 5
GAIN ACCESS TO PUMPING STATION 1

THINGS ARE REALLY STARTING TO HEAT UP The Strogg are definitely on to your plan, so you've got to hurry to the pumping stations. Unfortunately, Pumping Station One is utterly unaccessible from the station itself. Even more unfortunately, the area where the opening switch is located is swarming with cyborgs. Time to show 'em how it's done.

Objective Summary

1. Start; Shells, Stims, Berserkers, Hyperblaster, Ammo
2. Machine Gun Guards, Bullets, Shells, Cells
3. Gunner, Shells, First Aid
4. Grenade Launcher, Guards
5. Iron Maidens, Berserkers, Stims
6. Guards, Tank
7. Gunners, Combat Armor
8. Iron Maidens, Berserkers, Gladiator, Shells, Medkits
9. Railgun, Gunners, Environmental Suit, Secret Area #1: Invulnerability, Stimpacks, Shards; Secret Area #2: Cells, Shards, Environmental Suit
10. Gladiator, Gunners, Switch (to slide floor back), Icaruses, Ammo, First Aid
11. Gunners, Exit (to Pumping Station 1)

Mission 6

V1   V4

V2   V5

Quake II

Field Report

1

At your entry point, snag the **Shells** and **Stimpacks**, and then proceed down the tunnel walkway. Waste the Berserker coming at you, then hop out and snag the Hyperblaster and **Ammo** on your right. Watch out for the green stuff. It's toxic waste and that stuff is, well … toxic.

2

Continue down the tunnel, shoot the three Guards who make the mistake of charging at you from the right. Collect the **Bullets**, **Shells**, and **Cells** they drop.

3

On your right, a Gunner will be lobbing grenades at you. Use the entryway as cover while you take him out. Proceed down the tunnel. Step out onto the "dock" and turn right. Grab the **Shells** and ride the eleva-

tor up to the next level. Don't miss the two **First Aid** kits. You're going to need them.

4

Follow the walkway around past another door toward the **Grenade Launcher**, which you will want to add to your inventory in a few minutes. For now, get ready to blast the Guards who attack as you pass the door. Don't get caught in the corner by the Grenade Launcher! You won't have any room to maneuver, and you'll have the wrong weapon in your hands. Take out the Guards and then grab the gun. Stash it in your inventory for now and get your Rocket Launcher ready.

5

Open the door and blast the Iron Maidens waiting for you inside, high and to the right. Switch to another weapon and enter. Shoot the howling Berserker behind the stairs. Grab the **Stimpacks** along the left wall. (There are more through the opening to the right of the stairs), and head up

6 the stairway.

Three Guards will come at you. Take them out and back off; a Tank is on its way to back them up. Luckily, he's slow. Switch to a more powerful gun, take a Quad Damage, and wait until he comes **7** around the corner to take him out.

Head for the lift at the end of the walkway. A Gunner will be shooting down at you, so you'll have to hang back until you've taken him out. Your position sucks, but it's better to shoot them from down here than ride up and get nailed in the open. When the Gunners are down, ride up on the lift and grab the goodies up here, including the **Combat Armor** on your right. Much

8 needed protection there! Proceed down the corridor to the door at the end.

Beyond the door is a high, open area with a hell of a welcoming committee. (Or a welcoming committee from Hell, depending on your point of view.) Berserkers, a Gladiator, and a pair of strategically distant Iron Maidens are waiting for you in an exposed area. Open the door and back off, drawing the Berserkers and Gladiator in after you one at a time so you can waste them separately. Now get out a Rocket Launcher or Railgun. Use the crouch-and-fire technique to eliminate the Iron Maidens. Watch yourself; their rockets can and do slip past the door before it closes. If you aren't careful, at least a few will follow the Berserkers right down your throat. When the front is clear, collect the **Shells** and **Medkits** outside and cross the walkway. Careful, there's a sniper Iron Maiden **9** to your right and below.

Head down the walkway and grab the **Railgun** ahead of you. Switch quickly to a spraying weapon for the coming festivities, and enter the corridor and turn left. Several Gunners are waiting for you on both sides of the entrance. Hug the wall, crouch, and shoot. Take your time to

note make sure you've cleared them all out. **10**

There are two Secret Areas down in the slime in front of you. They'll yield all kinds of useful goodies. The only problem is, going after them will create quite a detour. If you chose to go, here's what you do. Walk toward the far end of the walkway. Shoot the Guard on your right and grab the **Enviro-Suit**. Enable your E-suit and jump into the toxic green stuff. Swim down and to your left to find the **Secret Area #1** (9a). Collect the **Invulnerability** power-up, **Stimpacks**, and **Shards**.

Surface and crawl up under the space under the walkway you jumped from. It's covered with slime, but you can walk on it. Move fast and follow the shallow tunnel straight ahead until you have to turn right, then ride the sludge down the slew and into the **Secret Area #2** (9b). Grab the **Cells**, **Shards**, and fortuitously, another **Enviro-Suit** (yours has just given out). Go back to where the duct came out into the open. Jump down and walk back around and up to the hallway that took you to the place where you first jumped into the slime. (It's quite a walk, but you've wasted all the bad guys, so it'll be a quiet one.)

Go past the right corridor and get ready to turn left. (Down at the end of the right corridor is a door you can't enter from here. Two Maidens and an Icarus guard it.) A Gladiator and Gunner are guarding the area to the left and you'll have to take them out. When you've killed the cyborgs, shoot the barrels near the bars on your right. The explosion will blast one of the bars away, allowing you access to the switch. Hit the switch and a long section of the floor on the other side of the area will open. This is how you'll get to Pumping Station One, but first you'll have to eliminate the two Icaruses that have appeared suddenly to block your way. Use the bars for cover and blast them to pieces. Next collect the

11 **Ammo** and **First Aid** kit.

When those strange birds are history, jump down into the opening you created. You'll land in a spacious passageway. Collect the goodies you find here, but watch out for a Gunner who will attack from the other end of the passage. There are two more around the corner doing their best to convince you to stay. Decline their offer with your trigger finger, grab the ammo behind the stairs, and take the Exit to Pumping Station One.

Mission 6

V1

V4

V2

V5

PUMPING STATION 1

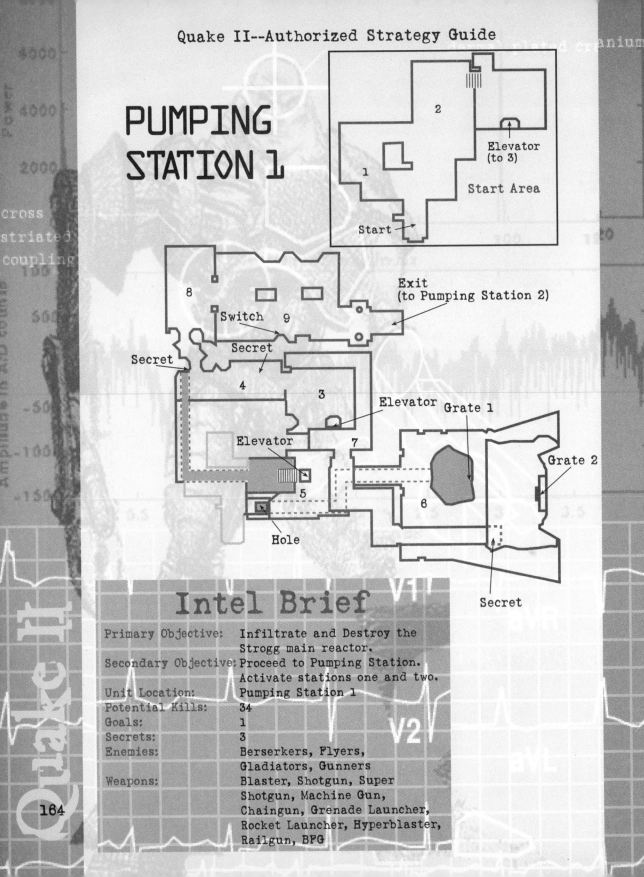

2

Elevator
(to 3)

1

Start Area

Start

Exit
(to Pumping Station 2)

8

Switch   9

Secret

Secret

4   3

Elevator   Grate 1

Elevator

7   Grate 2

5

6

Hole

Secret

Intel Brief

Primary Objective:	Infiltrate and Destroy the Strogg main reactor.
Secondary Objective:	Proceed to Pumping Station. Activate stations one and two.
Unit Location:	Pumping Station 1
Potential Kills:	34
Goals:	1
Secrets:	3
Enemies:	Berserkers, Flyers, Gladiators, Gunners
Weapons:	Blaster, Shotgun, Super Shotgun, Machine Gun, Chaingun, Grenade Launcher, Rocket Launcher, Hyperblaster, Railgun, BFG

Quake II

Objective 6
ACTIVATE PUMPING STATION 1

THIS IS A BAD TRIP, BUT ONE YOU'VE GOT TO MAKE, MARINE. Going through the Toxic Waste area is the only way to gain access to the first pumping station. And you have to activate the first pump before you can go to the second one. (Got that?) It's a dirty job, and you're the one who gets to do it.

Objective Summary

1. Start; Chaingun, Gunners, Stimpacks, Gladiator, Grenades, First Aid, Bullets, Shells, Slugs
2. Gunners, Shards, Medkits, Shards
3. Guards, Gunners, Shells, First Aid, Rockets
4. Berserkers, Grenade Launcher, Secret Area: Adrenaline; Secret Area (access to lower level)
5. Technicians, Cells, Adrenaline, Hole (entrance to outer courtyard)
6. Flyers, Secret Area: Quad Damage, Gladiator
7. Gunners, Stimpacks, Adrenaline, Armor
8. Gunners, Ammo, Medkits
9. Gladiator, Switch (activates the pumps), Exit (to Pumping Station 2)

Mission 6

Toxic II

Field Report

1 Go through the door and grab the **Chaingun.** Use it on the Gunner who attacks from the left. Grab the **Stims** and hit the three Gunners coming up around the corner on your right. Go back around to the left and take out the Gladiator. He's a ways away so you can nail him with your Railgun from a distance. Gather the stuff in the halls: **Grenades**, **First Aid** kits, **Bullets**, **Shells**, and **Slugs**.

2 Enter the room the Gladiator was guarding. Three Gunners will snipe at you from the room to the right of the crates. Hug the wall and work your way over and blast them. You'll have to go up the short stair and into the room to get all of them. (The cowards!) Grab the **Shards** to the right of the doorway and the **Medkits** next to the lift and in the far corner. Be sure to blast the barrels on your right to reveal some more **Shards**, then take the elevator up to the next room.

3 Put your back to the wall so you can come off the elevator firing. Guards and Gunners will come at you from all sides and above. Be fast and use the corner to the left of the elevator as cover if you need to. When you've cleared the room be sure to pick up the **Shells**, **First Aid** kits, and **Rockets** in the corners.

4 Go up the ramp and take out the two Berserkers. (Avoid blasting the barrels to the right of the entrance—you'll need them in a second.) Next, head for the **Grenade Launcher** twirling above the stack of crates. Grab it and look to your right (between the vertical pipes) into the next room, which is full of Gladiators, Gunners, and Berserkers. Lob a bunch of Grenades into the next room to soften things up (you don't have to go in there, yet), then turn around and shoot the flickering florescent light to the right of the doorway behind you. A crate on the left side will explode, revealing **Secret Area #1** with some **Adrenaline**. If you didn't destroy the explosive barrels earlier, you can climb down and use them to get it. Next, take a shot at the crack in the pipe closest to the crates; you'll blow a large hole in it and reveal **Secret Area #2**, which will give you access to the next leg of your mission.

5 Take out your favorite gun, then climb into the hole and drop down into some fast-moving water. In short order, the water will dump you into a chamber guarded by two Technicians. Take them out from underwater if you can. Grab the **Cells** they dropped, take the stairs up out of the water, and ride the nearby elevator up to the ledge. Upstairs, snag the **Adrenaline**, and look down over the edge. Below you'll see another pipe. Through the hole in it, you'll see more running water. Take a deep breath and drop down into the hole.

6 The rushing water will sweep you out into an open area. Notice the grate in front of you. Shoot it, and then climb up out of the water, but stay down on the rocks. A swarm of Flyers will attack suddenly and you can use the hollow under the walkway as cover while you take them down. When the air is clear again, jump up on the walkway. Notice the grate high up in the gray structure. Aim carefully and shoot that grate to complete a sequence that reveals **Secret Area #3** at the end of the walkway where a **Quad Damage** power-up is hidden. When you go to collect it, a

Gladiator will emerge from the door behind you and start shooting. Blast him quickly or he'll do a lot of damage.

7 Proceed to the door the Gladiator came from, and shoot the Gunner inside. Follow the corridor. You'll quickly come to a door leading to a balcony. Shoot the two Gunners who come at you, and then grab the **Stimpacks**, **Adrenaline**, and **Armor** around the corner to your right. Drop down and head back up the ramp into the room through which you gained access to the underground water system.

8 Head for the next room. If you followed our advice earlier and lobbed some Grenades into this room, you won't be facing a tough battle. Take out any remaining resistance and collect the **Ammo** and **Medkits**.

9 Turn right and into the room with the pumps. Another Gladiator is guarding this area. Blast him, then hit the switch on the wall past the pump on the right to activate the pumps. (It's in that first large mass of conduits.) You can now head for the Exit to Pumping Station 2.

167

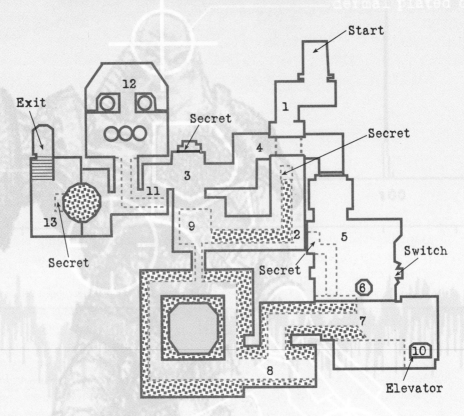

Start

12

Exit

Secret

1

Secret

4

3

11

Secret

13

9

2

5

Secret

Switch

6

7

10

8

Elevator

PUMPING STATION 2

Intel Brief

Primary Objective:	Infiltrate and destroy the Strogg main reactor.
Secondary Objective:	Proceed to Pumping Stations. Activate stations one and two.
Unit Location:	Pumping Station 2
Potential Kills:	43
Goals:	2
Secrets:	4
Enemies:	Tanks, Berserkers, Gladiators, Technicians
Weapons:	Blaster, Shotgun, Super Shotgun, Machine Gun, Chaingun, Grenade Launcher, Rocket Launcher, Hyperblaster, Railgun, BFG

Objective 7
ACTIVATE PUMPING STATION 2

ONE DOWN, ONE TO GO. You're really making them sweat. The whole joint is coming apart, and the bad guys know it's your doing. And they will do anything to stop you. The forces between you and your final objective are formidable ... and all because of one little Marine. HOO-rah!

_____Objective Summary

1. Start; Cells, Stims, Gunner, Gladiator
2. Berserkers, Gladiator
3. Secret Area: Body Armor
4. Gunners, Shards, Ammo
5. Guards, Tanks, Switch (to activate the pump)
6. Hole (to Blue Keycard), Guards, Technicians
7. Secret Area: Invulnerability
8. Ammo Pack, Gunners, First Aid
9. BFG, Technicians, Secret Area: Adrenaline
10. Gunner, Blue Keycard
11. Guards, Berserkers
12. First Aid, Rockets, Enviro-Suit, Gunners, Technicians, Stims, Body Armor
13. Secret Area: Quad Damage, Shells, Medkits, Exit (to Toxic Waste Dump)

Mission 6

Field Report

1 From your entry point, grab the **Cells** and **Stims** in front of you and get ready for an attack from the right. A Gunner will come around the corner, spoiling for a fight. Go ahead and give him one. Hang back and wait for the Gladiator backing him up.

2 Collect all the dropped ammo and head up the ramp. Move fast and be ready to shoot. Two Berserkers will hit you from the right, and another Gladiator will gun you from the walkway above and behind you. Run and gun! Take out the Berserkers first, and then come back for the back-shooting Gladiator—your Rocket Launcher should do the trick.

3 Go down the walkway until you come to a closed blue door on your right and an open doorway on your left. Shoot at the alien symbol embossed on the wall in front of you to open **Secret Area #1** and score some **Body Armor**. You can't open the door on your right without the Blue Keycard, so go through the open doorway on your left.

4 Follow the corridor, taking out the two Gunners you meet and grabbing the **Shards** and **Ammo** on the walkway from which the Gladiator sniped you.

5 When you get to a closed door, get out your heavy artillery. This is the second pump room, and two Guards and two Tanks guard it. You should be able to get most of them from the doorway. When the room has been cleared, go to the switch on the left to start up the pump. Your field computer will advise you to proceed to the reactor core for the final phase of your mission. The exit lies behind the locked door out in the hallway. So you need to get to the Blue Keycard that is twirling beyond your reach in a room adjacent to the pump room. (You can see it through the window in front of you.)

6 Blast the barrels underneath the window to open a hole in the floor. Step close to the edge and drop a few grenades to clear out the crowd of Guards waiting to shoot you to pieces. From the right angle, you'll be able to see them and they won't know what hit them. When you drop down, you'll still be facing two Technicians, so be ready to fire.

7 Turn right and head for the corridor at the far end of the walkway. Before entering the corridor, look to the right. You'll notice a closed metal door. Shoot it and follow the narrow passage to **Secret Area #2** and an **Invulnerability** power-up.

8 Retrace your steps and proceed through the corridor and around the corner. Collect the Ammo Pack and blast the Gunners at the far end to the right.

9 Follow the walkway around the structure in the center of this room and through a narrow tunnel to a chamber. You'll see another BFG—and you'll have to use it on three Technicians who attack at three o'clock when you take it. Down the slime-filled corridor from which they struck is **Secret Area #3** and some **Adrenaline**. If you think you need it, you'll have to spend some of your Invulnerability to get to it. (Be sure to save at least one.)

10 Return to the area where you dropped down and take the elevator around the corner up to the room that holds the **Blue Keycard**. You'll have only one Gunner to deal with to get the key. Take the key and jump through the window down into the pump room. Go back out the door and head for the hallway to the locked door and open it.

11 Beyond, you'll have a real fight on your hands. Berserkers attack at close quarters while Guards take pot shots at you from across a vat filled with toxic slime. Deal with the Berserkers first, then pick off the Guards.

12 Turn right in front of the toxic pool and follow the passage to a room with pipes. Grab the **First Aid** kits and **Rockets** to the left and right of the entrance, then continue around the pipes to a ramp. Below, you'll see an **Enviro-Suit** and two Gunners. Shred the Gunners then head for the suit. As soon as you grab it, a pipe behind you will explode, releasing three Technicians. Put a short in their systems, then head around the pipe to a ramp that leads into another oozy pool. Put on your Enviro-Suit and jump into the pool. Swim around the pipes and toward a tunnel entrance. Enter and follow the tunnel to a row of **Stims** and some **Body Armor**. Grab the goodies and hurry back to the vat of toxic slime.

note

When you shoot the grate behind the Armor, you can drop into the room where you picked up the BFG. You may want to keep this in mind for some deathmatch fun.

13 If you're fast enough, you'll make it safely to **Secret Area #4** and a **Quad Damage** nestled in a niche in the vat's side wall (on the far side nearest the exit doors) without taking too much damage. Grab it and climb out the other side. Collect the **Shells** and **Medkits** in the room, then head up the stairs to the Exit that leads back to the Toxic Waste Dump.

Mission 6

Quake II

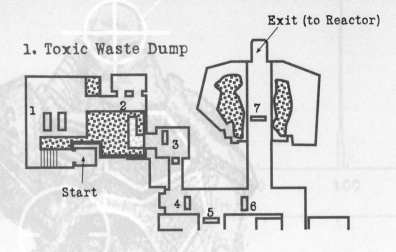

1. Toxic Waste Dump

Exit (to Reactor)

1   2   7

3

Start

4   5   6

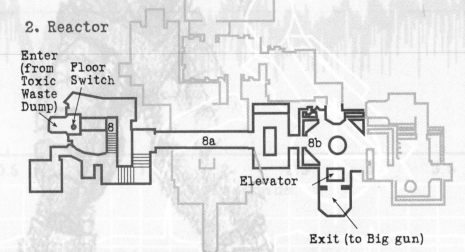

2. Reactor

Enter (from Toxic Waste Dump)

Floor Switch

8

8a

8b

Elevator

Exit (to Big gun)

Intel Brief

Primary Objective:	Return to the Reactor and Gain Access to the Big Gun
Secondary Objective:	Make it out alive
Unit Locations:	Toxic Waste Dump/Reactor
Potential Kills:	18/61
Goals:	1/2
Secrets:	0/2
Enemies:	Tanks, Berserkers, Gunners, Iron Maidens
Weapons:	Blaster, Shotgun, Super Shotgun, Machine Gun, Chaingun, Grenade Launcher, Rocket Launcher, Hyperblaster, Railgun, BFG

Objective 8
GET OUT ALIVE

MISSION ACCOMPLISHED... except for the part where you survive. Now this is the way to rock 'n' roll! Thanks to you, the Stroggos empire is about to shake rattle and roll away! But don't pull a muscle patting yourself on the back. You've got to make your way safely through a slime-filled Reactor facility teaming with pissed-off aliens. If you succeed, there's the mission you've been waiting for on the other side. Good luck, Marine.

Objective Summary

1. Start; BFG, Tank, Berserkers, First Aid, Stimpacks, Rockets, Cells, Slugs, Medkits
2. Icaruses, Rockets, First Aid, Cells, First Aid
3. Gunners
4. Gunner, Guards, Iron Maidens
5. Gunner
6. Gunner, Rockets
7. Iron Maidens, Rockets, First Aid, Exit (to Reactor)
8. Reactor Entrance, Slime, Exit (to Big Gun)

Mission 6

V1

V2

V4

V5

Field Report

1 Grab the **BFG** on the landing in front of you. Use the weapon to make quick work of the Tank firing at you below and to your right. The shot will probably take out the Berserkers as well. When the smoke has settled, grab the **First Aid** kit and **Stims** on the landing. There are also some **Rockets**, **Cells**, **Slugs**, and **Medkits** in this courtyard. (The slime pool next to you, by the way, is where you found the secret area with the Invulnerability power-up.)

2 Head up the ramp and cautiously proceed to the next room. Shoot the two Icaruses on your left. Grab the **Rockets** and **First Aid** kits, then head for the small alcove to the left. Snag the **Cells** and **First Aid** kit and hit the switch to extend a walkway.

3 Follow the walkway around the corner. There are two Gunners around the corner, hiding behind barricades. Using the corner as cover, try taking out the first one without taking too much damage. Then use your Grenade Launcher to go after the second one, ducking behind a barricade in the second doorway.

4 When they're both history, jump across the barricades and cautiously proceed down the corridor. Another Gunner is hiding behind a barricade around the corner. Again, try taking him out with a few Grenades. Now go up and crouch behind his barricade. Down the walkway, tucked securely behind another barricade, are some Guards and two Iron Maidens. If they haven't already, the Maidens will begin firing rockets at you. (Geez, chics!) Get out your Rocket Launcher and return fire. With careful aim and judicious ducking, you should be able to get them out of your way.

5 Jump the barricade and hug the right wall. There's a Gunner around the right corner. Run across the open space and leave him there. (You should be able to make it without taking a hit if he hasn't seen you.)

6 The exit to the Reactor is down the left corridor, but it is heavily fortified. Stick to the right wall and wait for the Gunner. When he's history, jump across the barricade, grab the **Rockets** and hug the wall to the left of the corridor.

7 Get your Rocket Launcher ready and blast the two Iron Maidens behind the barricade at the far end (in front of the exit). Drop them fast and go to the door, collecting the **Rockets** they so graciously left behind. For a little relief, grab the **First Aid** kits in front of the Exit and proceed to the Reactor.

8 As soon as you enter the Reactor area, you'll notice the earth shaking. The whole area is being rocked by deep, rumbling explosions. If you're not fast and cautious now, your handiwork might be your undoing. Step out onto the floor switch to extend the ramp. Traverse the ramp and head down he stairs and to your right. Grab the shells in the corner and brace yourself. You have to make it to across the slime to the red door at the far end (8a). Do your best to get there by tiptoeing along one of the curbs on either side without stepping into the slime. (It'll be a neat trick.) Walk through the door and follow the walkway to the lighted door and into the reactor room (8b). Take the elevator to the right up to the Exit to the Big Gun.

Mission 6

II Strigg

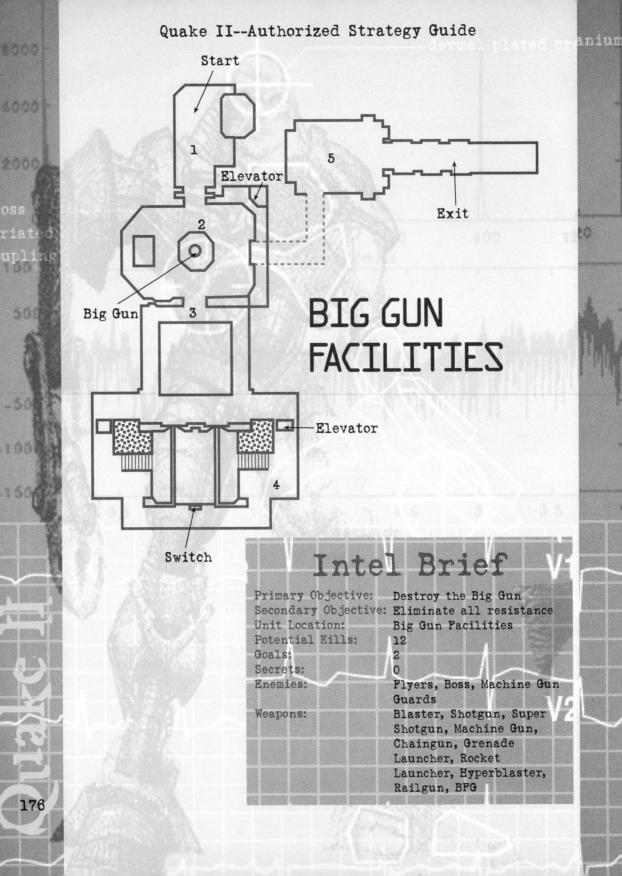

Start

1

5

Elevator

Exit

2

Big Gun

3

BIG GUN FACILITIES

Elevator

4

Switch

Intel Brief

Primary Objective:	Destroy the Big Gun
Secondary Objective:	Eliminate all resistance
Unit Location:	Big Gun Facilities
Potential Kills:	12
Goals:	2
Secrets:	0
Enemies:	Flyers, Boss, Machine Gun Guards
Weapons:	Blaster, Shotgun, Super Shotgun, Machine Gun, Chaingun, Grenade Launcher, Rocket Launcher, Hyperblaster, Railgun, BFG

Special Assignment
DESTROY THE BIG GUN

THE REAL OBJECT OF ALL YOUR SCURRYING through dark alien tunnels is upon you, Marine: the Big Gun, that great monstrous exterminating machine you flew by during the initial assault. A lot of good men and women won't be going home because of that damned cannon. Take it down!

Assignment Summary

1. First Aid, Stimpacks, Rockets, Combat Armor
2. Big Gun, Elevator (to upper walkway), Shells, Boss, Flyers, First Aid, Bullets
3. Guards, Elevator (to Control Room)
4. Guards, Switch (destroys Big Gun)
5. Exit

Mission 6

177

Field Report

1 From you entry point, grab the **First Aid** kit on the left and the **Stimpacks** ahead of you. You're gonna need 'em. There are some **Rockets** and **Combat Armor** by the crates on left. Get ready for this final assault with your Railgun or Rocket Launcher. If you've got at least four shots left in your BFG, that would be even better. Go into your inventory and queue up whatever is your next biggest gun. Doesn't hurt either to have a Quad Damage on you.

2 Go through the door and in the Gun Room. That's it—the Big Gun—right there in the center of the room. Be careful of the blue fluid surrounding it. It's deadly. Go directly to your left to the elevator bay and ride the elevator to the top. At the end of the walkway, you'll notice some **Shells**. The moment you grab them, an alarm sounds off, and the Boss is coming to get you—with Flyers flanking him. You'll need all the cover you can get or he'll blast you with a flight of four rockets at a time. It's virtually impossible to tangle with him without taking some serious damage. Run back down into the elevator bay for cover and try taking this big, ugly, dangerous firefly. Let him have it with everything you've got. The Flyers flanking him will make your job even tougher. Strike hard and strike again until he goes down, then clean up the gnats that came with him. When the Boss goes down, he'll drop some goodies, which you should grab. And you will also want to check the room for supplies—especially **First Aid** kits to heal your big boss battle scars. With the Boss out of the way, you now have access to the Big Gun's laser guard. Your field computer will advise you to seek these out and lock them down.

3 Proceed through the door across from the one through which you came. Waste the Guards that try to stop you, and go right, down the ramp. Go right again and up the elevator.

4 Blast your way through the Guards and follow the walkway to the right and up a short stairway into the control center. Hit the green button to lock down the lasers. It's only a matter of seconds now before the whole thing blows up. You've got to get to the escape pod, or you're dead.

5 Run, don't walk, back to the Big Gun room. A new door is open on the right. Go for it, fast, and dive into the pod in the next room. Hit the keyboard to shut the door and launch yourself to safety.

Mission 8

V1   V4

V2   V5

Crypt II

179

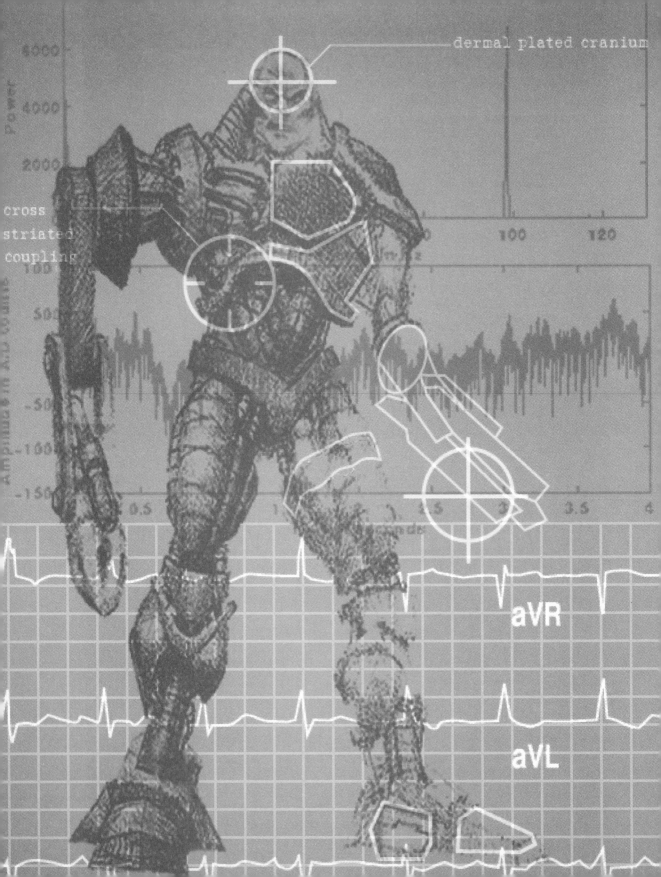

dermal plated cranium

cross
striated
coupling

aVR

aVL

Mission 7
CLOSE THE MAIN HANGAR BAY DOOR AND DESTROY THE BLACK HOLE GENERATOR

With the Big Gun offline, the most dangerous piece of equipment on Stroggos is the black hole generator. Your primary goal during your next mission is the destruction of this machine. It must be disabled at any cost. Mankind will never be safe while the Strogg have a means of reaching Earth. You must find a way into the main hangar installation, navigate the Strogg research lab, and deactivate the main CPU core. Your final objective is the airstrike marker. Retrieve and activate this device before you evacuate to your next mission.

Mission 1 by Unit Locations

1. Outer Hangar
2. Comm Satellite (Secret Level)
3. Outer Hangar
4. Research Lab
5. Outer Hangar
6. Inner Hangar

Secret
(Lower Level)

Start

Elevator

Secret/Exit

1

2

3

6

5

4

Secret

OUTER HANGAR

Intel Brief

Primary Objective:	Close the main hanger door. Destroy blackhole generator.
Secondary Objective:	Find a way into the main hangar bay installation.
Unit Location:	Outer Hangar
Potential Kills:	12/28
Goals:	1/1
Secrets:	0/3
Enemies:	Gunner, Icarus, Enforcers, Barracuda Sharks, Tank
Weapons:	Blaster, Shotgun, Super Shotgun, Machine Gun, Chaingun, Grenade Launcher, Rocket Launcher, Hyperblaster, Railgun, BFG

Quake II

Objective 1
FIND A WAY INTO THE MAIN HANGAR BAY INSTALLATION

JUST STAYING ALIVE IN THIS MEATGRINDER IS ONE HELL OF AN ACCOMPLISHMENT, Marine. Congratulations. The injury you've inflicted on the enemy is turning the tide. No one really has the right to ask more of you than you've already given, but that's just what we're going to do. We need someone to shut down the black-hole machine and keep these biomechanical bastards from ever getting to our world again. First, however, we're going to show you the entrance to this mission's secret level, Comm Station, where you can inflict some serious damage on the enemy's space station.

Objective Summary

1. Start, Medkits, Stimpacks, Gunner, Icarus, Shells, Rocket Launcher, Elevator (to lower level)
2. Enforcers, Gunner, Medkit, Ammo Pack, Shells, Bullets, Rebreather, **Secret Area:** Adrenaline
3. Combat Armor, Bullets, Shards, Barracuda Sharks
4. Barracuda Sharks
5. **Secret Area:** secret canyon; Icaruses, Combat Armor, Shells, Cells, Stimpack
6. Tank, Teleporter (access to **Secret Area:** the secret level, Comm Satellite)

Mission 7

Chapter 6

Field Report

1 From your starting point, grab the **Medkits** on your right, and collect the **Stimpacks** in the far left corner by the door. Careful, when the door opens you have to fight off a Gunner and an Icarus. Take them out from the doorway. There are also some **Shells** and a **Rocket Launcher** to the right of the door on the other side of the Pod. Next, head for the elevator behind the pod and ride it down to the lower level.

2 Shotgun the three Enforcers and the Gunner who rush you. When the grunts are history, look around the room and grab the **Medkit** to the right of the elevator, the **Ammo Pack** up on the crates, and the **Shells** to the right of the door. Around and behind the crates are some well-hidden **Bullets**. There's also a **Rebreather** to the left of the door, and over the pipe on the left is **Secret Area #1** hiding some **Adrenaline**. (You have to jump over the pipe to get to it.)

3 Through the door is an open deck next to a pool of water. You may have already killed the attackers who would have dogged you from above, but you have some nasty fishies waiting below. Before you dive in to play with them, collect the **Combat Armor** and **Bullets** to the right of the door, and then jump over the pipe on the left to score some **Shards**. You won't be able to jump back, but that's okay; you're going for a swim. Before you dive in, blast as many of the half dozen Barracuda Sharks swimming in the pool as you can. Most of them will give you the opportunity, but at least a few will hang back. Dive in and continue blasting.

4 When the sharks are cat food, swim down to your right toward the platform with the manhole. Dive in front of the platform and shoot out the power fuse adjacent to the whirling pump blades to disable the fan. Swim back up again, climb on the platform and drop into the manhole. At the far end, you'll notice two Barracuda Sharks. Follow the water-filled pipe (you might need your Rebreather here) to the end and have some shark sushi. Then surface into **Secret Area #2:** a little secret canyon.

5 Don't get too cozy, though. When you surface, you'll have to fight off two Icaruses attacking from above as you swim to the platform extending from the door in the structure ahead on your left. Be sure to grab the **Combat Armor**, **Shells**, **Cells**, and a **Stimpack** out on the platform.

6 Inside, a Tank patrols the circular hallway. Get out your heavy artillery and blast and retreat until he goes down. Find the teleporter inside, and step into it to be transported to **Secret Area #3:** this mission's secret level, Comm Satellite—another blast feast.

Mission 7

dermal plated cranium

COMM SATELLITE

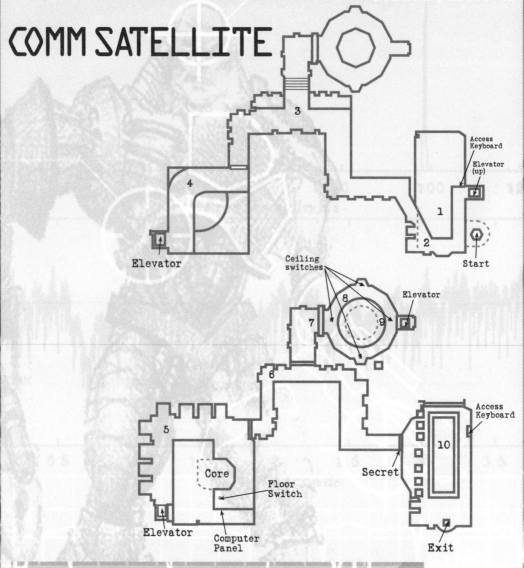

Access
Keyboard

Elevator
(up)

1

2

Start

Elevator

3

4

Ceiling
switches

8

8

Elevator

7

6

Access
Keyboard

5

10

Core

Floor
Switch

Secret

Elevator

Computer
Panel

Exit

Intel Brief

Primary Objective:	Close the main hangar door. Destroy blackhole generator.
Secondary Objective:	Find and disable the Power Core and destroy the Comm Satellite.
Unit Location:	Comm Satellite
Potential Kills:	43
Goals:	3
Secrets:	2
Enemies:	Icaruses, Tanks, Flyers, Technicians
Weapons:	Blaster, Shotgun, Super Shotgun, Machine Gun, Chaingun, Grenade Launcher, Rocket Launcher, Hyperblaster, Railgun, BFG

V2

Secret Level
FIND AND DISABLE THE POWER CORE AND DESTROY THE COMM SATELLITE

THIS SECRET LEVEL GIVES YOU AN EXTRA OPPORTUNITY to do some serious damage, Marine. It'll also give you a little vacation from gravity in the weightlessness of space. But it's a working vacation…make that killing vacation. You'll be facing all of Stroggos' airborne demons, as well as the ever present possibility of slipping into the cold, dark vacuum. It's a hell of a way to die, Marine, so watch your step, but use the lack of gravity to your advantage.

Objective Summary

1. Start; Access Keyboard (closes bay doors), Medkit, Power Shield, Slugs, Shells, Rockets, Grenade, Elevator (to 2nd Floor)
2. Bullets, Flyers, Shells, Cells, Rockets, Stimpacks
3. Blocked Door, First Aid, Shells
4. Icaruses, Technicians, Flyers, First Aid, Secret Area: Adrenaline, Shells, Bullets, Rockets, Elevator (to 3rd Floor)
5. Flyers, Shards, Rockets, Stimpacks, Slugs, Bullets, Floor Switch (exposes computer panel)
6. Technicians, Icarus, Bullets, Slugs, Stimpacks
7. Bullets, Cells, Medkits, Boss
8. Medkit, Bullets, Rockets, Ceiling Switches (crash satellite)
9. Shells, Slugs, Railgun
10. Secret Area: Adrenaline; Access Keyboard (closes bay doors), Armor, Shells, Medkits, Bullets, Exit/Teleporter (to Outer Hangar)

Mission 7

187

dermal plated cranium

Field Report

1 As soon as the teleporter deposits you on the satellite, go to the computer console on your right and close the bay doors. This will make it safe to collect the **Medkit, Power Shield, Slugs, Shells, Rockets,** and **Grenades** out past the safety line. (If you don't close the door, there's a good chance you'll end up dead in the vacuum of space.) Also, watch the low gravity up here. Your jumps will carry you quite a distance. Now go to the elevator to the right of the console and ride up to the next level.

2 Step out of the lift and turn left. Collect the **Bullets** and follow the corridor around to the right and get ready to rock and roll. As you follow the corridor around to the left and then the right, you will be attacked by Flyers and Icaruses at random points. Use the corridor support structures for cover and pick them off as you go. Don't miss the **Shells, Cells, Rockets,** and **Stimpacks** you'll find along the way.

note All of the enemies you will face on Comm Station are airborne. Consequently, your longer-range weapons are preferred here: Rocket Launcher, Railgun, and BFG. But save the heaviest artillery for the end of the mission. The first attack will come from a swarm of Flyers. Hang back and pick them off as they come around the corner one at a time.

188

3 Eventually you'll come to a doorway on your left that is blocked by a force field. Grab the **First Aid** kit and the **Shells** sitting in front of the doorway and proceed down the corridor. Go left and then through the door at the end of the hall.

4 This area is patrolled by Icaruses, Technicians, and Flyers (look to your right). You will have to fight them as you go. Don't miss the two **First Aid** kits on your left. Head right. If you look below, you'll see a series of supports holding the core structure. Carefully (that's hard vacuum below the supports) jump down and hop to each one until you reach the **Adrenaline** in **Secret Area #1**. Jump back up, grab the **Shells** and **Bullets,** then collect the **Rockets, Bullets,** and **Shells** in the next alcove. Enter the door on your right and ride the elevator up to the next level.

5 As you step off the elevator, a swarm of Flyers will attack from two sides. You'll have to run and gun. Grab the **Shards** and **Rockets** at the end of he corridor and turn right. Turn right again at the doorway (don't miss the **Stimpacks, Slugs** and **Bullets**). You'll come to a landing beside the computer core with a large floor switch. Step on the floor switch to expose the computer panel in the wall on your right. Blast the panel to disable the computer core. The lights will go out and your field computer will advise you to take out the satellite dish.

5 Go back to the door you just passed and go through it. On the other side, two Technicians and an Icarus will attack. Blast them and scoop up the **Bullets**, **Slugs**, and **Stimpacks** ahead of you. Follow the corridor to your right to a glowing doorway. Blasting the computer panel has deactivated the force field.

6 Go through the door and nab the **Bullets**, **Cells**, and **Medkit**. Stop and get out your heaviest artillery. Around the corner, a Boss is waiting. He won't be able to fly in after you, but he will throw a lot of heavy-duty fireworks down the hall. Hang back and use the walls as cover while you whittle him down and kill him.

7 Step out into the circular chamber and collect the **Medkit**, **Bullets**, and **Rockets** scattered around the walkway. Now is when the weightlessness of space comes in handy. With relative ease, you should be able to jump up and hit the four ceiling switches above you, nestled in niches. But be careful; if you misjudge your landing, you'll float out into space and die. When you've hit all four switches and completed the sequence, the satellite dish will crash out into space. Now you have to get back down to the planet to continue your mission.

8 Before you head back, look over the edge to the level below. You'll notice a **Railgun**, **Shells**, and **Slugs**. Float down, collect the goodies, then take the elevator back up again.

9 Go back to the corridor, turn left and continue until you come to a closed door. Before you open it, look down and to your right. In the dark corner below, there's an **Adrenaline** pack in **Secret Area #2**. Jump down to it, then jump back up. Open it and step into the hangar. Head for the access keyboard at the wall across from the entrance. Push the keyboard to close the bay doors. Now that it's safe again, collect the **Armor**, **Shells**, **Medkits**, and **Bullets** you find here, then step into the teleporter on the wall opposite from the bay doors to exit Comm Satellite and resume your mission in the Outer Hangar.

Mission 7

Quake II

189

dermal plated cranium

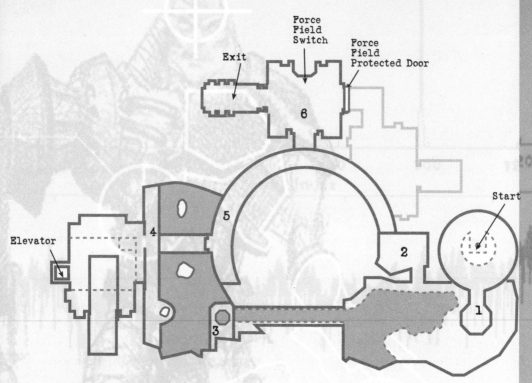

OUTER HANGAR

Intel Brief

Primary Objective:	Close the main hanger door. Destroy blackhole generator.
Secondary Objective:	Find a way into the main hangar bay installation.
Unit Location:	Outer Hangar
Potential Kills:	16/28
Goals:	1/1
Secrets:	3/3
Enemies:	Gunner, Icarus, Enforcers, Door
Weapons:	Blaster, Shotgun, Super Shotgun, Machine Gun, Chaingun, Grenade Launcher, Rocket Launcher, Hyperblaster, Railgun, BFG

Quake II

Objective 1 (continued)
FIND A WAY INTO THE MAIN HANGAR BAY INSTALLATION

BACK DOWN TO EARTH AND BACK TO WORK, MARINE. (Gravity sucks, doesn't it?) You're going back into the water for a quick swim, then into the main facility. All the usual bad guys are waiting to get a piece of you. Before you're finished with this leg of your mission, you will literally be going after a piece of one of them.

─── Objective Summary

1. Start, Secret Canyon, Ladder
2. Health, Shells, Bullets
3. Outer Hangar
4. Gunner, Flyer, Icarus, Grenades, Rockets, Cells
5. Enforcers, Mekit, Bullets, Medic, Shards
6. Tank, Stimpacks, Bullets
7. Exit (to Lab)

Mission 7

Gryst II

Field Report

1 Back in the Outer Hangar, step out of the teleporter and go back to the secret canyon. Go through the door and turn right. You'll notice a ladder against the wall.

2 Climb the ladder and enter through the hole on top into a small chamber stocked with Health, Shells, and Bullets. Grab the goodies, climb down the ladder, and jump into the water.

3 Follow the water-filled pipe back to the platform with the manhole in it. Then swim across to the platform. Reenter the room and ride the elevator up to the original Outer Hangar starting area.

4 Go through the door and, if you haven't killed him before, take advantage of the Gunner out on the walkway. You'll also be attacked by a Flyer and an Icarus (unless you took them out earlier) coming at you from the right. Use the doorway as cover and knock them out of the sky. Grab the **Grenade** the Gunner dropped, the **Rockets** on your left, and the **Cells** on your right, then step on the floor switch by the Cells to extend the walkway.

5 Through the door is a corridor curving to the left. Four Enforcers are waiting to charge you. Hang back and toss in a few Grenades to clear the way. You'll probably have to come in and clean up a bit, but they'll be wounded and weaker. Don't miss the **Medkit** inside the door, or the **Bullets** the Enforcers drop when they die. There's a Medic lurking in there who won't strike until you pass the doorway at the end of the corridor to collect the **Shards** stashed there. Be ready for him with some heavy artillery.

6 Inside the room beyond the corridor, a Tank stands guard, but you can lure him out and whittle him down. Pelt him with Grenades as you backtrack down the corridor. He won't last long. When you enter the room you'll find lots of **Stimpacks** and **Bullets** along the walls and in the corners. Hit the force field switch in the center of the room and you will get a message telling you that you can't get through the force field blocking the doorway on your right—you'll need the Tank Commander's head. (You'll get the same message when you go to the door itself.)

7 The one place you're likely to find one of these jury-rigged jalopies disassembled is in some kind of repair shop. In the case of the Stroggs, that would be the Research Laboratory. Go to the doors on the left, and head for the head in the Lab.

Mission 7

V1

V2

V5

Quake II

193

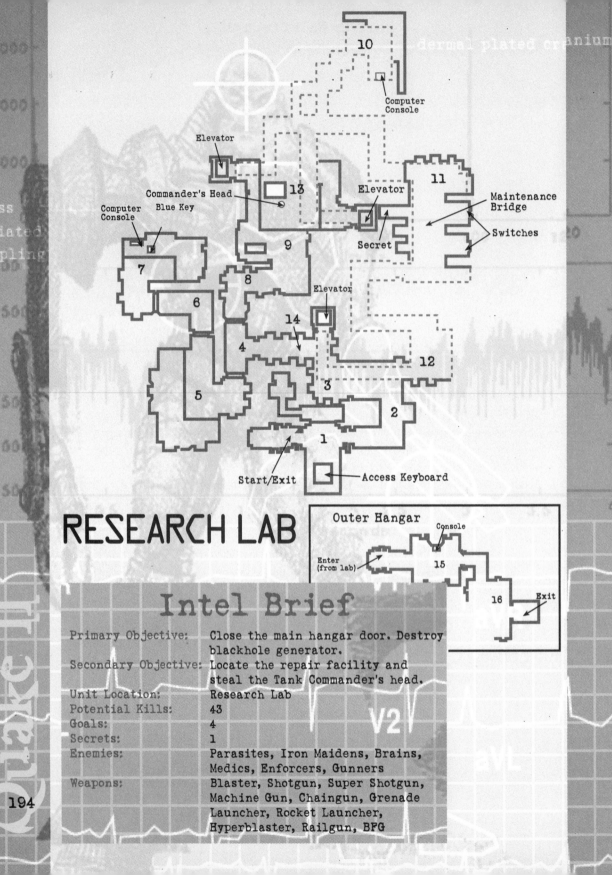

dermal plated cranium

10

Computer
Console

Elevator

Commander's Head
Blue Key

11

Maintenance
Bridge

Computer
Console

Elevator

Switches

13

Secret

7

9

8

6

Elevator

5

14

4

12

3

2

1

Start/Exit

Access Keyboard

RESEARCH LAB

Outer Hangar

Console

Enter
(from lab)

15

16

Exit

V2

Intel Brief

Primary Objective: Close the main hangar door. Destroy blackhole generator.

Secondary Objective: Locate the repair facility and steal the Tank Commander's head.

Unit Location: Research Lab

Potential Kills: 43

Goals: 4

Secrets: 1

Enemies: Parasites, Iron Maidens, Brains, Medics, Enforcers, Gunners

Weapons: Blaster, Shotgun, Super Shotgun, Machine Gun, Chaingun, Grenade Launcher, Rocket Launcher, Hyperblaster, Railgun, BFG

Objective 2
LOCATE THE REPAIR FACILITY AND STEAL THE TANK COMMANDER'S HEAD

AFTER YOUR MISSIONS THROUGH THE STROGGOS PRISON AND TORTURE CHAMBER, and your work in the hideous Strogg processing plant, the Research Lab shouldn't rattle you much. But it probably will. You're tough, Marine, but nobody can watch their comrades being dismembered and used for spare parts without a shudder. At least you can proceed knowing that you'll be using one of their parts to further their own destruction.

————Objective Summary

1. Start; Slugs, Medkits, Parasites
2. Parasites, Body Armor, First Aid
3. Grenade Launcher, Iron Maidens, Rockets
4. Iron Maidens, Grenade, Shells, First Aid, Rockets
5. Iron Maidens, First Aid
6. Parasites
7. Brains, Shells, First Aid, Body Armor, Hyperblaster, Console (brings up Blue Key), Blue Keycard
8. Parasites, Medic, Bullets, First Aid, Shells
9. Brain, Parasites, Stimpacks, Bullets, Grenades, Elevator (to lower level)
10. Brains, Parasites, Medic, Stimpacks
11. Switches (deactivate force field), Secret Area: Quad Damage, Slugs
12. Super Shotgun, Shells, Cells, Parasites
13. Tank Commander's Head, Stimpacks
14. Iron Maidens, Rockets, Exit (to Outer Hangar)
15. Enter (from Lab), Console (disengages force field)
16. Enforcers, Grenades, Shards, Exit (to Inner Hangar)

Mission 7

Field Report

1 The first ruined Marine you meet will give you **Slugs** when you put him out of his misery. Grab the **Medkits** on your right, and then shove the computer console to gain access to the lab. Back into it with your weapon pointed at the door on the right; the instant the door is unlocked, two Parasites will spring into the room and attack you. Hit them quick and keep in mind that this kind of group attack will be the norm throughout the Lab.

2 Enter the Lab and follow the hallway around to your left. Put the Marines you meet out of their misery with your blaster. (You've got to save your high-caliber stuff for the mission.) Watch out for a sudden attack from three Parasites, who will burst out of a hidden alcove in the wall on your right. When you've dispatched these creeps, collect the **Body Armor** and **First Aid** kits stashed in their hiding place.

3 Further along the hallway you'll find a **Grenade Launcher**, which will come in very handy when you have to deal with the two Iron Maidens around the next corner. Hang back and lob bombs at the biomechanical bitches, then snag the **Rockets** they drop.

4 Next you'll pass an elevator blocked by a force field. Make a note of it—you'll be using it in a bit. Ahead, you'll see another Marine in agony, but be careful. When you go to help him, two more Iron Maidens will come at you from the hallway ahead. Give them the same treatment you gave the others, then enter the hallway and gather up the **Grenades**, **Shells**, and **First Aid** kits you'll find there. (Don't forget the **Rockets** the Maidens drop.)

5 The door on your right is open to you, but to get to the room beyond it, you will need the Blue Keycard. For now, go to the door on your left. Watch yourself as you enter—the room is guarded by two Iron Maidens who will burst up from the floor when you enter. You can back out and use the doorway as cover while you blast them. Don't mess around with anything else in this room. Activating the consoles starts torture programs that will ring screams from your trapped comrades. Do the humane thing instead—shoot 'em with your Blaster. Be sure to grab the two **First Aid** kits before you go through the door on your right.

6 In the hallway, you'll be attacked by two more Parasites. It's too close to take them head on, so retreat as you shoot. This kind of gang attack in close quarters will only increase as you make your way through the Lab. To help break up these attacks, use your grenades. You'll find them to be very useful here in the Lab. And always keep your next weapon queued up and ready to go; the grenades won't be much use at closer quarters.

7 The room beyond the door at your left is swarming with Brains. Despite their slow, crippled movements, they will be very tough to kill in this number. And there ain't much room to move. Hang back and toss grenades at them while using the hallway as cover. When you've terminated the Brains, enter the room and collect the **Shells**, **First Aid** kits, **Body Armor**, and **Hyperblaster** you find there. Push in the first computer console you come to and the **Blue Keycard** will rise from a compartment in the floor on your right. The console on the other side of the room activates another torture program, though the poor bastard on the table wouldn't notice. Grab the keycard and head back to the hallway beyond the previous room (4).

8 As you proceed, two Parasites will drop from the ceiling above and attack, so be ready to put them away. You'll also encounter a Marine who could use your help, but watch it. Two more Parasites are using him as bate.

9 Further into the room, a Medic stands guard over a gruesome operation of torture. The screams of your comrades ring off the walls here, but there's little you can do beyond fragging the Medic. Grab the **Bullets** and **First Aid** kits you see and go to the door on your right. Your Blue Keycard will unlock it and let you into a short hallway leading to an elevator. Grab the **Shells** and then take the elevator down to the floor below.

10 As you step off the elevator and round the corner going left, a Brain and two Parasites will attack you. This is a truly deadly combination, so use those grenades and keep moving. Eliminate the Parasites first, and then go after the slow-moving Brain. Follow the hallway around, bearing left, until you come to another computer console. Push in this console to activate the Maintenance Bridge in the next chamber. Before you leave, be sure to collect the **Stimpacks**, **Bullets**, **Grenades**. Watch yourself in here. More Brains, Parasites and Medics are ready to ambush from around every corner.

Mission 7

Quake II

11 Beyond the red door, the way is blocked by a force field, so continue down the corridor to the next door. Brains, Parasites, and a Medic will attack. Bomb them, blast them, and then proceed to the next red door. Enter, grab the **Stimpacks** in the corner, and then step out onto the clear Maintenance Bridge on your right. Stay within the lighted borders or you will fall into a trench filled with acid. Look left and you will see two switches in two separate pockets in the wall. It's a tricky jump, but you must hit both of these switches to deactivate the force fields in this area.

note Save your game before jumping and after each successful jump.

Directly opposite these switches, you'll see some men crawling around in agony behind some barred cubbyholes. Shoot the one on your right to open a **Secret Area.** Inside you'll get a **Quad Damage** power-up and some **Slugs.**

12 Proceed across the Maintenance Bridge and through the red door on the other side. Follow the corridor and collect the **Super Shotgun** and the **Shells** you'll see in front of the next red door. Grab the **Cells** up on the raised area in the next room, and then go around to your right to another red door at the top of a short stair. A pack of Parasites is waiting on the other side of this one, so get ready to drop some grenades and fall back shooting. When the slavering mutant dogs have been dispatched, go on through the door and take the elevator back up to the previous level. At least two Medics and several Parasites are still wandering around, so watch yourself.

13 Return to the area beyond the Blue Keycard door; enter the first red door to the elevator that was blocked by a force field earlier. Ride the elevator up to the second level, follow the corridor around, and enter the repair room. When you take the **Tank Commander's Head**, alarms will sound and your field computer will prompt you to return to the Outer Hangar area. Hustle back the way you came and get out of the Lab, fast. And don't leave without grabbing the **Stimpacks** along the wall.

14 Get out your big guns. As you hurry down the hallway where you saw the elevator with the first force field, two Iron Maidens will rise up out of the floor to ambush you, one in front and one in back. Two more will be waiting at the entrance to the Outer Hangar. Be sure to grab the **Rockets** they drop when you waste them.

15 Exit the Lab and reenter the Outer Hangar. With the Tank Commander's Head in hand, so to speak, you will now be able to disengage the force field blocking the progress of your mission. Put the head in the fixture in the center of the room and the force field will collapse. Your field computer will prompt you to move on to the main hangar bay installation. Enter the door to the right of the console and proceed.

16 Inside, two Enforcers will attack. Put them down fast and grab the **Grenades** and **Shards**, as well as any ammo they drop. Now you can proceed to the Exit which will take you to the Inner Hangar.

Mission 7

199

dermal plated cranium

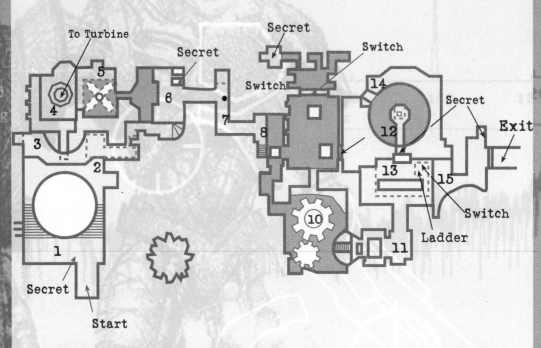

To Turbine

Secret

Secret

Switch

Switch

Switch

5

14

Secret

6

Exit

4

7

12

3

8

13

15

2

Switch

10

Ladder

1

11

Secret

Start

INNER HANGAR

Intel Brief

Primary Objective:	Close the main hangar door. Destroy blackhole generator.
Secondary Objective:	Locate hangar control and close main hangar bay door.
Unit Location:	Inner Hanger
Potential Kills:	44
Goals:	2
Secrets:	5
Enemies:	Gunners, Brains, Berserkers, Icaruses, Boss
Weapons:	Blaster, Shotgun, Super Shotgun, Machine Gun, Chaingun, Grenade Launcher, Rocket Launcher, Hyperblaster, Railgun, BFG

Quake II

V3

V2

V2

Objective 3
LOCATE HANGAR CONTROL AND CLOSE MAIN HANGAR BAY DOOR

THE TANK COMMANDER'S HEAD GOT YOU INTO THE INNER HANGAR AREA. You have a lot to do in here, Marine. That hangar door must be closed to truncate the enemy's air capabilities. But there are plenty of cyborgs around this very high security area who would rather you took up knitting—and they can be very convincing. Watch for the secret areas, and watch your ass!

Objective Summary

1. Start; Shards, Gunner, Secret Area: Adrenaline; Cells, Power Shield
2. Brains, Berserker, Icaruses
3. Bullets, Slugs, Megahealth, Berserkers, Bullets
4. Icaruses, Cells, Shells, Medkit, Combat Armor, Berserker, Console (shuts off turbine), Stimpacks, Gunners, Grenade, Rockets
5. Switch (retracts conveyor belts), Shards, Bullets
6. Icarus, Berserkers, Gunners, Secret Area: Quad Damage; Rockets, Grenades, Shells, Bullets, Medkits
7. Berserkers, Medkits
8. Icarus, Switch (activates platform), Switch (lowers walk way), Shards, Rebreather
9. Secret Area: Body Armor, Medkit; Power Shield, Stimpacks
10. Icaruses, Power Shield, Gunners, Shells, Bullets
11. Gunners, Berserkers, Shells, Stimpacks, Medkits
12. Boss, Guard, Shells, First Aid, Secret Area: Adrenaline
13. Stimpacks, Combat Armor, Gunner, Shells, Switch (raises ladder)
14. Stimpacks, Shards, Switch (lowers elevator), Gunner, Cells, Bullets, First Aid, Shells, Lever (closes hangar door)
15. Berserker, Brain, Medkit, Slugs, Shards, Gunner, Secret Area: Body Armor; Medkit, Bullets, Exit (to Launch Command)

Mission 7

dermal plated cranium

Field Report

1 As you enter the Inner Hangar, notice the **Shards** on your right. Don't grab them yet. Instead turn left and take out the Gunner lurking by the crates, then nail the one that comes up the stairs to avenge his buddy. Now grab the Shards and position yourself in front of the mainframe unit on the left. Shoot at the crack in the center block to reveal **Secret Area #1** and some **Adrenaline**. Snag the **Cells** and **Power Shield** up on the crates and head down either staircase.

2 Get ready to rumble. Two Brains and a Berserker are waiting for you, and two Icaruses will attack from behind. Blast and run, keep moving. Take out the Berserker first, then clip the Icaruses wings and go after the slower Brain. Grab the ammo they drop then climb up the crates on the right.

3 Jump onto the ledge. Find the **Bullets**, **Slugs**, and a **Megahealth** power-up stashed up there. When you go for the power-up, a Berserker will burst from a hiding place in the wall and come out swinging. Be prepared to take him on, then jump back down and take care of two more Berserkers that rush you as you're heading for the hatch to your left. (They were hiding out in the wall straight ahead.) When all is clear, make one more round, to make sure that you

haven't missed any goodies, including the **Bullets** behind the crates, then open the hatch and enter.

4 Beyond the next hatch is a huge Turbine Cover grid positioned over the floor. You can drop into the hole and ride the air being pumped by the turbine. Don't get too thrilled, though, two Icaruses are warmed up and ready to you. Take 'em down (you may have to jump off the air stream first to improve your aim), and grab the **Cells** they drop when they die. Look out the window, and you can see the Strogg city. If its occupants weren't monsters, it would almost be beautiful. Collect the **Shells** and **Medkit** stashed in the room. Notice the **Combat Armor** down on the lowered section, but watch out—there's a Berserker waiting down there. Shoot him first, then go after the armor. Push the keyboard in the computer console to shut off the turbine, then jump back down the hole onto the grid, and then down into the turbine room. Follow the corridor leading out of the turbine room. Grab the **Stimpacks** lined up outside the door. At the end of the hall, two Gunners are waiting, one on each side. Shoot the one on the right (he will attack first), but then move back quickly and nail the one on the left. (He's hiding in a cubbyhole.) Grab the **Grenade** and the **Rockets** in the corner.

Quake II

5 Hit the green switch to retract the conveyor belts. Drop down into one or the other of the openings to a beam below. Grab the **Shards** and **Bullets** stashed around the ledge, then drop down into the water. Time it so you don't hit the revolving paddle wheel. The water is shallow, so you can just walk ahead of the paddle wheel until you come to an opening into another room. (You could jump down onto the paddle wheel, ride it to the opening, then jump down.)

6 The next room is full of bad guys: an Icarus, two Berserkers, and two Gunners. The Berserkers come at you down the stairs and right into the water, so blast them first. Then hit the Icarus and the Gunner shooting at you from above and to your right. Blast the right of the two containers on the left-hand side of the ledge to reveal **Secret Area #2** and **Quad Damage** power-up. You'll also find **Rockets**, **Grenades**, **Shells**, **Bullets**, and **Medkits** around the room. Don't forget to look up the stairs in the area up and around the corner. (Behind the crates up there is a lift what will take you back to where you started.)

7 Next, enter the corridor in front of you. As soon as you round the corner, turn around and blast the two Berserkers who burst from a hiding place in the wall behind you. Grab the **Medkits** in their hiding place and follow the corridor until you come to two moving platforms.

8 An Icarus will shoot at you from the chamber ahead. Blast him and go to the moving platforms. The water is shallow in most areas, but if you jump down, you won't be able to get back up. (Unless, of course, you've mastered the fine art of rocket jumping, which you will need during the next leg of your mission.) To continue your mission, you must jump across the platforms to a niche in the wall on the other side and hit the green switch. This starts a third platform moving. Watch the timing of the movements for a moment, then jump onto the first platform, then over to the second one. Jump to the niche, hit the switch on the wall, and wait for the platform to return. Jump on it again, then ride the third moving platform to another switch, which lowers a walkway from the ceiling and a set of ledges down from the wall on your right. Collect the **Shards** and **Rebreather**.

Mission 7

203

9 Just below this ledge, the water is deep. If you put on the Rebreather, dive down and swim to your left, then surface, you'll come to **Secret Area #3** and some **Body Armor** and a **Medkit**. In the opposite corner, near some dead Marines, is a **Power Shield**. Grab the goodies and swim back to the surface. You'll have to return to the far alcove, climb the ladder, and jump your way back to the moving platform in front of you. Then hop over to the walkway and jump onto it and into the tunnel. Scoop up the **Stimpacks** lined up there and follow the tunnel to its end, where you can drop down to a tiny alcove.

10 Outside this alcove, you'll see a huge, rotating gear. You'll also see two Icaruses hovering in blast-a-Marine position. You're a sitting duck here, so shoot them fast and move out. Jump down onto the gear, and then jump to get the **Power Shield** in the corner. Then cross over the gears to reach the landing across the room on your right. Two Gunners are waiting for you there, so be ready to run and gun. Kill the cyborgs, then, collect the **Shells** and **Bullets** they drop.

11 Continue back into the next room. Another Gunner and a Berserker will attack. Waste them and then move down the hallway on your left. Don't miss the **Shells** in the right corner. Another Berserker will attack in the hallway, followed by another Gunner. Ice them and follow the hallway around either direction. Collect the **Stimpacks** on the floor on the left, and the **Medkits** beside them.

12 Go to the window and look down. You'll see blue pool with a platform running out over it at water level. There's a floor switch in the center of the platform. You will be jumping down to the platform, but first you have a hovering Boss to deal with. You should have plenty of cover. Shoot him down, and then drop a few grenades down on the Guard below. Jump down to the platform and hit the switch to extend a bridge above you. Grab the **Shells**, and **First Aid** kits out on the platform and walkway. In the shallow water, just under the end of he platform, is **Secret Area #4**, where some **Adrenaline** is hidden. Dive down quickly and grab it. Then surface, climb out, and go through the doorway.

13 Inside you will find a row of **Stimpacks** on your left and some **Combat Armor** on your right. When you go for the Stims, a Gunner will attack from the right. Be ready to blast him. Grab the **Shells** stashed behind the techno-cubes, then go to the back of the room and hit the switch. This raises a ladder through the floor. Climb the ladder and cross the bridge on your right.

14 On the other side, you'll see **Stimpacks** to the right and **Shards** to the left. Scoop them up and head left to another green switch. Hit the switch to bring the lift. When you get on the lift, put your back to the wall and get ready to shoot. One Gunner will be on patrol right in front of you in the room above, and another will come at you from around the corner on your left. Except for those two, the room is very quiet. Collect the supplies scattered around up here: **Cells** on your left; **Bullets** along the wall to your right; **First Aid** kits, and **Shells** tucked in a corner. Go to the lever with the pale blue flashing handle and throw it to close the main hangar door. Your field computer will advise you that the first half of your objective is complete. You should now proceed to the surface to complete the next leg of your mission.

15 Open the door at your right, but get ready for a Berserker attack. There's only one, but a Brain backs him up. Kill them, and then grab the **Medkit** on the crate inside the door, the **Slugs** around the corner further right, and the **Shards** on the left. As you round the corner and head for the lighted doorway, another Gunner will attack from behind the crates on the left. When you shoot him chances are you'll hit the wall behind him, to the left of the doorway, and reveal **Secret Area #5**. Go in and get the **Body Armor**. Be sure to grab the **Medkit** and the **Bullets** dropped by the Gunner, then take the elevator to the surface.

Mission 7

205

dermal plated cranium

LAUNCH COMMAND

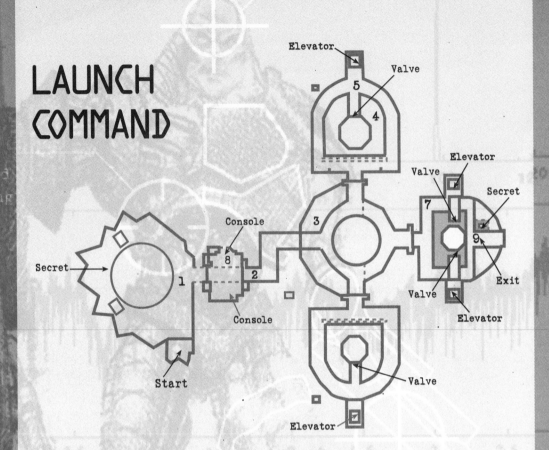

Elevator

Valve

Elevator

Valve

Secret

Console

Secret

Console

Valve

Exit

Valve

Elevator

Start

Valve

Elevator

Intel Brief

Primary Objective:	Close the main hanger door. Destroy blackhole generator.
Secondary Objective:	Shut off the coolant to the CPU Core.
Unit Location:	Launch Command
Potential Kills:	33
Goals:	6
Secrets:	2
Enemies:	Gunners, Iron Maidens, Tanks, Technicians
Weapons:	Blaster, Shotgun, Super Shotgun, Machine Gun, Chaingun, Grenade Launcher, Rocket Launcher, Hyperblaster, Railgun, BFG

Objective 4
SHUT OFF THE COOLANT TO THE CPU CORE

WELL, MARINE, YOU ARE IN FOR THE FIGHT OF YOUR LIFE. The CPU Core is heavily guarded and the big guns are arrayed against you. But you'll be able to use speed and know-how to get you through. This is no time for macho posturing. Even you can't kill everybody. Keep your ego in check and your mission objective foremost in your mind. Move out!

Objective Summary

1. Start; Rockets, Body Armor, Secret Area: BFG, Cells, Medkit
2. Gunner, Shells, First Aid
3. Iron Maidens, Rockets, Bullets, Stimpacks
4. Tanks, Gunners, Iron Maiden, Gladiator
5. Valve, Iron Maiden, Gladiator, Gunner
6. Tanks, Technicians, Valve, Iron Maiden, Gladiator, Gunner
7. Technicians, Valves
8. Technicians, Guards, Power Shield
9. Secret Area: Shells, Bullets, Slugs, Cells, Rockets, Grenade; Exit (to Outlands)

Mission 7

Quake II

dermal plated cranium

Field Report

1 You'll emerge from the elevator before a white gyro, rotating on a wide platform. Planes will be flying overhead, and the sound of radio communication fills the air. Go to your right and grab the **Rockets** and **Body Armor**, then approach the door to your right.

If you have mastered the fine art of rocket jumping, you can leap up onto the platform to **Secret Area #1**, where you will find a **BFG**, some **Rockets**, and a **Medkit**. On your way back out, climb the small ladder in the back, cross the platform, and jump back down in front of the entrance.

2 Open the door and lob a few Grenades down the corridor—your business card for the Gunner who's rushing you from the far end—then back out around the corner. When he's history, enter and grab the **Shells** the Gunner dropped, as well as the two **First Aid** kits inside.

3 Follow the passageway left, then right to another door. Inside, two of our favorite biomechanical bikini babes attack from either side of the central structure. Hang back and send them a missile or two. Grab the **Rockets** they drop and the **Bullets** and **Stimpacks**. Notice the doors; one on your right, one on your left. Beyond each door, the Stroggs have dispatched some of their finest, including Tanks, Iron Maidens, and Technicians. Start with the door on your left.

note

In fact, Iron Maidens, Gunners, Technicians and even more Tanks heavily guard this whole complex. Your best strategy from here on in is blow-and-go. Don't try to take everybody out, especially the slower, more powerful cyborgs. Whenever you can, just hustle past them—and don't forget to pick up the Bullets, Shells, Rockets, and Medkits wherever you go.

4 Enter and throw a rocket at one of the Tanks on either side. Keep hitting him as you blow past. If you can't get past him, kill him as quickly as you can. Around the corner you also have to fight off Iron Maidens, Gunners, and a Gladiator trying to nail you from above and from the ground floor. Run and gun and blast the place cyborg-free. Try reaching the entrance to the elevator at the far end of the room without attracting too many hits, and then ride it up to the next level.

5 Step out of the elevator and turn off the first valve. Watch out for the Gladiator and Iron Maiden team guarding the walkway. Fight any resistance and follow the walkway to a door guarded by a Gunner. Shotgun him, then proceed through the door into a circular corridor that is guarded by Tanks and Technicians.

Quake II

6 Run along the corridor to the left (or right) and go through the second left-hand (or right-hand) entrance. Take out the Gunner behind the door. Then carefully peek around the corner. There is another Iron Maiden and a Gladiator guarding this upper-level walkway. Watch their positions, then run for the second valve in front of the upper elevator entrance. If you have to, kill them, just don't stop and challenge them if you don't have to. Turn off the valve and return to the circular corridor you just came from, collecting whatever goodies you find.

7 Next, find the locked door. The one to the right of that door leads back to the valve you just shut off. The left one leads to the other valve. The door beneath the pipe with the exposed section showing blue, swirling water is the one you want. Enter and follow the walkway around to the left (or right) to the first elevator on your left (or right). Blast the Technicians hovering nearby, then ride the elevator up to the next level and turn the third valve. Jump down and run around to the other side—you'll be passing the exit; make a note of it—and do the same thing with the forth (and final) valve to complete this sequence that will disable the force field security.

8 Your field computer will prompt you to take out the black hole generator computers. Go to the formerly locked door, and follow the now accessible corridor to the next room. The sign above the door reads "Computer Systems." Enter, kill the Technicians and Guards, and then blast the computer console on your left. Jump up into the hole you've just created to recover a **Power Shield** from inside the hidden alcove. Then turn around and blast the console on the opposite wall. Your field computer has another message for you: "Launch systems destroyed. Force field disabled. Proceed to exit."

9 Return to the circular corridor and take the second door on your left (or right). You're back in the room with a water pool. Follow the walkway to the door marked Exit. Enter the short hallway and shoot the glass pane to your left. Jump through the window and dive into the water to retrieve some **Shells**, **Bullets**, **Slugs**, **Cells**, **Rockets**, and **Grenades** from **Secret Area #2**. When you've bagged the goodies, proceed through the Exit to the Outlands and the final objective of your mission.

Mission 7

209

dermal plated cranium

Start

1

2

Fuel Pod

Receptacle

Exit

3

Airstrike
Marker

OUTLANDS

Intel Brief

Primary Objective:	Close the main hanger door. Destroy blackhole generator.
Secondary Objective:	Retrieve the airstrike marker.
Unit Location:	Outlands
Potential Kills:	56
Goals:	2
Secrets:	0
Enemies:	Guards, Enforcers, Gunners, Flyers
Weapons:	Blaster, Shotgun, Super Shotgun, Machine Gun, Chaingun, Grenade Launcher, Rocket Launcher, Hyperblaster, Railgun, BFG

V2

Quake II

Objective 5
RETRIEVE THE AIRSTRIKE MARKER

THIS IS THE HOME STRETCH, AND IT'S A HUMDINGER. No cover. Big guns. And miles to go before you sleep. Ah hell, Gyrenes don't sleep! The trick here is to keep your head down and keep moving. Come to think of it, that's the trick everywhere.

Objective Summary

1. Start; Guards
2. Guards, Enforcers, Big Gun
3. Guards, Bullets, Flyers, Airstrike Marker
4. Fuel Pod, Guards
5. Guards, Gunner, Bandolier, Silencer, Slugs, First Aid, Exit

Mission 7

Field Report

1 As you go through the doors at the end of the Exit hallway, some Light Guards will attack from down a stairway. After what you've just been through, Guards are small potatoes, but the open area beyond the stairs is something else, so don't get cocky. Take out the Guards and get ready to rumble.

2 Use the rock cover to whittle down the number of Guards and Enforcers arrayed against you in the open area to your left. Watch out for that big gun; you've got to hit the gunner from behind to take him out, but you don't need to if you clear a path to the caves ahead. When you've thinned the opposition, break for the caves. You'll be running and gunning the whole way, past dozens of Guards and Enforcers. Just follow the wall on your left and keep moving!

By the way, the water makes lousy **note** cover. It's full of Barracuda Sharks, once you're in it, it's tough to climb out, and the enemy can shoot you down there anyway.

3 Don't stop until you come to a heavily guarded open area with some **Bullets**, **Health**, and a strange-looking object laid out on the ground. The **Airstrike Marker** is right around the corner. Grab it and keep going in the same direction, blasting away at the Guards dogging you.

4 When you come to the fuel pod, insert the Airstrike Marker into the blue receptacle between the pod and the door. You now have ten seconds to get back into the cave before the airstrike begins.

5 After the airstrike is over, reemerge from the cave and take out the Guards that have no idea what hit them. Turn right and enter through the door into a small chamber stocked with a **Bandolier**, **Silencer**, **Slugs**, and **First Aid** kits on either side of the consoles. (You may have to fight off a Gunner on your way in.) Take all you can carry and head for the Exit, fighting off any resistance that is left. Congratulations, Marine. You've turned the tide!

Mission 7

V1

V4

V2

V5

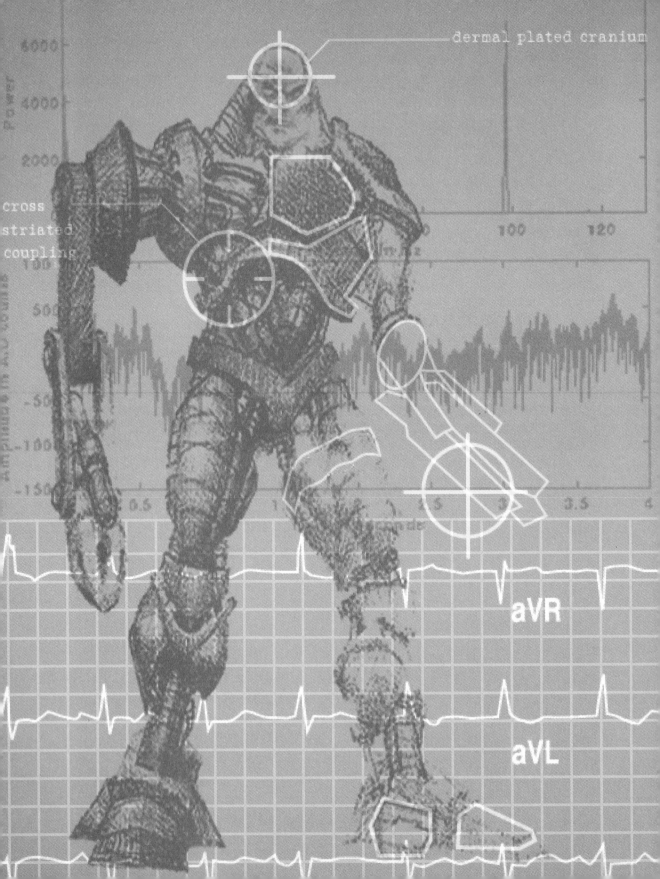

Mission 8
NEUTRALIZE THE STROGG LEADER'S COMMUNICATION SYSTEM

Your final objective is the so-called Makron, the leader of the Strogg empire. This powerful creature may be found within the walls of the central Palace. To get to the Makron's Inner Chamber, you must first penetrate the outer courts and lower levels of the palace. While you are inside, disable the comm system to further isolate the Strogg leader. To accomplish this, you will need a key, a data CD, and a security pass, all of which may be found within the overall palace grounds. When you have located the Makron, terminate with extreme prejudice.

Mission 8 by Unit Locations

1. Outer Courts
2. Lower Palace
3. Upper Palace/Lower Palace
4. Inner Chamber
5. Final Showdown

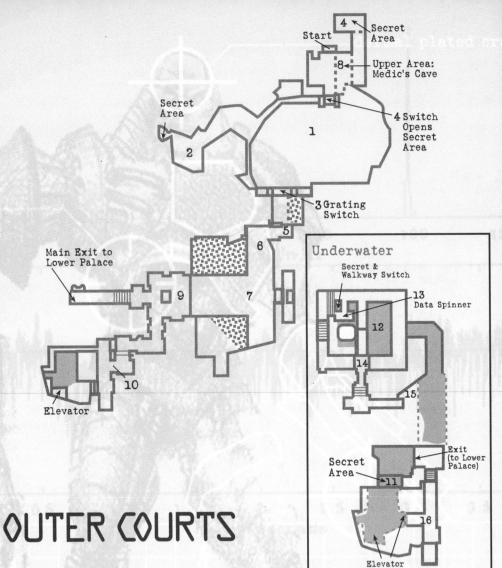

OUTER COURTS

Intel Brief

Primary Objective:	Neutralize the Strogg Leader's communication system
Secondary Objective:	Find functioning Data Spinner in Outer Courts
Unit Location:	Outer Courts
Potential Kills:	67/68
Goals:	1
Secrets:	4/5
Enemies:	Icaruses, Tanks, Tank Commanders, Guards, Medics
Weapons:	Blaster, Shotgun, Super Shotgun, Machine Gun, Chaingun, Grenade Launcher, Rocket Launcher, Hyperblaster, Railgun, BFG

Objective 1
FIND A FUNCTIONING DATA SPINNER IN THE OUTER COURTS

YOU'RE HEADING FOR THE HOME STRETCH, MARINE, but the Strogg will be out in force to stop you. As you get nearer to your final mission, they get that much tougher. This time, they'll come at you in groups and swarms and they won't give you a break. You've got to be tough, but you've also got to be smart. Use your equipment and your brain and you'll make it through in one piece.

Objective Summary

1. Start; Icaruses, Bullets, First Aid, Shards
2. Machine Gun Guards, Gladiators, Icaruses, Slugs, First Aid, Bullets, Shells, Rockets, **Secret Area:** First Aid, Power Shield; Combat Armor
3. Bullets, First Aid, Invulnerability, Floor Switch (opens gate below)
4. Switch (opens door to secret area), Ladder (to Secret Area), **Secret Area:** Rockets, Slugs, Shells, Grenades, Body Armor; Adrenaline
5. Machine Gun Guards, Bullets, First Aid
6. Tank Commander, Icaruses, Rockets, Bullets, Shells
7. Machine Gun Guards, Icaruses
8. Medics, **Secret Area:** First Aid
9. Rockets, Tank Commanders, Rockets, Bullets, First Aid, Shells, Combat Armor, Stimpacks
10. Gladiators, Shells, Grenades, Icaruses
11. Rebreather, Medkit, **Secret Area**
12. Machine Gun Guards, Gladiator, Bullets, Cells, Rockets, Medkit
13. Data Spinner, Guards, First Aid, Floor Switch (opens Secret Area), **Secret Area:** Adrenaline
14. Icaruses, Shells
15. Medkits, First Aid, Shells, Rockets
16. Guards, Gladiator, Shells, Power Shield, Rockets, Grenades, Medkits, Exit (to Lower Palace)

Mission 8

217

Field Report

1 From your starting point, open the door and start blasting the half a dozen Icaruses dropping down from the sky on all sides. (An endless stream of Icaruses will dog you wherever you go in the Outer Courts—they will even follow you into caves and corridors—so keep listening for that little screech and the hum of their power packs.) When you've cleared out the first wave of Icaruses, go out and collect the ammo they dropped. You'll also find **Bullets** around the corner on your left and right as well as directly in front of you. Don't miss the **First Aid** kits on your right and in the far corner ahead. Grab the **Shards** and head down toward the cave on your right.

2 As you move out into the open, several Machine Gun Guards will charge out from the cave. Two Gladiators hiding in a cubbyhole beside the cave will join them. You'll have to retreat and gun them as you run. When you've taken them out, go back to the cave and cubbyhole and collect the ammunition and supplies. Be careful! There's another Gladiator in the cave, and he's not so shy that he won't come charging out after you. Expect at least one and maybe two more Icarus attacks during this skirmish. When all your enemies are down, collect all the **Slugs**, **First Aid** kits, and **Bullets** outside the cave. Inside the cave, you'll find a **First Aid** kit, **Shells**, **Rockets**, more **Bullets**, and

Secret Area #1. Shoot the wall just across the lava on the right to find the **First Aid** kit and **Power Shield** hidden there. The cubbyhole contains a **Combat Armor.**

3 Exit the cave, but do not rush into the large entryway. As you approach it, the floor will drop away, and if you're on it you'll end up in a pool of lava. You can easily enter by hugging the wall and walking in on the wide edges of the open trap doors. You can't enter yet due to the large gate blocking your way, so before you go that way, follow the terrace up past the entryway. Stay close to the wall and follow the ramped path up and back right. (Along the way collect **Bullets** and **First Aid** kits.) Follow it around to the narrow ledge, and then hop down onto the stone lintel above the entryway. Collect the **First Aid** kit, **Bullets**, and **Invulnerability** power-up, then hit the floor switch to open the gate below.

4 Jump to the next ledge and keep following the ledges around to the doorway over the start room. At the end of the ledge, hop onto the stone above the entryway. Some of this will be tricky going, so be prepared to climb back up. Hit the green switch. This opens the door to a secret area inside near your starting point. Notice the doors in the darkened alcove above the switch. You'll be getting back to them later. For now, make your way down and back to the room you started in. Kill the two Machine Gun Guards who rush you as you head toward

Quake II

the entrance. Continue down the hallway on your right and you'll come to a Ladder. Grab the two **First Aid** kits at the foot of the ladder and climb up into **Secret Area #2**. Collect the **Rockets**, **Slugs**, **Shells**, **Grenades**, and **Body Armor** waiting there. Walk along the narrow ledge and get the **Adrenaline** before jumping down.

5   Exit and head down to the main entryway. Shoot the two Machine Gun Guards who attack you in the alcove and grab the **Bullets** and **First Aid** kit.

6   Go through the door into the inner courtyard. You'll see a Tank Commander coming toward you. Waste him from a distance with your Railgun or Rocket Launcher. Hang back in the corridor; more Icaruses are on the way and you'll need the cover. Blast the mechanical harpies out of the air, and grab the **Rockets**. Notice the doors on your left. When you go down toward the doorway on your right, an alarm will sound and half a dozen Machine Gun Guards will burst through those doors, guns blazing. At the same time, more Icaruses will descend from the sky and hang in front of the entryway, shooting. Triggering this onslaught is unavoidable, but you can get through it. For now, stick to the upper walkway and take out the Tank Commander that will shoot at you from the lower doorway, then shoot down the Icaruses that arrive to back him up. Collect the **Bullets** and **Shells** along this upper area.

7   Now, take out your Hyperblaster, queue up your Chaingun, and get ready to rumble. Turn and face the doors the Guards will be charging out of and back down the ramp slowly. The instant the alarm starts, begin hurling bombs toward the doors. Once the Guards expire, dive into their hiding place and pull out your Rocket Launcher. Icaruses will already be shooting at you from behind, and you will take a few hits, but they will have to drop down low to get at you in the alcove. Wait for them to show in the opening and then drop them with your rockets. Grab the ammo the Guards and Icaruses have dropped and go back out into the open area you started in. Watch out for the lava trap!

8   As you enter the courtyard, some Medics will attack you. Once you've wiped them out, follow the ledges back to the switch above your entryway. Those doors above it are open now, and you'll find a **First Aid** kit inside **Secret Area #3**. (The truth is, this one is hardly worth the trip, but now you know what was behind those doors.)

9   Go back inside and head for the door at the bottom of the ramp. Grab the **Rockets** dropped by the dead Tank Commander in the doorway. Around to your left, a Tank Commander is guarding the stairs; around to your right two Tank Commanders are guarding the stairs. Your best strategy here is to lure them down and pick them off from

Mission 8

219

around the corners in the entry. Use the halls for cover as you dodge in and out, firing rockets as they come into view. When the Tank Commanders are out of the way, you'll hear the radio recon report of "access through the sewers." Collect the ammunition and supplies strewn around the halls (**Rockets**, **Bullets**, **First Aid** kits, **Shells**, **Combat Armor**.) Don't miss the **Stimpacks** line up on the middle staircase. (Those doors lead to the Lower Palace.)

10 Go up the staircase on the left. Through the doors, a Gladiator and a Shotgun Guard will charge you, so get ready. Several Icaruses will back them up. Use the hallway as cover while you take them out. Don't charge out into the open right away—more Icaruses are coming. And after a few seconds, more will follow them. Your best strategy here is to run out and jump directly into the water. (You can come back for the supplies and ammo later.)

11 Under the water you'll notice two lifts on your left. One takes you back up to the ledge you jumped from; the other you'll come back to. For now, swim to your right. Surface in the next alcove and grab the **Rebreather** and the

Medkit. The door on the ledge is blocked by a red force field (you can see the goodies inside, but can't touch), so you'll have to keep swimming. Remember this location—it's **Secret Area #4**.

12 Dive back in and swim down the pipe until you get to a broken grating blocking your way. Shoot the bars and the grate will open. Enter the vertical pipe and you will rise up to the next level. Machine Gun Guards and a Gladiator guard the open area at the end of the next pipe. You'll be exposed if you let yourself float out into the open. Instead, stay submerged and swim to your left (grab the **Bullets** and **Cells** you pass) to a nook in the far corner. Take the **Rockets** stashed there and put your back to the wall. This should give you enough cover to toss a few grenades out and soften up the bad guys. You'll take a few hits when you come out to clean up. Collect the ammo the cyborgs dropped, pick up the **Medkit**, and go into the next room at the top of the stairs.

13 There you'll find the **Data Spinner** you've come for. Kill the Guards who attack you, snag the **First Aid** kits, shoot the glass and grab the spinner. Your field computer will advise you to find the communications laser Data CD in the Upper Palace. To get there you'll have to go through the Lower Palace.

tip   Before you leave the room, shoot the wall panel beside the Data Spinner niche, and it will move back, revealing a floor switch. Step on the floor switch and **Secret Area #5** will be revealed behind you. Hit the green wall switch (which lowers a walkway outside the room), grab the **Adrenaline**, and exit the way you came.

14 In the hallway, go right, then right again. Proceed down the stairs, but watch out for the Icarus who will be shooting at you from the left. Blast the biomech bird, then snag the **Cells** and go to the end of he corridor. There's another Icarus waiting for you, so be ready to fire.

15 Hop down to the pipe and ledges below, and grab the **Medkit**, **First Aid** kit, **Shells**, and **Rockets** stashed there. When you've gathered the goodies, drop to the water below. Swim back down the pipe to the first pool you jumped into and take the elevator on the left up into another hallway.

16 Three Guards and a Gladiator will be waiting for you, so be ready. When you've taken them out, scoop up the ammo they dropped and the **Shells**, **Power Shield**, and **Rockets** stashed there in the hallway. When you do this, another Gladiator will come out of a hiding place behind you. Waste him, take his shard, and go back to his hiding place for the **Grenade** and **Adrenaline**. Go up the stairs, take the **Medkits**, and then enter the red doors to exit to the Lower Palace.

Mission 8

II tɪɐq

221

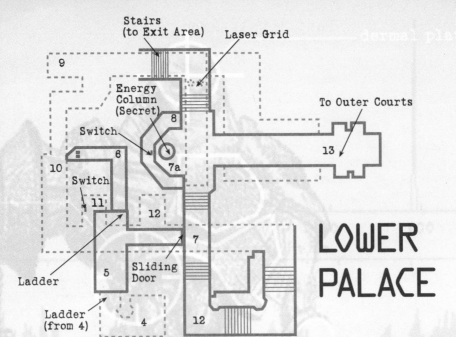

Stairs
(to Exit Area)

Laser Grid

Energy
Column
(Secret)

Switch

Switch

To Outer Courts

13

LOWER
PALACE

Ladder

Ladder
(from 4)

Sliding
Door

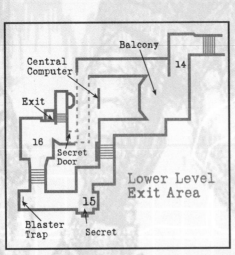

Central Computer

Balcony

Exit

Secret
Door

Blaster
Trap

Secret

Lower Level
Exit Area

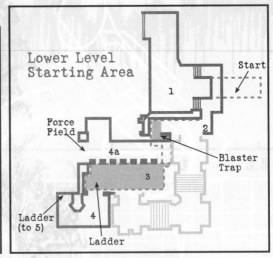

Lower Level
Starting Area

Start

Force
Field

Blaster
Trap

Ladder
(to 5)

Ladder

Intel Brief

Primary Objective: Neutralize the Strogg Leader's
                      communication system
Secondary Objective: Find the communications laser data
                      CD in Upper Palace
Unit Location: Lower Palace
Potential Kills: 54/89
Goals: 1/3
Secrets: 4/6
Enemies: Guards, Berserkers, Technicians,
                      Brains, Tanks, Tank Commanders
Weapons: Blaster, Shotgun, Super Shotgun,
                      Machine Gun, Chaingun, Grenade
                      Launcher, Rocket Launcher,
                      Hyperblaster, Railgun, BFG

Quake II

222

Objective 2
FIND THE COMMUNICATIONS LASER CD IN THE UPPER PALACE

YOU'RE GOING TO THE PALACE, MARINE, but don't expect to meet the queen. You've made it to the center of the city and you're on your way to your final showdown. But first, you have to navigate the labyrinthine lower and upper palaces. This leg of your mission will require more brain than brawn—especially since you're outmuscled in the brawn department. The key to your success lies in a strategy that will thin the cyborg herd. Time to rope and ride!

Objective Summary

1. Start; Guards, Berserkers, Stimpacks, Rockets, First Aid
2. Secret Area: Power Shield, Adrenaline
3. Blaster Trap, First Aid, Ladder
4. Machine Gun Guard, Guards, Berserker, Tank Commander
5. Ladder, Berserker, Guards, Tank Commander
6. Ladder, Guard, Rockets, Bullets, First Aid, Invulnerability, Technician, Secret Area
7. Guards, Tank Commander, Switch (opens gate)
8. Machine Gun Guards, Stimpacks, Laser Grid
9. Rockets, First Aid
10. Brain, Machine Gun Guards, Technicians
11. Brains, Switch (deactivates red force fields), Medkit, First Aid
12. First Aid, Bullets, Secret Area: Quad Damage; Technician, Berserkers, Tank Commander
13. (Outer Courts) Secret Area: Rockets, Cells, Slugs, Grenade, Power Shield, Medkit, Red Key
14. Berserker, Tank Commander
15. Berserker, Tank, Machine Gun Guard, Secret Area: Wall (shoot to disable Blaster Trap)
16. Berserker, Tank Commander, Guards, Technicians, First Aid, Body Armor, Bullets, Secret Area: Rockets, Medkits, Tank Commander; Switch (activates elevator), Exit (to Upper Palace)

Field Report

1 You'll enter the Lower Palace at the low end of a ramp leading up into a hallway where one Guard is waiting for you behind two explosive barrels. Two Berserkers and two other Guards are poised behind a stone barricade in an alcove right above you. Blast the barrels to vaporize the rookie Guard, then charge up the ramp and around the corner to your right. Fight off the Berserker that follows you, then, using the corner as cover, launch a few Grenades over the barrier into the alcove. The barrels up there will amp up the explosion and take everyone out.

note If you accidentally open the door to your left while seeking cover, you'll also have to deal with a hovering Technician in the hallway beyond—in addition to the Berserker who is rushing you.

A Berserker may be the only one to survive, so be ready for a killing shot with another weapon. When nobody is left, collect the ammo and supplies scattered around the area: **Shells** next to the door, **Stimpack** on the steps, **Rockets** and a **First Aid** kit up behind where the Guards were standing.

2 Midway up the stairs to the left of your starting point, low in the wall on your right, you'll see a small, square opening. Shoot the crooked bars, then crouch down and enter the narrow corridor.

Turn right and slide down the steep ramp into **Secret Area #1**. Grab the **Power Shield** and Adrenaline and go left. Put on your armor, take out a spraying weapon, such as a Chaingun, and get ready to get stung.

3 Around the next corner is a blaster trap that will hit you in the back as you pass. Slip past it and dive right around the corner. You should only have to take one shot. Around the corner, go directly to the platform and hug the right wall. Use the overhang for cover from the snipers above. (Don't worry, they'll get theirs.) Collect the **First Aid** kit, and run for the ladder on the other side.

4 Get up that ladder fast and dive through the sliding panel at the top with your gun pointed right and blasting. Two Machine Gun Guards are waiting for you inside, and several cyborgs on the walkway behind you are using your butt for target practice. When you've secured the room, go back to the panel. Get out your Grenade Launcher or Rocket Launcher (or both), and start lobbing bombs over to the hall across from you (4a). Stay back to keep from getting hit, but keep at it until you've cleared out the Guards, Berserker, and Tank Commander (if he shows) on patrol there. This will make it easier for you when you reach that corridor eventually.

5 Take out your Chaingun and climb the next ladder. At the top, run forward, turn right, and begin firing immediately at the Berserker rushing you. It's a tight space so hit him quickly.

6 When the monster goes down, go to the next ladder and climb up. A Guard will charge you from the left, but he'll be the only enemy in the room. Waste him and grab the **Rockets**, **Bullets**, and **First Aid** kit, then open the door the tiny alcove on your left. Inside you'll find an **Invulnerability** power-up. Snag it.

tip   Take this opportunity to shoot down the Technician floating by in the high-ceilinged room beyond the bars. Take him out and you'll have one less reason to look up when you get to that room.

The area behind the ladder protected by the red force field is **Secret Area #2** (you'll access it later). Remember to come back for it after you de-activate the yellow force fields later.

7 Climb back down the ladder and turn left. Cautiously approach the sliding door and get your Grenades or Rockets ready. Open the door and throw some bombs into the hallway. About a half dozen Guards will be anxious to pile in from the hallway outside. Hang back far enough that you can handle the few who do. (If you've got the ammo, you could probably just stand there and spray the

space as the lame-brained Guards swarm into it.) After you've killed all the Guards, a Tank Commander will follow their example. If you open the panel, jump back, and blast him from a corner, he should never make it through. When you've taken out most of the baddies, make a mad dash for the hallway. Turn left, run down the stairs, and head for the blue energy column on your right. (Careful, a Technician is following you, so keep your eyes open.) Drop down over the edge next to the column and hit the switch below (7a) to open a small gate to your left.

8 Inside the narrow room are two Guards. Take them out quick, then crawl through the small opening inside. To your left, you'll notice a door blocked by a shifting blue laser grid. Grab the **Stimpacks** inside the room, then, when the grid lines go vertical, slip through into the corridor.

9 Turn left (turning right and through the door takes you back to the starting area) and go down the hallway. At the end (past the two barrels) is a low-ceilinged room with some crates in it. Climb the crates and grab the **Rockets** and **First Aid** kit stashed above the door.

Mission 8

Quake II

225

10 Jump down and continue down the hallway to your right. Go up the short stairway. Stop and get out your Grenade Launcher; you're about to get caught in a squeeze play. Just past the door outlined with lights (it's inaccessible right now), a Brain waits to ambush you on the right. When you move past him, Machine Gun Guards will charge from ahead and simultaneously two Technicians will burst up from the floor behind you. Be prepared. At the lighted door, turn around and face the opposite direction. Now run down the hallway backward. You'll see everybody coming. Ice the Guards first and then use their hiding place (now on your left) for cover. Bounce Grenades off the walls to get around the Brain's force field, and lob them at the Technicians to bring them down before they get to you. This is a tricky maneuver, but it'll work if you don't go around the corner and open the double doors. If you do, two more Brains will join the party.

11 When you've dealt with your ambushers, open the double doors, drop back and waste the Brains inside. Go to the security panel and hit the red button. This deactivates the red force fields throughout the Palace, including the one blocking the computer console for the Data Spinner and Data CD.

note

Remember that last secret area back in the Outer Courts that was protected by a red force field? Now you can reach it.

If you cleared the walkway behind the bars from the top of the ladder earlier,

there will be no one coming from the hall on your left to deal with. (Chances are, you'll still be stalked by a Tank Commander.) Grab the **Medkit** by the security panel, scoop up any ammo dropped during the battle (don't miss the **First Aid** kits back where first Brain was hiding), and then head down the hallway past the disengaged force field.

12 Snag the **First Aid** kit and **Bullets** inside the doorway on your left, and follow the hallway up the stairs (more **First Aid** kits on a landing). Follow the stairs down to the central hall with the blue image on the floor. To your right is a blue energy column. On top of it sits a **Quad Damage** power-up (technically, in **Secret Area # 3**). To get it down, shoot the demon's face behind the column, and the one across from it above the hallway. The beam will disappear and the Quad will drop to the platform. As soon as you shoot, two Berserkers will attack. Run up the opposite stairs to get some room and shoot the Berserkers. Use the Quad to nail the Tank Commander coming down the stairs to back up his cyborg buddies. (Don't forget to grab the **Rockets** the Tank Commander drops when he croaks.)

13 Now you have an errand to run—get ready for another swim. To access all areas of the Upper Palace, you must have the Red Keycard. You'll find it back in the underwater passageway you accessed in the Outer Courts. Use the door opposite the Quad Damage hiding place, and retrace your steps to the Outer Courts. Go directly to the water (upon entering turn right and right again, go up the stairs and through the door), dive in, and swim to the room outside the pipe (see Underwater map on page 216). This Secret Area is open now, and it's full of goodies: **Rockets**, **Cells**, **Slugs**, **Grenades**, a **Power Shield**, a **Medkit**, and the thing you really came for: the **Red Key**. Scoop it all up, dive back into the water and take the elevator on your left up to the next level. Follow the corridor to the exit to the Lower Palace.

14 You arrive back in your original starting area. Retrace your steps to the hallway with the energy column and go to the end of the hall. If you didn't take him out earlier, a Tank Commander will be waiting for you around the corner to your left—so have your Rocket Launcher ready. Also, there are two Berserkers waiting for you at the top of the stairs. Once they're gone, you can open the double door to a large hall.

15 Take out the two Technicians near the door, then enter through the door. (Notice the large computer console in the room below you as you pass through the red double doors. You'll be coming back here later.) Follow the red carpet through the next set of doors and kill the Berserker and Tank on the other side. Continue up the stairs and shoot the Machine Gun Guard. At the top of the stairs, turn right and then left, but before you turn right again, shoot the wall ahead of you to discover **Secret #4** and permanently disarm the blaster trap waiting for you around the corner.

16 Follow the hallway to the end. Around the corner, a Berserker, a Tank Commander, and several Guards are waiting for you at the top of the stairs. Lure them down so you have some room to move and kill them quickly before they overwhelm you. When they're history, go upstairs. Straight ahead is an elevator that takes you to the Upper Palace. Before exiting, however, look around the corner on your right. Two Technicians are hovering in front of a door at the end of the flight of stairs. Bring them down, then climb the stairs and grab the **First Aid** kits, **Body Armor**, and **Bullets** on the next landing. Go back downstairs and shoot the computer panel on the wall to your right to open a passage to **Secret Area #5,** which contains some **Rockets** and **Medkits**. Ready your Rocket Launcher and jump down. At the end of the narrow corridor, there's a Tank Commander anxious to make your acquaintance. Don't disappoint him. When he's dead, drop down and walk up the stairs ahead. Turn right through the door and right again to return to the balcony from which you saw the computer panel. (You might have to put up with another Berserker.) Follow the red carpet to return to the room with the elevator. Hit the switch to your right to call the elevator and take it to the Upper Palace to find the Data CD.

Mission 8

Quake II

227

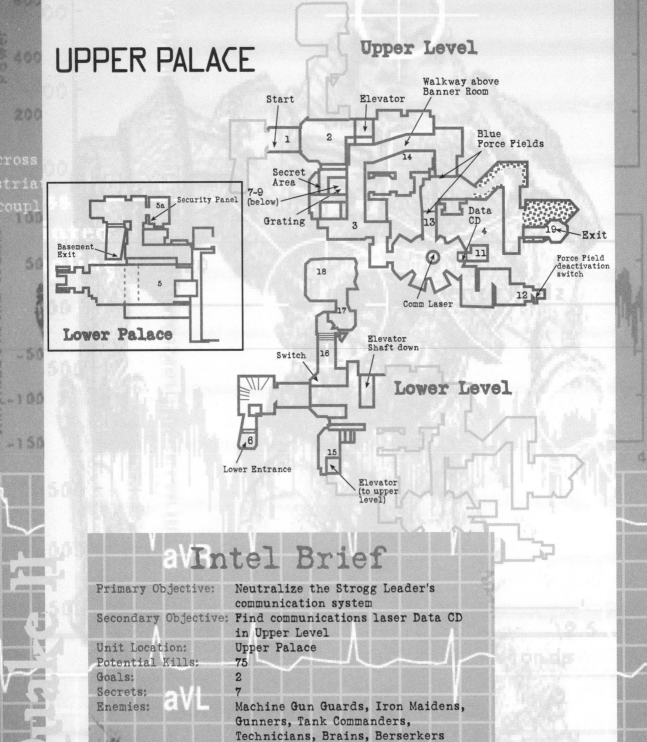

UPPER PALACE

Upper Level

Lower Palace

Lower Level

Intel Brief

Primary Objective:	Neutralize the Strogg Leader's communication system
Secondary Objective:	Find communications laser Data CD in Upper Level
Unit Location:	Upper Palace
Potential Kills:	75
Goals:	2
Secrets:	7
Enemies:	Machine Gun Guards, Iron Maidens, Gunners, Tank Commanders, Technicians, Brains, Berserkers
Weapons:	Blaster, Shotgun, Super Shotgun, Machine Gun, Chaingun, Grenade Launcher, Rocket Launcher, Hyperblaster, Railgun, BFG

Objective 3
SHUT DOWN THE COMMUNICATIONS LASER

THIS LEG OF YOUR MISSION WILL HAVE YOU running back and forth between the upper and lower palaces. You'll be dodging Tank Commanders, Berserkers, and Iron Maidens all along the way, with a few Technicians wandering around to make your life even harder. Listen to your field computer and keep your head down. It's all in a day's work, Marine. Move out!

Objective Summary

1. Start; Machine Gun Guards, Silencer, Shells, Switch (turns off force field), **Secret Area:** Adrenaline, Cells, Slugs
2. Iron Maidens, Rockets, Bullets
3. Guards, Gunners, Iron Maidens
4. Comm Laser Platform, Data CD, Tank Commander, Technician
5. (Lower Palace) **Secret Area**, Medkit, Technicians, Tank Commander, Central Computer, Brains, Guards, Security Panel, Switch (deactivates force field), **Exit** (to Upper Palace)
6. (Upper Palace basement) Machine Gun Guards, Iron Maidens, Stimpacks, Bullets, Slugs, First Aid, Gunners, Medkit, Shells
7. Machine Gun Guards, Shells, Shards, Medkit, **Secret Area:** Power Shield, Slugs, Invulnerability, Bullets
8. Gunner, Guard, Grenade, Shards, Medkit, First Aid, Ammo Pack
9. Ladder, Bullets, Gunners, Technician, First Aid, Silencer, Shard, Grenades, Security Pass
10. (Lower Palace) Technicians, Berserkers,
11. (Upper Palace) Keyboard (deactivates Comm Laser)
12. Switch (deactivates yellow force fields)
13. (Lower Palace) **Secret Area:** First Aid, Medkit, Bullets, Shells, Grenades, Rockets, Cells, Slugs; Quad Damage
14. Gunners, Guards, Iron Maiden, Technicians, Medkits, First Aid, Shells, Cells
15. Elevator (to other side), Elevator (down)
16. Light Guards, Switch (lowers stairway)
17. Technician, **Secret Area:** Body Armor, Slime Pool
18. **Secret Area:** Carmack's head
19. Iron Maiden, Technician, Keyboard (extends bridge), **Exit** (to Final Showdown)

Mission 8

Quake II

Field Report

1 At your entry point into the Upper Palace, half a dozen Machine Gun Guards are on duty. But they're not expecting anyone, so you can take them by surprise and mow them down fast. Grab the **Silencer** and **Shells**, and then hit the red switch on the left to turn off the force field. (Leave the other one on for now to discourage pursuers.)

tip Step into the hall. Look up and shoot the indentation in the ceiling to reveal **Secret Area #1**. The wall slides open to reward you with **Adrenaline**, **Cells**, and **Slugs**.

2 Take the elevator on the left up to the next level. Go through the doors and blast the two Iron Maidens guarding the next door. Grab the **Rockets** they drop and the **Bullets**.

3 Go through the door and blast your way through the half dozen Guards, Gunner, and Iron Maiden blocking your way. Use a Quad Damage power-up if you've got one. The corridor on your right will take you to the Communications Laser and the Data CD.

4 You'll have to fight your way through another Iron Maiden and two Gunners to get it. Step onto the Comm Laser platform and grab the **Data CD**. Your field computer will advise you to repro-gram the Data Spinner at the Central Computer. You'll find that computer in the Lower Palace. Head back to the ele-vator. You'll have a Tank Commander and a Technician to deal with. Take the elevator down and retrace your steps to the Lower Palace.

5 When you step off the second elevator onto the red carpet in the Lower Palace, look left. Shoot the computer panel to access the secret area again. This time, jump down and go downstairs to access the Central Computer room behind the red doors below. Blast the two Technicians floating above, and then shoot down the Tank Commander on guard. Place the Data Spinner in the left side, and the CD in the right side of the computer to be reprogrammed. Shove the central keyboard to get the **Reprogrammed CD** and **Spinner**. (It'll rise up out of the floor behind you.) Grab it and head back to the Upper Palace through the doors opposite the ones you used to enter the Central Computer room. Kill the Brains in the passageway and enter the small room on your right (5a). Fight off the Guard and Brain inside, then push the red button to deactivate the force field in the Central Computer room. Now you exit through the red doors to the Upper Palace.

When you press against the wall to the left of the control panel (the one that shut off the force field), a door opens in the nearby hall for a few seconds— another Secret Area stuffed with **Combat Armor**, **Grenades**, **Rockets**, and a **Mega-Health**. **tip**

6 Scoop up the **Stimpacks** on the stairs and climb up. You'll have to fight your way through Machine Gun Guards on the next landing, and an Iron Maiden will attack from the alcove on the right. This is a fierce battle so use the stairs for cover as you fight. Collect the **Bullets** the Guards drop, and the **Slugs** and **First Aid** kit back where the Iron Maiden was hiding. Proceed down the walkway and toss a few Grenades up the stairs to soften up the Machine Gun Guard, Gunner, and Iron Maiden waiting for you up there. Go up the stairs and snag the **Bullets** on the right. When you head down the corridor the other direction, an Iron Maiden will rise up and attack. Blast her, then take out the Guard ahead. Don't miss the **Medkit** down the hall on your right. Grab the **Shells** the Guard drops, then go up the stairs through the lighted doorway.

> **tip**
>
> While still in the basement area of the level, descend down to the dirt-wall excavation, and stand in front of the force field until you hear an explosion to your left. Kill the Technician trapped in the ceiling hole and an Enviro-Suit will drop down into your lap—**Secret #2**.

7 Shoot the Machine Gun Guards who charge you at the top of the stairs. Grab the **Shells** and **Shards** they drop and the two **Medkits** against the right wall. Take the lift up to the next level. Go through the grating (it will open for you) and shoot the wall on the left to expose **Secret Area #3**. Go inside and collect the **Power Shield**, **Slugs**, and **Invulnerability** power-up. Don't miss the **Bullets** on the ledge by the ladder.

8 Drop down to the level you can see below. Shoot the Gunner and the Guard. Collect the **Grenades**, **Shard**, **Medkit** and follow the walkway around. Shoot the Gunner at the end of the hall and collect the **Shard** he drops, plus the **First Aid** kit and **Ammo Pack** hidden here.

9 Take the ladder down to the lower level. Follow the lights in the ceiling around (don't miss the **Bullets**). Blast the two Gunners and Technician on guard at the end. Grab the **First Aid** kit and **Silencer** on the left, the **Shard** one of the Gunners drops, the **First Aid** kit and **Grenades** in the next room, and, of course, the **Security Pass** on your right.

10 Drop down to the walkway below and retrace your steps back to the basement entrance to the Lower Palace. Watch out for the Technicians roaming the halls. When you reenter the Lower Palace, two Berserkers will be there to greet you. Say howdy with your Hyperblaster and head upstairs. Find the red carpet and follow it back to the elevator. Take the elevator back up to the upper floors of the Upper Palace. You should now have everything you need to complete your mission.

Mission 8

Quake II

231

11 Go directly to the Comm Laser. Stand on the platform on which you found the CD and a door will open for you there. Go inside and push the keyboard to deactivate the Comm Laser. Your mission is now complete. You can head for the exit.

12 Before you exit the Upper Palace, however, there's one more secret area you won't want to miss. To get to it, drop off the edge of the walkway surrounding the now disabled Comm Laser, and find the gray door. Your security pass will let you in. Go inside and hit the switch on the central console. This will deactivate all the yellow force fields in the Palace. Grab the **Stimpack** and return to the Comm Laser.

> **tip** Remember to return to the Lower Palace and access the **Secret Area** (see Objective 2, Point 6) that was behind a yellow force field. This will gain you two **First Aid** kits, a **Medkit**, some **Bullets**, **Shells**, **Grenades**, **Rockets**, **Cells**, and **Slugs**—well worth the trip back. Grab the Stimpack and return to the Comm Laser.

13 Go through the red door. At the bottom of the stairs, a half dozen Guards will attack. Blast them, then shoot the impact switch above the panel on your right to disable the blaster trap temporarily (you'll have about four seconds). Scoop up the **Cells** and **First Aid** kit and hustle down the hallway. At the end of the hall, drop off the ledge to your right and run through the lava to find **Secret Area #4** and a **Quad Damage** power-up and some Health. Ride the elevator up to the hall above, shoot the impact switch (to stop the blaster trap again), and follow the walkway to the right to the Hall of Banners.

14 Inside, Gunners, Guards, and an Iron Maiden are waiting to attack, so you'll have to run and gun. You'll probably take a lot of hits, so be sure to collect the **Medkits** and **First Aid** kits scattered around the room, along with the **Shells** and **Cells** on the ledge surrounding the room.

15 Go down the sloping ramp and climb the stairs into the main entry hall. (You have to hit the switch first before you can enter.) Take the elevator on the other side. When you get to the top, go through the first and second set of red doors, then turn right. When you get to the end of the hallway, instead of turning left to go to the Comm Laser, go through the red door on the right. With the force fields deactivated, you can access the sub-basement level from here. Take the elevator down, follow the hallway around to your right, down the stairs, around left, to a hallway with an open shaft on the right.

16 Drop down the shaft into the sub-basement level. Shoot the Light Guards that dog you, then proceed through the lighted doorway. Hit the green switch to lower a stairway in the ramp ahead of you. Shoot the attacking Light Guards and grab the ammo and supplies they drop.

17 Go down the stairs and frag the Technician that suddenly appears above the slime pool. In a breach in the brick wall ahead of you is **Secret Area #5** with some **Body Armor** hidden inside. Grab it and get ready to swim in some slime. An Enviro-Suit would work best, but you can use Invulnerability (your visibility isn't as good). Slide along the ledge to your right until you hear a click, then dive down and swim through the opening doorway to your left.

18 Surface into **Secret Area #6**—the ultimate secret area. Go to the dusty computer console and push in the keyboard. Fluid will drain from the clear container on the right, revealing… revealing… John Carmack's head! Blast the glass and crawl in to grab your prize, Marine. Then shoot the lighted spot on the wall behind you and get back to work! Take this exit back to the elevator and return to the Comm Laser.

19 From the Comm Laser upstairs, go through the wide, red doors, turn right and follow the hallway around to the end. You'll have to kill an Iron Maiden who appears just past the first lava pit, and a Technician who attacks at the end of the walkway. Kill these monsters quickly and go to the computer console. Push in the keyboard and a bridge will extend to the pod across the lava on your left. Enter the pod to go to your final objective—killing the Makron.

tip

Secret Area #7 can be accessed from the upper-level walkway in the Hall of Banners. Look down and to your right as you pass under the archway. You should see a dark, square opening to the side of the pathway. Drop down into the darkness. The cramped space below contains combat armor, health, and ammo. Drop through the hole in the floor to exit the secret chamber. Be warned! You'll dropping into the path of the blaster trap next to the Hall of Banners.

Mission 8

233

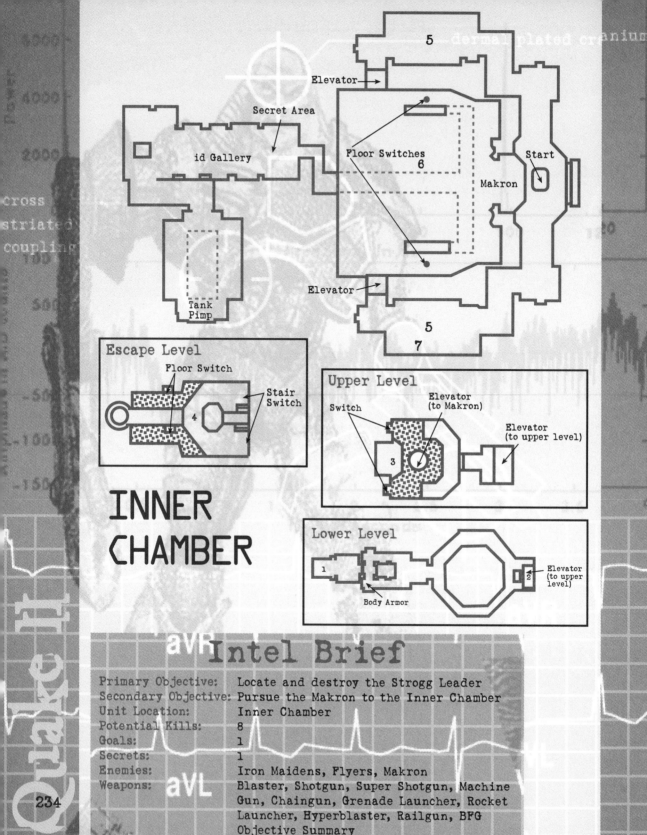

5

Elevator

Secret Area

id Gallery

Floor Switches

6

Start

Makron

Tank
Pimp

Elevator

5

7

Escape Level

Floor Switch

Stair
Switch

4

INNER CHAMBER

Upper Level

Switch

Elevator
(to Makron)

Elevator
(to upper level)

3

Lower Level

1

2

Elevator
(to upper
level)

Body Armor

aVR Intel Brief

Primary Objective: Locate and destroy the Strogg Leader
Secondary Objective: Pursue the Makron to the Inner Chamber
Unit Location: Inner Chamber
Potential Kills: 8
Goals: 1
Secrets: 1
Enemies: Iron Maidens, Flyers, Makron
Weapons: Blaster, Shotgun, Super Shotgun, Machine
                       Gun, Chaingun, Grenade Launcher, Rocket
                       Launcher, Hyperblaster, Railgun, BFG
                       Objective Summary

aVL

Quake II

Objective 4
KILL THE MAKRON

THIS IS IT, MARINE, YOUR FINAL OBJECTIVE, your final showdown with the Big Biomechanical Kahuna. The Strogg of Stroggos. The Makron. You've got this bad boy hiding out in his inner chamber, but that shouldn't comfort you much. Remember, a beast is never more dangerous than when it's cornered. And you're on this beastie's home turf. Keep your wits about you and let your training keep your alive. If you pull this one off, victory is ours. Good luck!

———Objective Summary

1. Start; Body Armor
2. Stimpacks Shells, Rockets, Slugs, Bullets, Cells, Switch (activates elevator)
3. Iron Maidens, Switches (open way to elevator)
4. Floor Switches, Switches (extend stairs), Flyers, Teleporter
5. Stimpacks, First Aid, Shards, Rockets, Medkits, Grenades, Slugs, Elevator (to chamber)
6. Floor Switches (open hatches), Safety Chamber, Makron
7. Escape Pod, Secret Area, Exit

Mission 8

Quake II

Field Report

1 From your entry point, follow the red carpet out to the walkway in front of the smiling demon relief. Grab the **Body Armor** on your left and continue around to the tall engraved door. Push on the door and stand back while it is blasted away from the inside by powerful lasers.

2 Enter and follow the curving corridor in either direction. (There are some **Stimpacks** on the left.) Keep going around to the elevator. Grab the **Shells**, **Rockets**, **Slugs**, **Bullets** and **Cells** stashed in the corner. (You are going to need them.) Hit the switch and ride the elevator up to the next level.

3 Open the door ahead of you and enter another circular corridor. In front of you, behind a force field, you'll see a piston-like elevator. Go around to the right, and then the left, and blast the two Iron Maidens who will shoot at your from across the lava. You'll have to get quite close to the moving walkways, but they won't be able to resist shooting at you, so you'll have a shot. With Maidens out of the way, your task is a little easier (and quieter). You have to ride each walkway out to the switches, hit the switches, then ride back. The only trouble is, you have to jump the last few feet over lava. Hitting the switches opens the way to the elevator you saw when you entered this chamber.

4 Climb on and it will take you up for your first glimpse of the Makron. You'll only see him for a moment at the end of the walkway, standing on a platform, before he teleports to his Inner Chamber. To go after him, you must hit both floor switches—without being fried by the lasers. It's a timing game you can win if you're careful. The game gets a little tougher when Flyers show up to dog you. Try to ignore them until you've activated the floor switches, then blast them. Now hit the two switches on the wall behind the platform. Stairs will emerge at the base of the platform. Climb up, and you'll vanish up the pipe to the Final Showdown.

5 When you arrive at the teleport terminus, look around and start gathering supplies. Look out the windows and you'll see that you're on some kind of space ship or station. You'll find **Stimpacks**, **First Aid** kits, **Shards**, **Rockets**, **Medkits**, **Grenades**, and **Slugs**. Find the elevator. Before you take it up, notice the three sealed escape pods.

6 The elevator will deposit you on a wide, open expanse. On either side of this final battlefield you'll find floor switches that open hatches to a large chamber below. Each switch opens the hatch on the opposite side. The chamber is full of ammo, but mostly it will just give you a place to hide. The guy you'll be hiding from is standing around the pillar on your left. The Makron's mount—Jorg—is a massive killing machine. Huge. Ugly. Deadly. His dual Chainguns will shred you with an endless supply of ammo. To kill him, you'll need your BFG and a Quad Damage power-up; to keep him from killing you, you'll need Invulnerability or fast feet-or both! When you do finally kill this monstrous bastard, he will shatter, collapse… and the Makron will jump up out of the rubble to kill. The Makron is much deadlier than his mount. He can move faster, he fires a cutting blaster stream, and his arms fire BFG blasts and railgun slugs! If your BFG runs out of ammo, your next choice should be your Railgun. Keep moving, keep firing, and keep your head down.

7 When you've dispatched both versions of the Makron, take the lift back down and jump into the open escape pod. In a matter of moments, you'll be sailing through space to safety. You've come a long way, Marine. The Strogg won't be bothering Earth anytime soon. With their leader dead, Stroggos will be immersed in civil war until a new Makron is selected, and even then, their infrastructure is in ruins thanks to your efforts. You deserve a medal—assuming you can make it back home. Good job, Marine!

DON'T MISS THIS ONE. To get a look at the id Software crew who put this game together, drop down into the safety bunker and shoot the cracked wall. The very last **Secret Area** will open, and you'll get a look at the folks behind *Quake II*. Be sure to go down the shaft to get a look at what the locals will be doing with the Makron in toaster heaven.

tip

Mission 8

Quake II

Part III
MULTIPLAYER QUAKE II

DEALING DEATH ON THE STROGG is all well and good, but at the end of the day, all it takes to triumph over them--when you have this guide by your side--is time. Once the Makron is blasted into gibbets, what do you do? Easy, go find a friend and kill each other! *Quake II* is the fourth of id Software's titles in which head-to-head play takes the game to another level. (In case you've been on another planet, the other titles are *Doom*, *Doom II*, and *Quake*.) Enjoy.

MULTIPLAYER BASICS

In this section, you'll get the scoop on how to set up your match, choose your ordinance, and advance into the alien territory.

Getting Started: Control Configuration and Game Setup

Multiplayer setup in *Quake II* is handled from the Multiplayer menu—the Main Menu's second option. Once you're in the Multiplayer Menu, you'll be given three options:

- Join Network Server
- Start Network Server
- Player Setup

Join Network Server enables you to join a game in progress, whether it's on your local network or on the Internet. (Check out the sources listed at the end of this section for good lists of Internet *Quake II* servers.) You can add IP addresses (or URLs) to your address book and have *Quake II* automatically search them for active games to join.

Start Network Server enables you to host *Quake II* Deathmatch. If you select to go this route, you'll be able to choose the following play options:

- **Initial Map**—Choose the map in which the game will start. You can choose any of the 39 levels that come with the game. If you want to load up a custom level, you need to use the Console. More on that later.

- **Time Limit**—How long will the fragging go on? It's up to you. Leave this alone if you don't want a time limit for the match.

- **Frag Limit**—The game will end/switch to the next map when a player reaches this frag count.

- **Falling Damage**—This option toggles damage from long falls on or off.

- **Weapons Stay**—Instead of disappearing when picked up, weapons stay in the game so that every player can get them if you set this setting to YES.

- **Instant Powerups**—If you set this option to YES, then power-ups work as soon as they are picked up (replace i.e. you don't store them in Inventory and wait to use them later).

- **Allow Powerups**— Allows/disallows power-ups in the game.

Quake II

- **Allow Health**—If you set this one to NO, then there will be no Health in the match. This makes it an all-out frag fest, where the player who can kill the fastest should win.

- **Allow Armor**—If you set this option to NO, things can get rather painful. At a minimum, it would curb rocket jumping a bit.

- **Spawn Farthest**—Assures that players will re-enter the game after they die at a point as far away from another player as possible. This makes it easier to get back into the game, and avoids people who like to hide behind spawn points and kill new arrivals.

- **Same Map**—Keeps the server in a particular map, even after the game ends. A new game will start in the same map as soon as the previous one ends.

- **Force Respawn**—This option keeps things moving. Everyone has five seconds to re-enter the game before the Server will force them to respawn. So don't head for the kitchen to take a break when this option is set. This is a good option for tournament play, especially with the Spawn Farthest option set.

Player Setup enables you to choose your gender, appearance, and your handedness preference.

Quake II Resources: Where to Go for More Info

There are hundreds of good *Quake/Quake II* sites on the World Wide Web. Here are some of the more popular ones that have links to most others:

- **Blues News (http://www.bluesnews.com)**—The #1 *Quake II* news site on the net. If you can't find what you're looking for here, chances are this site has a link to it.
- **Planet Quake (http://www.planetquake.com)**—Another great site that also hosts many *Quake II*-related pages.
- **Stomped (http://www.stomped.com)**—This one's been around awhile. Still a good resource.

There are also several good USENET newsgroups for *Quake*-related stuff:
- rec.games.computer.quake.announce
- rec.games.computer.quake.quake-c
- rec.games.computer.quake.editing
- rec.games.computer.quake.misc
- rec.games.computer.quake.playing
- rec.games.computer.quake.servers

If these sites don't contain enough info about *Quake II*, then check for their *Quake II* equivalents.

Multiplayer Basics

Kicking Ass: Deathmatch Tips and Tricks

There are as many strategies for Deathmatch as there are players. That's the beauty of it—you can customize your approach any way you like. However, even though you can do things any way you like, there are a few things that you need to do well in order to come out on top.

- **Set your controls up properly**—The best Deathmatch players use a Mouse/Keyboard combination for control. Setup your keyboard so that you can easily reach everything (inventory, weapons keys, use key, and so on). Most people use the left side of the keyboard, since this allows easy access to the weapons keys without too much movement.

- **Master the art of circle strafing**—Circle strafing allows you to keep a bead on your target while circling it. To do it, use your strafe keys (STEP LEFT and STEP RIGHT, to be exact). While pushing STEP LEFT, move the mouse away from you to circle a central point. Do the reverse when pushing STEP RIGHT. Master this technique—you're dead without it.

- **Learn the levels**—Even though you've been through all the levels in *Quake II* in single player mode, things are different in multiplayer mode. There are new areas open, extra teleporters, and different weapon placements. Be sure you know the lay of the land before jumping into a match. If you enter a level you don't know well, spend a few minutes looking around and develop a strategy for the map.

- **Pay attention and use your head**—Listen and look for clues to your enemy's whereabouts. Elevators, weapon pickups, and pain sounds can all give away your prey's location. Also, be aware of nearby spawn points, and make sure no one can appear behind you. (If Spawn Farthest is set to ON, no one will be re-spawning near you.)

- **Learn to rocket jump**—Rocket jumping enables you to jump higher than normal. This is extremely useful in taking shortcuts to reach upper ledges. To perform a rocket jump, ready your Rocket Launcher and aim at the ground. Let a rocket fly and jump up just as the explosion occurs. You can perform this running forward, backward, or by jumping sideways. A word of caution: rocket jumping will eat up your health in a hurry. Armor helps, but will eventually wear out. Make sure you are healthy enough to blow up a rocket under your feet.

- **Use patterns to control the level**—In every level, there is an optimal path that will take you by a power-up (quad damage, invulnerability, megahealth) and at least one weapon, and allow domination of the level if you can control this pattern. Look for areas where fighting is heaviest, then work a pattern that takes you through there at regular intervals.

- **Don't get cornered**—If you prefer to find a nice, quiet place to blast everyone from, make sure you have a way out. What you need for this type of strategy is a defendable approach that also enables you to grab ammunition when you need it. Don't make the mistake of setting up shop in an easily accessible area.

- **Get used to every weapon**—Everyone has his/her favorite (or least favorite) weapon, but in Deathmatch you don't have the luxury of always using what you like. You've got to be able to finish someone off with everything in your arsenal. In addition, homing in on one weapon all the time makes you predictable—a big mistake. Learn to kill with whatever's nearby until you can get into a pattern that makes sense to get what you want.

- **Running isn't always good**—To survive in Deathmatch, you have to set Always Run in the OPTIONS menu to ON. The problem is that when you run, your footsteps can give you away. It's a trade-off that usually doesn't matter, but in a two-player match where things are much quieter, it can give you away. Be aware of it, and check out the Console Commands (Aliases) in the next chapter for a fix.

- **Don't ignore power-ups**—The best players always know when a power-up is going to re-appear, and they have a pattern that enables them to grab it as soon as it does. Get used to the timing of their re-appearance. The advantage of always being at 200 percent health is huge, as is the constant acquisition of quad damage power-ups.

Weapons Briefing

In the single player section of this guide you've got some basic information about each of the weapons available in the game. When you're playing multiplayer *Quake II*, you need to know each weapon's strengths and weaknesses. This section gives a brief run-down of what you need to know.

- **Blaster**—This weapon won't get you very far. Perhaps its biggest problem is that if you fire it at someone, chances are they'll turn and blast you with something more powerful. Only use this weak weapon when you have no choice, or against someone else who just respawned. The upside of the Blaster's weakness is that most players ignore it, so it's possible to get in several shots before they turn to swat you.

- **Shotgun**—A definite improvement from the Blaster, but with every weapon usually available in Deathmatch, this one won't cut it for long. You've got to keep moving if you take a shot with this slow-loading weapon. Its slower reload time will leave you vulnerable. The scattering effect of its projectiles make it a good choice for instantly damaging someone at close to medium range, but not for long-distance work

- **Super Shotgun**—Probably the most dependable Deathmatch weapon, the Super Shotgun can bring someone to their knees with two well-aimed shots. Damage is instant and the spread of the shot is guaranteed to injure your target. The extra-slow reloading time is a pain, but as long as you use it wisely and keep on the move, you won't have a problem.

- **Machine Gun**—A great choice for making quick work of someone at medium range. The key thing to know about this weapon is that in Deathmatch the barrel won't rise the longer you hold the trigger down. With that disadvantage out of the way, this becomes a much better weapon to use.

- **Chaingun**—This weapon is great for use in crowds, but don't waste it on individuals. It's power-up cycle and long spin-down time waste ammo and leave you vulnerable for too long. This is a great weapon to use at long distance, since the sound of it will be masked as you cause instant carnage a fair distance away.

- **Grenade Launcher**—A great crowd-tamer, the Grenade Launcher is best used from above. Many times you'll find them on ledges above the action where you can take advantage of the elevation to rain grenades down on everyone below. Using these against individuals is not recommended, as they are easy to dodge.

- **Hand Grenades**—Very similar to Grenade Launcher fire, but much slower. Your best bet with these is to drop them behind you as you head down hallways with someone in pursuit. Also send them up elevators to take out anyone waiting to come down.

- **Rocket Launcher**—In *Quake*, this was the weapon to have. In *Quake II*, there are several other good choices, but the Rocket Launcher is still a favorite. Good for use at medium to long range as well as rocket jumping to reach ledges (or hiding places) quickly. The rockets travel somewhat slowly, so they aren't the best choice for taking someone out in a hurry if they see you coming. Use something that does instant damage instead and aim for their feet—you'll do more damage that way.

- **Hyperblaster**—You want one of these in your backpack if you can get it. The Hyperblaster will cut through opponents like a hot knife through butter. It doesn't have a spin-up delay like the Chaingun, but it does take some time to spin down after you let up on the trigger. The biggest problem with this weapon is finding cells to feed it. Depend on a crowd gathering in any room with a Hyperblaster in it.

- **Railgun**—The ultimate sniper tool, the Railgun causes massive, instant damage to its target regardless of the distance to the shooter. The projectile is not at the end of that blue vapor trail—it was at the front. By the time you see the vapor trail, the target is already dead. Get good with this one—it's the only weapon guaranteed to give you a kill for every accurate shot. Of course, the downside is that you give away your position when you fire it. The best use of this weapon is to keep it ready in inventory, then switch to it in tight spots—they won't know what hit 'em.

- **BFG10K**—It's back! The BFG10K does massive damage with every shot. Most of the time, the problem is getting it, because someone usually sets up shop in the room where it is. Once you get it, be aware of how it works. In flight, the green ball will shoot out lasers and damage anyone nearby. Upon impact, anyone with a clear line of sight to the blast will be killed instantly. The blast also does radius damage, so don't fire it at close range—you'll get hurt to the tune of 60 percent to 100 percent of your own health. If you can control an open area that has plenty of Cells around (as in the Grid Control level), then the BFG is a killing machine.

MULTIPLAYER LEVELS AND CONSOLE BASICS

This section is intended to give you a feel for the way each of the 39 levels that comprise *Quake II* stack up in Deathmatch play. Needless to say, everyone has different preferences, so experiment with all of them to see if you agree.

Knowing Your Maps: Deathmatch Level Analysis

Table 1 presents a general guideline to the levels. The *Map* column has the name of the level that you would have to type into the console (or select from the Multiplayer menu) to reach that particular level (i.e. Outer Base = base1). The *QName* column has the "in-game" name of the level, such as Outer Base. The *#Players* column gives the number of players who can play comfortably in the level (based primarily upon weapon availability and placement), the *Hot Spots* column gives you a feel for the areas you need to control during play, and the *Analysis* column discusses info about the level.

Table 1. Level Analysis

MAP	QNAME	#PLAYERS	HOT SPOTS	ANALYSIS
base1	Outer Base	4–6	Rocket Launcher area, Quad Damage area	Good map for up to six players—a bit crowded with more. Count on massive battles in the Rocket Area courtyard, as well as some serious fighting near the Quad Damage power-up under the stairs near the Exit
base2	The Installation	6–10	Bridge, Entrance, and Exit	Play is similar to base1, but the level is a bit larger, allowing more players to go at it. Watch out for snipers near the bridge and entrance.
base3	Comm Center	10+	Near Machine Gun, Hyperblaster room, Comm Center area (Chaingun)	This map is more spread out than the previous two base levels. Four players will have to look around awhile to find one another, so this one is best with 10 or more. The BFG and Rockets are tough to get, so stock up when you get the chance.
train	Lost Station	4–6	Platforms, Secret Areas	This one makes for an odd Deathmatch—fighting will most likely be concentrated in a few areas. Not a good map for more than 6 players—weapons are too sparse. Plenty of underwater combat, though, so this might be a good one to try for a change of pace.

MAP	QName	# Players	Hot Spots	Analysis
bunk1	Ammo Depot	15+	All weapon areas	Huge level—20 could play comfortably here, but the weapons are very hard to come by. This one is a paradox—by the time you get enough players to make a good match, you can't get a weapon anymore. If you like to hunt for your prey, this is the level for you.
ware1	Supply Station	15–32	Near Quad Damage (spawn points nearby), and near the Rocket Launcher	Another of the sprawling warehouse levels, don't jump into a game here without more than 15 players—unless you need a breather from a fast-paced match. Expect fierce fighting around all weapons, but don't expect to find a weapon often if you're playing without "Weapons Stay" set to ON.
ware2	Warehouse	8–16	Railgun room, Quad Damage area, Hyperblaster chamber	This is the best of the warehouse levels, as far as Deathmatch goes. Plenty of action here, and good weapon balance. The Railgun is a popular target here, so get used to fighting for it/around it.
jail1	Main Gate	8–12	Ledge over Main Gate (Railgun), Machine Gun room, Grenade Launcher area near start, Chaingun area downstairs	Excellent fast-paced level. It's all here—if you love to snipe at people, then you can grab the Railgun and do that from the ledge over the Main Gate. If you want some quick frags, go for the Grenade Launcher area. For plenty of targets, keep an eye on the Machine Gun room—it's always crowded.
jail2	Detention Center	8–12	Cell block (Quad Damage, Machine Gun, Super Shotgun), area near Grenade Launcher	Another good level for a decent-sized crowd. Plenty of weapons, good weapon balance, and some cool places to fight your battles characterize this level. Watch your back, and stay on your toes when opening either door that leads from the central courtyard—chances are someone is slinging death behind it. Don't walk into it unprepared.
jail3	Security Complex	10–16	Courtyard near Willit's pod, BFG room under pyramid, Main Courtyard, Rocket Launcher area	Good, solid Deathmatch level. Plenty of open areas, and some good frag fest areas near the weapons. You usually spawn near a weapon, so expect plenty of action in this one.

Part 3: Multiplayer Quake II

Map	QName	# Players	Hot Spots	Analysis
jail4	Torture Chambers	10	Cell Block B, Bridge over Cell Block A, lava pool (stash at bottom)	Don't open a door if you aren't ready to blast whoever may be behind it. There are plenty of ledges and ways for other players to get the drop on you, so use your head in this level. Great level for snipers and BFG haters—the swim to the BFG is a killer.
jail5	Guard House	8–10	Hyperblaster/BFG areas, courtyard	This one degenerates into a battle to see who can get the BFG and/or Hyperblaster and keep them longest. Plenty of action in these areas, but not a lot in others. This makes it tough to support more than 10 players in this level.
security	Grid Control	10	Boss courtyard upstairs, BFG area	The Boss courtyard (which, for all you Doom players, is reminiscent of Doom II Level 7) is the key to this level. Grab the BFG, then control this area. There are multiple player respawns nearby, and chances are someone will enter the area constantly.
mintro	Mine Entrance	6–8	Rocket Launcher/BFG area, ledge near start (Hyperblaster)	Great map for 6–8; good weapon balance, plenty of areas to fight in. Very fast-paced match.
mine1	Upper Mines	10–20	BFG area near exit, all "fan" areas, Quad Damage area above start, Hyperblaster hall	Large level, but well connected with teleporters and passages. Great for up to 20 players. Plenty of action near the BFG, so use caution if you're going to get it. Lob a few Grenades down there first to clear a path.
mine2	Bore Hole	10	Grenade Launcher platforms (snipers), BFG area across ledge, Rocket Launcher room, Bore area (Hyperblaster)	Decent Deathmatch level, but you may get caught without a weapon a fair amount of the time—it's not all that large and most weapons are a short walk away from spawn spots. The BFG is worth getting, but keeping it will take some work.
mine3	Drilling Area	10–12	Exit room (Hyperblaster), Quad Damage underwater, Railgun and teleporter area, drilling area (BFG and Rocket Launcher)	10–12 players makes this a fast-paced frag fest. More than that would be too many. A good pattern here is: Hyperblaster, Machine Gun (on bridge), Quad Damage (underwater), Railgun. Watch those teleports—expect plenty of telefragging since they are your only connection to other parts of the level.

Quake II--Authorized Strategy Guide

Map	QName	#Players	Hot Spots	Analysis
mine4	Lower Mines	6–10	Quad Damage area, Rocket Launcher/Super Shotgun	A bit cramped for more than 10 players, this map isn't the best of Deathmatch maps—most areas are only accessible from one direction, making it easy for a player to dominate an area.
fact1	Receiving Center	6–10	Quad Damage/BFG area below, Rocket Launcher room, Chaingun bridge, Exit area (Hyperblaster)	Snipers heaven. This level has a lot of one-way entrances to room (you can only get to them one way). Control the Rocket Launcher room or Hyperblaster to rule this one.
fact2	Processing Plant	6–10	Hyperblaster room, Rocket Launcher/Quad Damage area, Railgun room	This one gets crowded with more than 10, but it's a fun map to play. Not loaded with weapons, so a defensive strategy works best in here—grab a weapon and defend it.
fact3	Sudden Death	4–8	Railgun/BFG/Rocket Launcher room and ledges around it, Hyperblaster near start	Count on plenty of action around the Railgun in the lava pit, as well as the Rocket Launcher and BFG above. You can have a field day picking off the players going for either of those weapons, assuming you've got enough firepower yourself. The BFG is a deathtrap—don't waste time trying to get it unless the area is completely clear.
power1	Power Plant	4–8	BFG room, both court-yards, Rocket Launcher ledge	This one has too few weapons to handle more than 8 players. There are areas where there will be no fighting, and areas where the fighting will be extremely heavy, due to the fact that a weapon is located there. This is what is meant when people say that the level isn't well balanced—it's slow paced for 4 players, and frustrating with more than 8.
power2	The Reactor	10	Rocket Launcher room, Railgun courtyard, ledges near other Railgun	Lots of room between weapons here. Look for stragglers in the halls that are looking for weapons and enter the area with the Megahealth and Grenade Launcher carefully—it's usually busy.

Map	QName	# Players	Hot Spots	Analysis
cool1	Cooling Facility	10	Grenade Launcher area, Rocket Launcher areas, BFG area	Not as fast-paced as some, but still decent, this level has a decent weapon supply, but they are spread throughout the level. Plan to load up and go in search of your prey if you're playing with fewer than 10 players.
waste1	Toxic Waste Dump	10	Railgun walkway, Rocket Launcher halls, and Hyperblaster courtyard	Four players will never find each other in this large level. You should be able to get a weapon, but you'll have to go looking for a fight in one of the hot spots if you want some action.
waste2	Pumping Station 1	6–8	Grenade Launcher areas, Crate area with BFG hidden inside, switch room (teleporter and Chaingun), near Quad Damage power-up	This is a fairly small map, which makes it a 6–8 player level. Expect tons of action near the Grenade Launcher up on the crates, as well as near the BFG around the corner. The only flaw in this level is that the teleporter to the Quad Damage power-up doesn't work both ways.
waste3	Pumping Station 2	6–8	Quad Damage area, Railgun room	This level plays smaller than waste2, so be prepared to open fire as soon as you round a corner. Unless you're careful, you'll spend plenty of time sucking slime, so do your best to avoid those areas.
biggun	Big Gun	6–8	Rocket Launcher hall, Grenade Launcher platform, BFG room (Exit), Railgun ledge.	Great small level—frags-o'-plenty here. Avoid the open pit and toxic water in the Boss chamber and use the Railgun above the chamber (and the handy supply of Slugs) to keep everyone out.
hangar1	Outer Hangar	6–8	Hyperblaster canyon, Grenade Launcher/Teleporter area,	Nice open areas to fight in, as well as decent weapon balance as long as there aren't too many players in the level.
hangar2	Inner Hangar	8–10	Rocket Launcher area, Quad Damage area	This level isn't really optimized for Deathmatch. There are still things you have to do to get it setup for play (like extend the bridge, close the hangar doors). Most of the fighting will be near the Rocket Launcher.

Map	QName	#Players	Hot Spots	Analysis
lab	Research Lab	6–8	BFG room, other open areas, Teleporter to Quad Damage	Slow-paced level. Areas aren't connected in more than one place, so if you don't have a weapon, you'll have to go through someone to get one most of the time.
command	Launch Command	6–10	Hyperblaster/Machine Gun/Super Shotgun room, Rocket Launcher/Quad area, courtyard near BFG/Hyperblaster	Two of the most desirable Deathmatch items—the Rocket Launcher and Quad Damage power-up area right on top of one another—this level plays a lot like king of the mountain—get that Launcher! Also expect serious fragging near the start due to the presence of the BFG and Hyperblaster there.
strike	Outlands	10	Grenade Launcher and courtyard beyond, Railgun area, Rocket Launcher ledge, Railgun/Machine Gun area	Good outdoor level—10 or more will have no problem playing in this map. Weapons are spread out, but easily reached. You can always dive into the water to avoid attacks, or sneak up on other players.
space	Comm Satellite	10–12	All weapons areas, circular chamber, Hangar bay areas	Low gravity makes this level a must-play for Deathmatch. Once you get used to it, you'll be able to make some jumps to shorten the path to the areas.
city1	Outer Courts	12–16	Entry courtyard and ledges, Hyperblaster area	Great sniper areas in courtyard outside entrance, especially the Railgun and Rocket Launcher ledges. If you go swimming inside, don't expect too much action—weapons are too spaced out in there.
city2	Lower Palace	8–10	Secret corridor (Hyperblaster), Central Computer room and ledge above with Grenade Launcher	Good level for a decent crowd. Stick to the main areas, with an occasional jog to get the Hyperblaster. The ledge over the Central Computer chamber is a great place to lob Grenades from, but it's not well protected. Expect company up there.
city3	Upper Palace	10	Hyperblaster area, lower level, banner room, Comm Laser area	Although there are several open areas throughout this level, much of your combat here will be in the halls—both upstairs and in the basement. Use the elevators and teleporters to your advantage, and work circles around your enemies.

Part 3: Multiplayer Quake II

MAP	QNAME	#PLAYERS	HOT SPOTS	ANALYSIS
boss1	Inner Chamber	4–6	Railgun ledge, hallways, Grenade Launcher room	Rather small for a Deathmatch level, but still a good one. The teleporter near the Railgun makes this one a circular layout—it takes you right back to the start. This one isn't a sniper's level. You've got to keep moving to score big here.
boss2	Final Showdown	6–10	Passages near Rocket Launcher, Makron's courtyard, downstairs near Exit/Start areas	The upper courtyard is a killing zone—don't even think about going up there without a weapon. Lurking in the passages below is usually profitable, but there will be plenty of action in the courtyard if you're ready for it.

Console Commands: Using Quake II's Command Line Interface

Chances are that there are a few things you'd like to change about the way *Quake II* is set up. The best way to make any change is to use the Console. The Console is a command line interface that gives you control over the variables that make up the *Quake II* world. While you can't use all the commands for Deathmatch play, you can make use of some of the more common ones to help you out. You can place several Console commands in a text file, give it an extension of **.cfg**, put it in your quake2/baseq2 directory, and load it from within the game by typing **exec myconfig.cfg**, where myconfig is the name of your file. This is useful for setting up your game differently on the fly. A complete list of Console commands is available by typing **cvarlist** from within the Console. Tables 2 and 3 list some of the commands most commonly used in the game.

Table 2. Console Commands

COMMAND	WHAT IT DOES
Bind	This command enables you to bind an action to a key. Every key setting that you chose from the OPTIONS menu is actually a binding. For example, the command line version of setting your "E" key for jumping would be: *bind e +jump*. Use bindings to toggle key commands you don't want active all the time.
Map	The map command enables you to skip to different maps, or load a custom map from the console. Just type *map newmap*, where newmap is the name of the map you want to load to switch maps. The map's *.bsp* file must be in the *quake2/baseq2/maps* subdirectory in order for the command to work.
Alias	This command is one of the most useful. An *alias* is a collection of commands that are grouped together. You can then *bind* that *alias* to a keyboard or mouse key. This allows a degree of in-game programming similar to macros in other programs. To make an *alias* work properly, each command must be enclosed in quotation marks, and each command has to be separated by semi-colons. For more details on alias commands see Table 3.
Kill	If you find yourself stuck—and it does happen from time to time—you can use this command to commit suicide. Don't do it often—suicide costs you a frag. Just type kill and you'll die.

Table 3. Alias Commands

COMMAND	WHAT IT DOES
alias +atleft "hand 1; wait; +attack" alias +atcntr "hand 2; wait; +attack" alias +atrigh "hand 0; wait; +attack" alias -atleft "hand 2; wait; -attack" alias -atcntr "hand 2; wait; -attack" alias -atrigh "hand 2; wait; -attack" bind mouse1 +atleft bind mouse2 +atrigh bind mouse3 +atcntr	Hand switching. Donít like the way you shoot from the right side all the time? This alias will enable you to fire from the left, center, or right side by using the three buttons of a three-button mouse.
alias +rj "rj1;rj2" alias rj1 "set rj_cl_pitchspeed$cl_pitchspeed;set cl_pitchspeed 100000;wait;+lookdown;wait;-lookdown;set cl_pitchspeed $rj_cl_pitchspeed" alias rj2 "set rj_hand $hand;hand 2;+moveup;+attack" alias -rj "-attack;-moveup;set hand $rj_hand;centerview" bind g +rj	Rocket Jumping. This alias will enable an automatic rocket jump with the press of one key.
alias walk "set cl_run 0; echo walking; bind v run" alias run "set cl_run 1; echo running; bind v walk" bind v "walk"	Run/Walk toggle. This alias turns auto-run off when you want to sneak up on someone.

There are hundreds of possible Console commands. For additional help with them, check out Fahrenheit 176's detailed listing at

http://www.planetquake.com/f176/

Quake II

APPENDIX

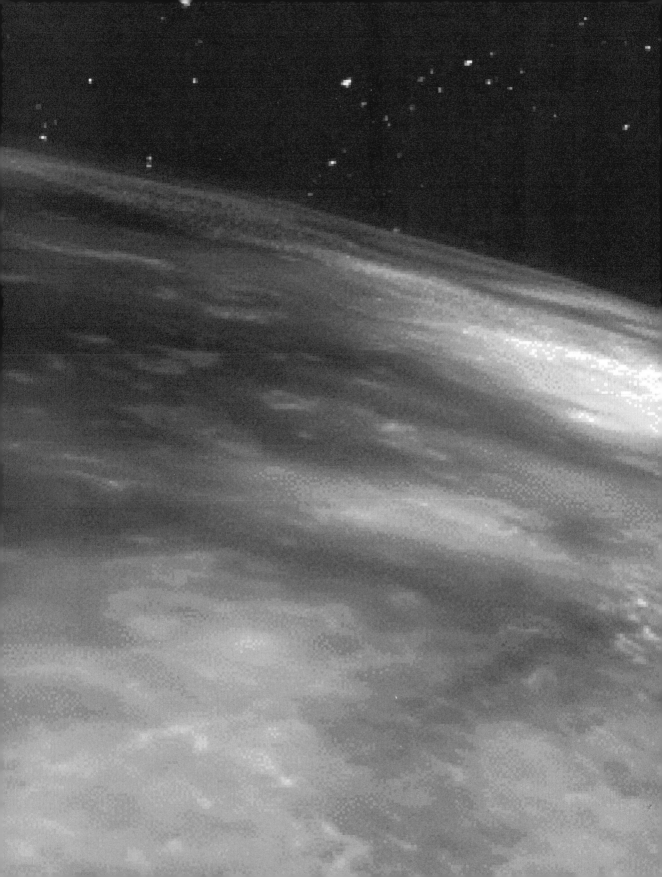

Appendix A
CHEAT CODES

We sure hope you have a very good reason to turn to this page. Be advised that being stuck in the game or wanting to stock up on supplies on the sly are not valid reason for a true Marine. So if you want to risk dishonorable discharge, go ahead, use these codes. Just don't let us catch you bragging about your victories. To use these cheat codes (which come to us courtesy of Kuhas and his Quake Marines), press "~" to open the game's console, then type the command at the prompt. Hit enter to accept your choice. Hit "~" again, and you're back in the game, cheater.

General Cheat Codes

COMMAND	ITEM	QUANTITY
give all	All Items	*See* Arsenal and Supplies Cheat Codes
give health	Health	100
give weapons	All Weapons	All - No Ammo
give ammo	All Ammo	100s/200b/200c/50g/50s/50r
give armor	Body Armor	200
give body armor	Body Armor	+1
god	God Mode	on/off
notarget	No Target Mode	on/off
noclip	No Clip Mode	on/off

NOTE: The following items are not activated by the "give all" command and require separate entry:

COMMAND	ITEM	QUANTITY
give airstrike marker	AirStrike Marker	1
give blue key	Blue Key	1
give red key	Red Key	1
give security pass	Security Pass	1
give commander's head	Commander's Head	1
give power shield	Power Shield	1
give armor shard	Armor Shard	1
give combat armor	Combat Armor	1

Arsenal Cheat Codes

COMMAND	ITEM	QUANTITY
give blaster	Blaster	1 - No ammo
give shotgun	Shotgun	1 - No ammo
give super shotgun	Super Shotgun	1 - No ammo
give machinegun	Machine Gun	1 - No ammo
give chaingun	Chaingun	1 - No ammo
give grenade launcher	Grenade Launcher	1 - No ammo
give rocket launcher	Rocket Launcher	1 - No ammo
give railgun	Railgun	1 - No ammo
give bfg10k	BFG10K	1 - No ammo

Supplies Cheat Codes

COMMAND	ITEM	QUANTITY
give shells	Shells	10
give bullets	Bullets	50
give cells	Cells	50
give grenades	Grenades	5
give rockets	Rockets	5
give slugs	Slugs	10
give jacket armor	Jacket Armor	1
give combat armor	Combat Armor	1
give armor shard	Armor Shard	1
give power shield	Power Shield	1
give silencer	Silencer	1
give bandolier	Bandolier	1
give ammo pack	Ammo Pack	1
give rebreather	Rebreather	1
give environment suit	Enviro-Suit	1
give quad damage	Quad Damage	1
give invulnerability	Invulnerability	1
give ancient head	Ancient Head	1
give adrenaline	Adrenaline	1

Part 3: Multiplayer Quake II

Access and Other Cheat Codes

COMMAND	ITEM	QUANTITY
give blue key	Blue Key	1
give red key	Red Key	1
give security pass	Security Pass	1
give pyramid key	Pyramid Key	1
give data cd	Data CD	1
give power cube	Power Cube	1
give data spinner	Data Spinner	1
give airstrike marker	Airstrike Marker	1
give commander's head	Commander's Head	1

Mission Cheats

To play a mission before you complete the ones that come before it, type one of these commands:

MISSION	COMMAND
Warehouse Unit	exec warehouse.cfg
Jail Unit	exec jail.cfg
Mine Unit	exec mine.cfg
Factory Unit	exec factory.cfg
Power Unit	exec power.cfg
Biggun Unit	exec biggun.cfg
Hangar Unit	exec hangar.cfg
City Unit	exec city.cfg
Boss Levels	exec boss.cfg

Appendix B
HOW TO USE THE CD-ROM

So you've killed the ultimate Strogg, the Makron. You've explored every nook and cranny of Stroggos and the world *Quake II* has to offer—both in single- and in multiplayer games. What you want now are new environments in which to continue to blast and have fun. Well, here they are: five exclusive add-on levels for registered users of *Quake II*. However, before you can access these new environments, you first have to perform a few simple steps.

Installing the Exclusive Add-On Levels

In Microsoft Explorer, doubleclick **d:\Levels.exe** (substitute the actual letter of the CD-ROM drive for d) and follow the onscreen instructions. Click OK in the WinZip Self Extractor pop-up window. Click Unzip to unzip the map files into the *c:\quake2\baseq2\maps* subdirectory (you may have to change the drive letter, depending on where you installed *Quake II*).

Playing the Exclusive Add-On Levels

To play any of these levels from *Quake II*, enter the console (press "~"), then type **Map mapname** at the command prompt, where mapname is the name of one of the following maps:

> crdoom
> depot
> eviscera
> solitary
> wicked

Note: For more information on the individual levels, read the TXT files in the *quake2/baseq2/maps* directory.

Quake II

Appendix C
EXCLUSIVE ADD-ON LEVEL MAPS

The following table presents a general breakdown of the exclusive add-on levels. The *Map* column lists the name you would have to type into the console (or select from the Multiplayer menu) to reach that particular level. The *QName* column lists the "in-game" name of the level. The *#Players* column gives the number of players who can play comfortably in the level.

MAP	QNAME	#PLAYERS
crdoom	Crack of Doom	2-14
depot	Depot	single
eviscera	Eviscerator	2-10
solitary	Solitary	2-6
wicked	Wicked	8-12

The following pages show the maps of these exclusive add-on levels.

CRACK OF DOOM

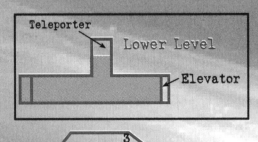

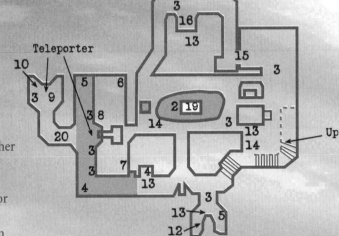

1 Body Armor
2 Power Shield
3 Grenades
4 Rocket Launcher
5 Shells
6 Shotgun
7 Combat Armor
8 Medkit
9 Super Shotgun
10 Rockets, Grenades, Shells
11 Machine Gun
12 Hyperblaster
13 First Aid
14 Cells
15 Bullets
16 Railgun
17 Grenade Launcher
18 Chaingun
19 Quad Damage
20 Armor

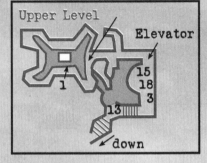

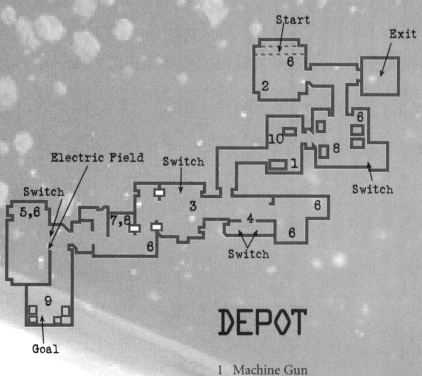

Start

Exit

Electric Field

Switch

Switch

Switch

6

2

10

8

1

6

6

3

7,8

5,6

6

4

6

6

Switch

9

Goal

DEPOT

1 Machine Gun
2 Shotgun
3 Super Shotgun
4 Chaingun
5 Rocket Launcher
6 Medkit
7 Secret
8 Grenade Launcher
9 BFG10K
10 Shells

EVISCERATOR

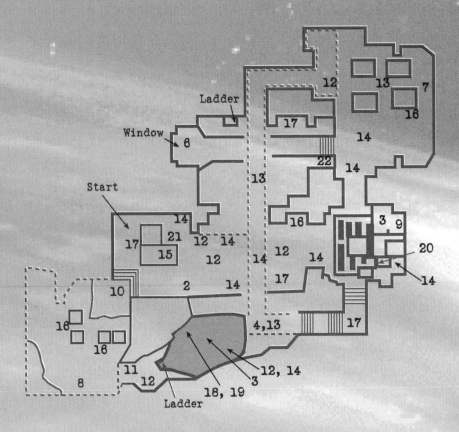

Ladder

Window

Start

Ladder

18, 19

12, 14

3

4,13

Power Shield — 20

1 BFG10K
2 Chaingun
3 Grenade Launcher
4 Machine Gun
5 Railgun
6 Rocket Launcher
7 Super Shotgun
8 Shotgun
9 Combat Armor
10 Armor Jacket
11 Adrenaline

12 Armor Shard
13 Bullets
14 Health
15 Quad Damage
16 Shells
17 Rockets
18 Megahealth
19 Grenades
20 Power Shield
21 Slugs
22 Cells

SOLITARY

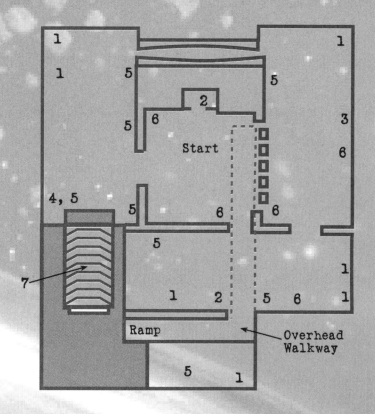

Ramp

Overhead
Walkway

Start

1 Health
2 Grenade Launcher
3 Super Shotgun
4 BFG10K
5 Grenades
6 Shells
7 Invulnerability

WICKED

1   BFG10K
2   Shotgun
3   Hyperblaster
4   Shells
5   Rockets
6   Quad Damage
7   Grenades
8   First Aid
9   Slugs
10 Cells
11 Armor Jacket
12 Rocket Launcher
13 Bullets
14 Machine Gun
15 Megahealth
16 Body Armor
17 Railgun
18 Grenade Launcher
19 Chaingun
20 Super Shotgun

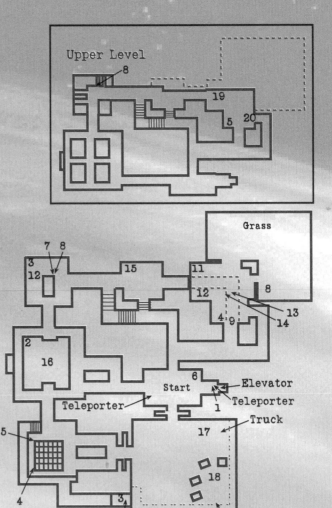

Did you survive the

Strogg onslaught?

Do you already know

all the levels for
Quake II inside out?

Are you ready for

more Quake II?

Then go ahead and
install the five

Exclusive Add-On Levels from the accompanying CD-ROM

(For installation instructions see Appendix B)

LICENSE AGREEMENT AND LIMITED WARRANTY

PLEASE READ THIS LICENSE CAREFULLY BEFORE USING THE SOFTWARE. THIS DOCUMENT IS AN AGREEMENT BETWEEN YOU AND THE WIZARDWORKS GROUP INC (THE "COMPANY"). THE COMPANY IS WILLING TO LICENSE THE ENCLOSED SOFTWARE TO YOU ONLY ON THE CONDITION THAT YOU ACCEPT ALL THE TERMS CONTAINED IN THIS AGREEMENT. BY USING THE SOFTWARE YOU ARE AGREEING TO BE BOUND BY THE TERMS OF THIS LICENSE. IF YOU DO NOT AGREE TO THE TERMS OF THIS LICENSE, PROMPTLY RETURN THE UNUSED SOFTWARE (INCLUDING ALL PACKAGING AND YOUR ORIGINAL, DATED SALES RECEIPT) WITHIN 10 DAYS OF PURCHASE TO **THE WIZARDWORKS GROUP INC, 2300 BERKSHIRE LANE, PLYMOUTH, MN 55441** AND YOUR MONEY WILL BE REFUNDED.

1. Ownership And License. This is a license agreement and NOT an agreement for sale. The software contained in this package (the "Software") is the property of the Company and/or its Licensors. You own the disk/CD on which the Software is recorded, but the Company and/or its Licensors retain title to the Software and related documentation. Your rights to use the Software are specified in this Agreement, and the Company and/or its Licensors retain all rights not expressly granted to you in this Agreement.

2. Permitted Uses. You are granted the following rights to the Software:
(a) *Right to Install and Use.* You may install and use the Software on a single computer. If you wish to use the Software on more than one computer, please contact the Company for information concerning an upgraded license allowing use of the Software with additional computers.
(b) *Right to Copy.* You may make and maintain one copy of the Software for backup and archival purposes, provided that the original and each copy of the Software are kept in your possession.

3. Prohibited Uses. The following uses of the Software are prohibited. If you wish to use the Software in a manner prohibited below, please contact the Company at the address, phone, or fax numbers listed above for information regarding a "Special Use License". Otherwise, you may NOT:
(a) Make or distribute copies of the Software or documentation, or any portion thereof, except as expressly provided in this Agreement.
(b) Use any backup or archival copy of the Software (or allow someone else to use such copy) for any purpose other than to replace the original copy in the event it is destroyed or becomes defective;
(c) Alter, decompile, or disassemble the Software, create derivative works based upon the Software, or make any attempt to bypass, unlock or disable any protective or initialization system on the Software;
(d) Rent, lease, sub-license, time-share, or transfer the Software or documentation, or your rights under this Agreement.
(e) Remove or obscure any copyright or trademark notice(s) on the Software or documentation;
(f) Upload or transmit the Software, or any portion thereof, to any electronic bulletin board, network, or other type of multi-use computer system regardless of purpose;
(g) Include the Software in any commercial products intended for manufacture, distribution, or sale; or
(h) Include the Software in any product containing immoral, scandalous, controversial, derogatory, obscene, or offensive works.

4. Termination. This license is effective upon the first use, installation, loading or copying of the Software. You may terminate this Agreement at any time by destruction and disposal of the Software and all related documentation. This license will terminate automatically without notice from the Company if you fail to comply with any provisions of this license. Upon termination, you shall destroy all copies of the Software and any accompanying documentation. All provisions of this Agreement as to warranties, limitation of liability, remedies or damages shall survive termination.

5. Copyright Notice. The Company and/or our Licensors hold valid copyright in the Software. Nothing in this Agreement constitutes a waiver of any rights under U.S. Copyright law or any other federal or state law.

6. Miscellaneous. This Agreement shall be governed by the laws of the United States of America and the State of Minnesota. If any provision, or any portion, of this Agreement is found to be unlawful, void, or for any reason unenforceable, it shall be severed from, and shall in no way affect the validity or enforceability of the remaining provisions of the Agreement.

7. Limited Warranty and Disclaimer of Warranty. For a period of 90 days from the date on which you purchased Software, the Company warrants that the media on which the Software is supplied will be free from defects in materials and workmanship under normal use. If the Software fails to conform to this warranty, you may, as your sole and exclusive remedy; obtain a replacement free of charge if you return the defective Software to us with a dated proof of purchase. The Company does not warrant that the Software or its operations or functions will meet your requirements, nor that the use thereof will be without interruption or error.

EXCEPT FOR THE EXPRESS WARRANTY SET FORTH ABOVE, THE COMPANY DISCLAIMS ALL WARRANTIES, EXPRESS OR IMPLIED, INCLUDING AND WITHOUT LIMITATION, THE IMPLIED WARRANTIES OF MERCHANTABILITY AND FITNESS FOR A PARTICULAR PURPOSE. EXCEPT FOR THE EXPRESS WARRANTY SET FORTH ABOVE, THE COMPANY DOES NOT WARRANT, GUARANTEE OR MAKE ANY REPRESENTATION REGARDING THE USE OR THE RESULTS OF THE USE OF THE SOFTWARE IN TERMS OF ITS CORRECTNESS, ACCURACY, RELIABILITY, CURRENTNESS OR OTHERWISE.

IN NO EVENT SHALL THE COMPANY OR ITS EMPLOYEES OR LICENSORS BE LIABLE FOR ANY INCIDENTAL, INDIRECT, SPECIAL, OR CONSEQUENTIAL DAMAGES ARISING OUT OF OR IN CONNECTION WITH THE LICENSE GRANTED UNDER THIS AGREEMENT INCLUDING AND WITHOUT LIMITATION, LOSS OF USE, LOSS OF DATE, LOSS OF INCOME OR PROFIT, OR OTHER LOSS SUSTAINED AS A RESULT OF INJURY TO ANY PERSON, OR LOSS OF OR DAMAGE TO PROPERTY, OR CLAIMS OF THIRD PARTIES, EVEN IF THE COMPANY OR AN AUTHORIZED REPRESENTATIVE OF THE COMPANY HAS BEEN ADVISED OF THE POSSIBILITY OF SUCH DAMAGES. IN NO EVENT SHALL LIABILITY OF THE COMPANY FOR DMAGES WITH RESPECT TO THE SOFTWARE EXCEED THE AMOUNTS ACTUALLY PAID BY YOU, IF ANY, FOR THE SOFTWARE.

SOME JURISDICTIONS DO NOT ALLOW THE LIMITATION OF IMPLIED WARRANTIES OR LIABILITY FOR INCIDENTAL, INDIRECT, SPECIAL OR CONSEQUENTIAL DAMAGES, SO THE ABOVE LIMITATIONS MAY NOT ALWAYS APPLY.

ACKNOWLEDGMENT

YOU ACKNOWLEDGE THAT YOU HAVE READ THIS AGREEMENT, UNDERSTAND IT AND AGREE TO BE BOUND BY ITS TERMS AND CONDITIONS. YOU ALSO AGREE THAT THIS AGREEMENT IS THE COMPLETE AND EXCLUSIVE STATEMENT OF THE AGREEMENT BETWEEN YOU AND THE COMPANY AND SUPERCEDES ALL PROPOSALS OR PRIOR ENDORSEMENTS, ORAL OR WRITTEN, AND ANY OTHER COMMUNICATIONS BETWEEN YOU AND THE COMPANY OR ANY REPRESENTATIVE OF THE COMPANY RELATING TO THE SUBJECT MATTER OF THIS AGREEMENT.

Quake II is a trademark of id Software, Inc.